The Lion and the Dragon

AUBREY SINGER

The Lion and the Dragon

The Story of
the First British Embassy
to
the Court of the Emperor Qianlong
in Peking
1792-1794

BARRIE & JENKINS
LONDON

First published in Great Britain in 1992 by
Barrie & Jenkins Ltd
20 Vauxhall Bridge Road, London, SW1V 2SA

A catalogue record for this book is available
from the British Library

ISBN 0 7126 5444 5

Typeset in Imprint by SX Composing Ltd, Rayleigh, Essex
Printed and bound in Great Britain by
Butler and Tanner Ltd, Frome and London

To my wife and family
and to the many Chinese friends who have helped
me with this book

Contents

List of Illustrations

SOURCES OF ILLUSTRATIONS

An Authentic Account of an Embassy by Sir George Staunton (1797): plates 1, 2, 14, 26, 27, 28, 35; British Library: 6, 7, 8, 10, 19, 20, 21, 23, 30, 39, 40; *The Costume of China* by William Alexander (1805): 4, 5, 15, 16, 18, 22, 24, 25, 29, 32, 33; Coutts & Co: 38; Natural History Museum, London: 36; Royal Archives, Windsor Castle: 17; J.H. Bourden-Smith: 37; Aubrey Singer: 3, 9, 11, 12, 13, 31, 34.

Preface

Contemporary accounts of the Macartney Embassy were written before attempts were made to produce a standardized transliteration from Chinese to English. In order not to pass on to the reader the problems encountered when dealing with more than one style of transliteration, the following compromise has been reached: within the text names have been transliterated into Pinyin; within quotations the original has been used with the Pinyin equivalent following in brackets. Exceptions have been made where Anglicization has produced familiarity – e.g. Peking for Beijing.

The published sources and the many documents that I have had access to in writing this book have provided a wealth of information, but they have at the same time caused difficulties, of both time and geography. Because some of the accounts were written after the Embassy returned to England, dates and places – and even events – as recorded by one participant have not always tallied with those recorded by another. Even the map used by the Embassy contains names not mentioned in any of the documents, and mysteriously omits others that were included in the itinerary. In addition, many landmarks have changed their names – and some even their position: the Yangtze River has wandered over some two hundred miles in the intervening years. And readers should be aware that the Grand Canal in parts of its length used the existing rivers; in 1793 the Hai River, for example, was regarded as part of the Canal.

My job has therefore been partly one of piecing together, and partly one of unravelling and making sense of discrepancies. But I have wanted to avoid imposing a spurious uniformity, and so inevitably some inconsistencies remain.

Acknowledgements

THIS BOOK DRAWS ON the diaries and accounts of seven people: Lord George Macartney of Lissanoure, the Ambassador; Sir George Leonard Staunton, Minister Plenipotentiary in the absence of the Ambassador; Dr James Dinwiddie, 'Machinest'; John Barrow, Comptroller; William Alexander, draughtsman; Aeneas Anderson, valet to the Ambassador; and J.C. Huttner, tutor to Master Staunton. It also draws on Chinese documents.

Thanks are due to many people: to Anthony Grey, who in February 1988 forgot to bring a hat whilst on a tour of the Forbidden City, and to Professor Yan Chongnian for inquiring during Anthony's absence about British intentions for the Macartney bicentennial. It was at this moment that the idea for this book was born.

In his support of the book and connected events, I gratefully acknowledge the generosity of the Midland Bank and Nicolas Wolfers. I am indebted to Her Majesty The Queen for gracious permission to reproduce the Imperial edict from Qianlong to George III preserved in the Royal Archives at Windsor. I would also like to record my gratitude to Professor J.L. Cranmer-Byng for allowing me to quote from his edition of the Macartney journals and his articles in the *Journal of Oriental Studies*; and to the India Office Library and the British Library for their help in finding illustrations and sources. I must also record with deep gratitude the generous grant made by Liu Ding Yih and The British Taiwan Cultural Institute towards the colour reproduction of the Alexander sketches and other illustrations.

Thanks are also due to Frances Wood of the Oriental Department of the British Library for reading the manuscript and for making helpful suggestions; to Sue Phillpott for her editorial support; to Stephen Hearst and Alasdair Milne; to Noble Wilson for his translation of Huttner's account of the Embassy; and last but by no means least to Judith Murrell and Jean Sedley, who laboured over the research notes and the manuscript in all its manifestations.

Dramatis Personae

The Embassy

Lord George Macartney of Lissanoure, Ambassador
Sir George Leonard Staunton, Secretary and Minister Plenipotentiary in the absence of the Ambassador
John Barrow, Comptroller
Jacobus Li ('Mr Plumb'), Interpreter, from the Chinese College at Naples
Dr William Scott, Surgeon
Dr Hugh Gillan, Physician and Natural Philosopher
James Dinwiddie, 'Machinest' and Experimental Scientist
Thomas Hickey, Painter
William Alexander, Draughtsman
Henry Eades, Metallurgist
John Haxton, Gardener and Botanist
David Stronach, Gardener and Botanist
Master George Thomas Staunton, Page to the Ambassador
Aeneas Anderson, Valet to the Ambassador
Herr J.C. Huttner, Tutor to Master Staunton
Victor Thibault, Mathematical Instrument Maker
Charles Henry Petitpierre, Watchmaker

Military Escort

Lieutenant-Colonel George Benson, Commander, Military Escort
Lieutenant Henry Parish, Commander, Artillery Detachment
10 Dragoons
20 Artillerymen
20 Infantry

Maritime Support

HMS *Lion* (64 guns); Captain Erasmus Gower, First Lieutenant; Lieutenant Campbell
Hindostan, East-Indiaman (30 guns); Captain William Mackintosh

The Chinese

The Emperor Qianlong

Heshen, Manchu Grand Secretary, Chief Minister of the Imperial Court and favourite of Qianlong

Zhengrui, Manchu Chief Conducting Mandarin, Salt Administrator at Tientsin

Wang (called Van-ta-gin by the Embassy), Han Chinese, Conducting Mandarin, Military Commander at Tongzhou

Qiao (called Cho-ta-gin by the Embassy), Han Chinese, Conducting Mandarin, Administrator at Tientsin

Songyun, Manchu Grand Councillor; after meeting at Jehol appointed to conduct Macartney to Zhoushan

Changling, Manchu, new Viceroy of Canton; travelled with Macartney on last stage of journey to Canton

Fuchang'an, Manchu, Second Minister; escorted Macartney round Jehol

Fukhang'an, Manchu, Viceroy of Sichuan, formerly Viceroy of Canton, who fought the campaign against the Gurkhas in Tibet in 1791.

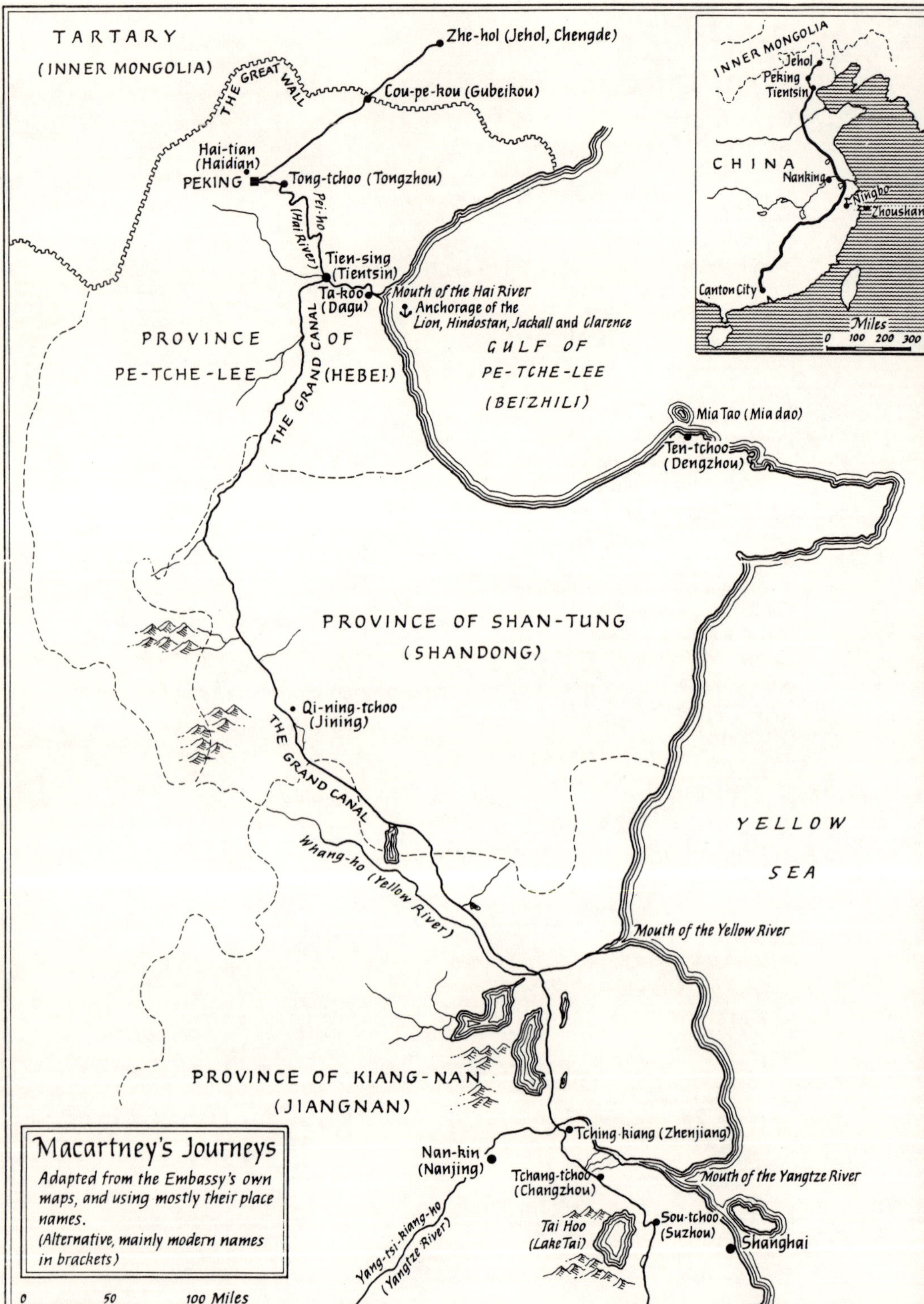
TARTARY
(INNER MONGOLIA)
THE GREAT WALL
Zhe-hol (Jehol, Chengde)
Cou-pe-kou (Gubeikou)
Hai-tian
(Haidian)
PEKING
Tong-tchoo (Tongzhou)
Pei-ho
(Hai River)
Tien-sing
(Tientsin)
Ta-koo
(Dagu)
Mouth of the Hai River
Anchorage of the
Lion, Hindostan, Jackall and Clarence
PROVINCE
PE-TCHE-LEE
OF
(HEBEI)
THE GRAND CANAL
GULF OF
PE-TCHE-LEE
(BEIZHILI)
Mia Tao (Mia dao)
Ten-tchoo
(Dengzhou)
PROVINCE OF SHAN-TUNG
(SHANDONG)
Qi-ning-tchoo
(Jining)
THE GRAND CANAL
Whang-ho (Yellow River)
YELLOW
SEA
Mouth of the Yellow River
PROVINCE OF KIANG-NAN
(JIANGNAN)
Tching-kiang (Zhenjiang)
Nan-kin
(Nanjing)
Tchang-tchoo
(Changzhou)
Mouth of the Yangtze River
Tai Hoo
(Lake Tai)
Sou-tchoo
(Suzhou)
Shanghai
Yang-tsi-kiang-ho
(Yangtze River)
Macartney's Journeys
Adapted from the Embassy's own maps, and using mostly their place names.
(Alternative, mainly modern names in brackets)
0 50 100 Miles
INNER MONGOLIA
Jehol
Peking
Tientsin
CHINA
Nanking
Ningbo
Zhoushan
Canton City
Miles
0 100 200 300

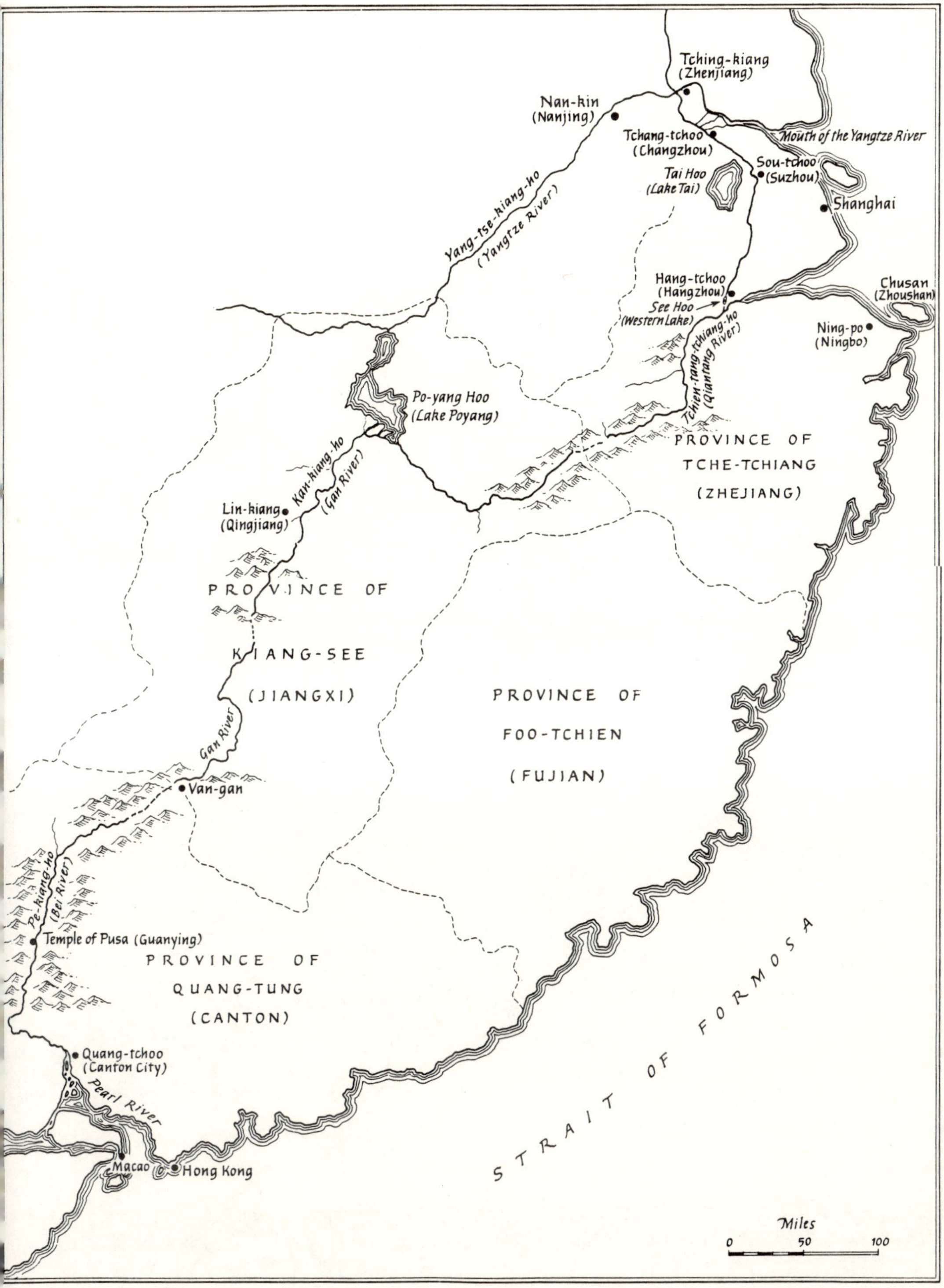

Tching-kiang
(Zhenjiang)
Nan-kin
(Nanjing)
Tchang-tchoo
(Changzhou)
Mouth of the Yangtze River
Sou-tchoo
(Suzhou)
Tai Hoo
(Lake Tai)
Shanghai
Yang-tse-kiang-ho
(Yangtze River)
Hang-tchoo
(Hangzhou)
See Hoo
(Western Lake)
Chusan
(Zhoushan)
Ning-po
(Ningbo)
Tchien-tang-tchiang-ho
(Qiantang River)
Po-yang Hoo
(Lake Poyang)
PROVINCE OF
TCHE-TCHIANG
(ZHEJIANG)
Kan-kiang-ho
(Gan River)
Lin-kiang
(Qingjiang)
PROVINCE OF
KIANG-SEE
(JIANGXI)
PROVINCE OF
FOO-TCHIEN
(FUJIAN)
Gan River
Van-gan
Pe-kiang-ho
(Bei River)
Temple of Pusa (Guanying)
PROVINCE OF
QUANG-TUNG
(CANTON)
Quang-tchoo
(Canton City)
Pearl River
Macao
Hong Kong
STRAIT OF FORMOSA
Miles
0
50
100

Prologue

Twentieth-century man knows within seconds what has just happened at the other side of the globe. This instant awareness of events thousands of miles away makes us different from our ancestors. Above all, it changes the data that go into making history. The man on the spot, for example, loses some of his status. For centuries he was of decisive importance. Being well aware of this, the most stable empire since the birth of Christ, the Celestial Empire of the Chinese, made sure that the barbarians – the peoples living beyond its sway – would have very few witnesses indeed of this extraordinary civilization that knew itself to be superior to human societies elsewhere.

By the eighteenth century, there was one other such institution that had fairly elevated ideas about its own excellence – the British Empire. Its leaders, wishing to further trade, were anxious to find out more about China. The outcome of that memorable attempt is the story of this book. But first, consider the unequal posthumous fates of the story's two protagonists.

There can be no greater contrast in vista or culture than that presented by the graveyard of Chiswick Parish Church alongside the River Thames in London and the Eastern Qing Tombs, seventy-four miles east of Peking, a walled enclave some twenty-one miles wide where are to be found, in isolated splendour, the burial sites of six of the Qing dynasty emperors of China. The crowded graveyard at Chiswick attracts few tourists. Of those who do visit, most want to see the grave of William Hogarth, the famous eighteenth-century artist. His tomb is well preserved and easily distinguishable, but inscriptions on the others have been eaten away by the atmospheric pollution from which London has suffered in varying degrees over the last two hundred years.

Thus, little attention is paid to grave no. E182, described as a 'chest tomb', whose blackened sandstone is almost indecipherable except for the barely visible name MACARTNEY. The registry of graves inside the vestry contains the inscription:

Sacred to the memory of
THE RIGHT HONOURABLE GEORGE
EARL OF MACARTNEY
PRIVY COUNSELLOR, KNIGHT OF THE HONOURABLE ORDER
OF THE BATH . . .

What the rest of the inscription contains are the gracious platitudes due to a career diplomat of stature. What it omits are any details of Macartney's career: his appointment as Envoy Extraordinary to the Court of Catherine the Great of Russia; his service in the West Indies, his capture by the French, his time in India as Governor and President of Fort St George, Madras; his Fellowship of the Royal Society; and his appointment as Ambassador to China and, finally, as Governor of the Cape of Good Hope.

In contrast, as befits one of the greatest rulers of China, the tomb of Qianlong, the fourth Qing Emperor, is magnificently preserved. It is a great attraction to tourists, who mill about among the stone animals and guardians of the Sacred Way, in the courtyards and the halls of audience. It is the more interesting because the doors of the tomb chamber itself and those of the neighbouring tomb of Empress Cixi were dynamited by the warlord Sun Tianying in 1928 – this sacrilege thus brutally exposing the Imperial way of death. Although the treasure has gone, the opulence of the buildings and the burial chamber with its bas-reliefs of Buddhas and their Manchu inscriptions is a continual source of reverential wonderment for those who crowd these halls and passageways.

Qianlong was twenty-five years old when he ascended the throne in 1736. He was not Chinese, but Manchu – a descendant of the Jurchen tribe of eastern Manchuria, who had conquered China in 1644. He believed in the warrior virtues of his forefathers, in superb horsemanship, and in archery and wrestling and the hunt as surrogates for war. He also believed in the benefits of intellect, of scholarship, literature and calligraphy. He wrote many poems in his own hand and surrounded himself with Confucian scholars as well as Jesuit missionaries skilled in the arts and sciences.* His reign proved the last period of stability for China, during which its frontiers reached their furthest point.

* The Jesuits arrived in China in 1583 following the establishment of the Portuguese trading base at Macao. After many difficulties learning the language and assimilating the customs of the country they established themselves in Peking where, with their knowledge and ability in mathematics, astronomy and mechanics and their artistic skills, they ingratiated themselves at Court.

What did Qianlong look like? There is a frontispiece portrait in the official account of the Embassy by Sir George Staunton, Macartney's Vice-Minister. Unfortunately, it is a co-operative effort, drawn by William Alexander, draughtsman to the Embassy, from sketches by Macartney and Lieutenant Henry Parish, commander of the artillery detachment accompanying the mission. Staunton writes:

> [The portrait] was made under unfavourable circumstances . . . the features of the face, which were taken by stealth and at a glance, bear a less strong resemblance [to the original] . . . To render the portrait of his Imperial Majesty more correct, it might have been proper to draw the eye more full and clear, and the countenance more open and cheerful. Such it was at least during the interview with the Ambassador . . .

The interview in question took place in 1793 in Jehol (today Chengde, two hundred miles to the north-east of Peking and then in Tartary, the Manchu homeland), where the reign of the Emperor and the career of the diplomat, after a voyage from England that had taken one year, briefly intersected in four short audiences. Of this Embassy to China, it has been observed that Macartney and his suite were received 'with the utmost politeness, treated with the utmost hospitality, watched with the utmost vigilance and dismissed with the utmost civility'. If it was the first direct contact between the British government and the Imperial Court, it was also the first link in a chain of events during which the Confucian inertia of the Middle Kingdom clashed disastrously with the thrust and vitality of the Age of Reason.

Between 1656 and 1753 six embassies had reached China – two Dutch, two Russian and two Portuguese. All but one had sought trading concessions from the Chinese, and in some degree or other they all failed. The impact of these unsuccessful adventures was not lost on the East India Company, for, like those earlier embassies, Macartney's was totally motivated by trade. Although under royal Letters of Accreditation, the enterprise was wholly financed by the East India Company. Thus it comes as no surprise that the story of these diplomatic failures and the history of Europe's relations with China were set out for Lord Macartney in a lengthy brief prepared in 1792 by a Mr Cobb of the Secretary's Office of East India House. The document carefully analysed Chinese xenophobia, pointed out that the Chinese were not expansionist, stressed that their aim was stability not change, and emphasized their fear of aggressive foreign traders. Chinese contact with the Portuguese, the Dutch and the English had provided them with many examples to justify their caution. The document also explained how the Chinese expected an embassy to behave: that no matter what might be the embassy's own perception, the Chinese, as a matter of face, would regard it as a *tributary* mission to pay homage to their Emperor, such homage to include the three deep bows and the nine knockings of the forehead against the floor – the kowtow.

The first British attempt to send an embassy had ended in 1788 when the Ambassador, Lieutenant-Colonel Cathcart, a consumptive, died at sea off Sumatra. He was a nominee of Henry Dundas, a member of the board of control of the East India Company. Since no successor had been designated, the embassy had returned without beginning its task. Then in 1791 the idea of an embassy was revived when Dundas, a friend of William Pitt, the Prime Minister, was made Home Secretary while retaining his seat on the East India Company board of control.

The reason underlying the new British Embassy was, like its predecessor, economic. By the end of the eighteenth century, trade with China was big business. Britain (and her Indian possessions) exported to Canton a wide variety of goods including cotton, broadcloth, beaver skins, glass, tin, lead, pepper, cloves, sandalwood and rattans. In turn Canton exported, in the same British ships, raw silk, nankin (a cotton cloth), chinaware, rhubarb, alum, mercury, sugar, cassia and tutenag (a form of Chinese zinc). But by far the biggest of all exports was black and green tea. Just as the British in the next thirty years were to make the Chinese addicts of opium, so the Chinese had already made the British regard tea as a necessity. In 1793 exports from England to China totalled £1,200,000, while exports from China to England were worth £1,527,775 – at eighteenth-century prices. But if British trade with China carried out under monopoly by the East India Company was lucrative, the conditions imposed by the Chinese made it particularly onerous. All trade had to be carried out from a compound of 'factories'* outside the city of Canton, and only during five months of the year. The rest of the time the traders spent cooling their heels at Macao, some twelve hours' sail away. The city of Canton was forbidden to them, and no women were allowed in the factories. No Chinese could teach them their language, under pain of death.

Worse still was the corruption built into the system. All trade had to be channelled through the Guild of Merchants, known to foreign traders as the Hong or Cohong. They were directly responsible to the Hoppo, the Collector of Customs – representing the Hubu (Minister of Finance), whose title the Hoppo was often given in error by foreigners. The post of Hoppo, in the direct gift of the Emperor, was usually given to a Manchu who, as conquerors, were disliked and distrusted by the Han Chinese, who constituted the mass of the population. The appointment was for a limited period, and the incumbent, apart from collecting the Emperor's taxes, extracted squeeze from the Hong and from the factories, and, as well as lining his own pocket, he protected his back by paying considerable bribes to the Court at Peking. The Hoppo also controlled lesser functionaries, such as the pilots who

* The 'factories' of Canton were the rented warehouses where foreign merchants lived and traded their goods.

accompanied the foreign convoys, the interpreters and the *compradores* (the ship's chandlers). At the same time, the Hoppo was answerable to the Viceroy or Governor-General of Canton province, usually a Han Chinese, whose word was law and whose edicts held sway over both Hoppo and European traders. Any appeal to the Emperor was firstly through the Hoppo and then through the Viceroy.

This system reduced the margin of profit, and made the market for British goods narrow and inflexible as well as making the foreign traders' living conditions intolerable. No wonder suspension of trade was often considered, but rejected as an option. After all, not only would a profitable and growing market be lost, but it would be left open to others. So it was decided to send an embassy from King George III, financed by the East India Company, to the Court of Emperor Qianlong at Peking – a direct appeal might succeed where local diplomacy had failed. Moreover, although it would go against Chinese wishes, the Embassy was to avoid Canton and go directly to Peking, thus making it more difficult for the Viceroy and the Hoppo to interfere.

The aims of the Embassy to China were, first, to negotiate a treaty of commerce and friendship; second, to establish an ambassador at the Court of Peking; third, to improve trading conditions in Canton; fourth, to extend British trade by opening new ports; fifth, to persuade the Chinese to cede an island base to Britain – this was to be further north, probably on the Zhoushan archipelago, closer to the tea-growing and silk-producing areas, thus reducing transport costs and provincial taxes; and sixth, to create new markets in China, especially Peking. The timing of the Embassy was chosen to coincide with Emperor Qianlong's eighty-third birthday.

The Ambassador selected, Lord Macartney of Lissanoure, was a close and trusted friend of Dundas and a diplomat of great experience who, as mentioned earlier, had served in Russia, the West Indies and India. He was a man who believed in diplomacy rather than force, though there were occasions when he accepted force of arms as a necessity. When the Embassy set out in 1792, Macartney was fifty-five years old.

To ensure a reasonable chance of success, Macartney stressed that the Embassy 'should be conducted with a certain pomp and dignity'. So he was given a ship of the line, the *Lion*, of sixty-four guns; an East-Indiaman, the *Hindostan*; and a brig, the *Jackall*. As well as various routine exports, he took with him a cargo of the most modern scientific instruments as presents for his Chinese hosts, the *pièce de résistance* being a magnificent planetarium – which was the reason he was to give for entering China via the port of Tientsin, for the overland journey could have damaged it. There was a Herschel telescope, various quadrants, a model of a man-of-war and a large lens. There were also sword blades, glass lustres, broadcloth, artillery pieces, diamond-encrusted watches, Wedgwood porcelain, two phaetons, portraits of King George and Queen Charlotte, and a book of pictures of the notables of

England and their estates.

No less impressive were the people chosen to accompany Macartney. All were highly educated products of the Age of Reason, carefully selected for the role they were to play. There was Sir George Staunton, the Vice-Minister who would take over if anything happened to Macartney, and who was to write the official account of the Embassy. His twelve-year-old son, a linguistic genius, accompanied him as Page to the Ambassador. Already fluent in Latin, Greek, French and German, Master Staunton was to learn Chinese during the voyage and use his knowledge to copy documents for the Emperor.

There were two medical doctors, Dr Hugh Gillan and Dr William Scott; two botanists, John Haxton and David Stronach; and a Scottish dominie named James Dinwiddie. His title was 'Machinest', and his role was to set up the scientific instruments and explain them to the Chinese who would take possession of them. Also included were two artists: Thomas Hickey, who was a friend of Macartney's and a portrait painter, yet was to paint only one picture throughout the trip – he was, however, rated a good conversationalist; and William Alexander, so underrated by Macartney that twice he was denied the chance to accompany the main body of the Embassy, yet made over nine hundred sketches in watercolour – almost a photographic record. There was also a mathematical instrument maker called Victor Thibault, and a watchmaker called Charles Henry Petitpierre.

In charge of the military detachments was Lieutenant-Colonel George Benson, and under him was Lieutenant Parish, who drew many plans of structures they were to encounter. J.C. Huttner, philologist, and tutor to young Staunton, because of his fluent Latin was to conduct much of the negotiation with the officials of the Court via the Jesuit missionaries. He was frequently to undertake the task of translating letters into Latin, which the Jesuits would subsequently translate into Chinese – or vice versa (from Chinese through Latin into English). There was also a band of six German musicians under one Joseph Zapfar, whose instrumentation comprised two violins, one viola, one violoncello, one hautbois, one bassoon, two basset horns, one clarinet, one German flute and one fife. Last, but not least, there were two interpreters, both Chinese Catholic converts sought out in Naples.*

In all, the Embassy consisted of ninety-five souls, the estimated cost to the East India Company being the then enormous sum of £78,000.

On Friday 21st September 1792, the Embassy boarded at Spithead off the

* Since there had been no one in England able to speak Chinese, Sir George Staunton had sent to Naples where, thanks to the intervention of Sir William Hamilton, two Chinese had been found, members of the Chinese College, who had been trained for the priesthood but who could interpret from Chinese into Latin or Italian.

Hampshire coast, the Ambassador and his suite in the *Lion* and the remainder of the Embassy in the *Hindostan*. Contrary winds detained them till the 26th, when they weighed anchor and set out down the English Channel. An equinoctial gale prevented the Ambassador calling on King George and Queen Charlotte at Weymouth, and separated the brig, the *Jackall*, from the *Lion* and the *Hindostan*, forcing the big ships to run for Torbay, where it was found that the *Lion* had sprung a leak. Not until 28th September were the shores of England left behind. The Embassy was not to return for another two years.

The outward passage reflected the measured progress of a long voyage. At the island of Madeira the Embassy's supplies of wine were taken aboard, and the expedition then sailed on to Tenerife, St Jago (capital of the Cape Verde Islands), Rio de Janeiro and Tristan da Cunha. At each port they went ashore, investigating the social life and everything and anything that caught their eye: convents in Madeira, the biology of the cochineal beetle and the prices of British goods in Rio de Janeiro, and the wingspan of the albatross at Tristan da Cunha. They continued their journey across the South Atlantic, then entered the Indian Ocean. Having called at the islands of St Paul and Amsterdam, they sailed on in a north-easterly direction towards Java. At the Straits of Sunda, after five months' sailing, to their surprise and delight they were rejoined by the missing *Jackall*, not seen since the gale in the English Channel. Next they called in at Batavia (modern Jakarta), where, in spite of stringent fumigation below decks and mixing antiscorbutic foods like sauerkraut with their regular diet, their crews came down with typhus and dysentery; the symptoms of scurvy would appear later on. On 24th May 1793, after eight months at sea, the squadron reached its first destination, Cochin China (now South Vietnam).

On 16th June they sailed from Tourane Bay (now Dà Nang) across the Gulf of Tonkin to the Ladrone Islands; then, skirting Macao and avoiding Canton, as planned, they reached the Zhoushan Islands. There they discovered two uncharted landfalls and, having named them after Staunton and Macartney, they sailed into the Gulf of Beizhili (Bohai Sea). Finally on the 20th, within two days' sail – given a good wind – of Tientsin, the ultimate destination of their sea journey, they anchored off Dengzhou in the Gulf of Beizhili.

Part One
Dagu to Jehol

1

O Brave New World!

At five o'clock on the afternoon of 20th July 1793, the flotilla – HMS *Lion*, the *Hindostan*, the *Jackall* and now the *Clarence* (another brig that had been purchased at Batavia) – anchored abreast of Dengzhou, a city of the first rank in the province of Shandong in China. Sailing up the low-lying coast, they had caught glimpses of well cultivated fields on the high ground. From their anchorage, they could make out a line of houses, crenellated walls about a mile and a half long, and a pagoda to the north of the town. Their two days of sailing from the uncharted waters of the Zhoushan Roads had been cautious and tentative. Fog on the previous evening had made them heave to for the night.

Sir Erasmus Gower, captain of the *Lion*, had little faith in the Chinese pilots who had been sent to meet them. Their inclination was to hug the shore, but the flotilla, whose draught was greater than the Chinese junks', needed to stand out to sea. What is more, the pilots were used to sailing before the wind; they had no experience of ships that could sail to windward. The anchorage, therefore, was a staging post that would give the flotilla a chance to reconnoitre the navigation of the surrounding waters, before sailing to Dagu on the mouth of the Hai River (Pei-ho), the entry to Tientsin.

Before setting foot in China, everyone on board the ships was mustered to hear a proclamation from the Ambassador: not only the sailors, soldiers, artillerymen and crews but all ninety-five members of the Ambassador's suite including the servants and musicians – fifty-six in the *Lion*, thirty-nine in the *Hindostan* – some six hundred men in all.

While the crew of the *Lion* was assembling on the foredeck, Lord Macartney of Lissanoure was in his state room preparing for the occasion. Aeneas Anderson, his valet de chambre, helped him with his dress: tight breeches and frock-coat, with sword, decorations and plumed hat. Looking at the Ambassador in the mirror, Anderson saw a handsome, tall man whose slight stiffness of movement betrayed the wear and tear of his fifty-six years. Recurring attacks of gout, two duelling wounds, the ravages of tropical climates and of eighteenth-century medicine, had all contributed to his poor health. The valet also saw, in spite of Macartney's bearing and presence, a lonely man with a cold and distant affection for his childless wife, the Earl of Bute's daughter, who for the twenty-five years of their marriage had stayed at home to look after her mother while the diplomat had travelled the world. Gossip had it that he had an eye for a pretty face. During his time at the St Petersburg Court of Catherine the Great, some scandal involving a chambermaid had reached England. But, in an age noted for corruption, Macartney had a solid reputation for integrity, probity and devotion to duty. On returning to England from Madras after serving as President and Governor of Fort St George, he was publicly praised for those virtues by both Charles James Fox and William Pitt, for his period in office was unmarked by the peculation and fraud which seemed to go with high office in the East India Company. This reputation was allied to a stolidity of character which, in turn, was leavened by considerable scholarship, political acumen and social grace. A Fellow of the Royal Society and a confidant of leading politicians, Macartney was welcomed at Court and in society – indeed, his greatest asset was his well earned popularity.

A short while later, on the deck of the *Lion*, the muster was nearly complete. The foredeck was crowded with expectant faces: nearly all had been selected or had volunteered for this voyage. As the sense of anticipation grew among the assembled ranks, Captain Gower appeared on the quarter-deck. Knighted a year earlier just before leaving Britain, he was a senior captain with twenty-eight years' worldwide service in the Royal Navy. In full naval uniform, he was more than a match for the civilian finery of the Ambassador, who stood alongside but slightly behind him. The Captain ordered his second-in-command, Lieutenant Campbell, to proceed. Raising his voice against the creak of the rigging and the slap of canvas, Campbell began to read the words that Macartney and his deputy had so carefully composed over the last few days:

> It is impossible that the various important objects of the Embassy can be obtained but through the goodwill of the Chinese, that goodwill may much depend on the ideas which they shall be induced to entertain of the disposition and conduct of the English nation, and they can judge only from the behaviour of the majority who come among us.

Macartney steadied himself against the movement of the ship. Listening to the words they had both drafted stood Sir George Staunton, doctor of medicine, amateur botanist – specimens that he sent back to Britain are still preserved in the Natural History Museum in London – fellow of the Linnean

Society and of the Royal Society, friend of Dr Johnson and of Edmund Burke, now Secretary to the Embassy and Minister Plenipotentiary in the case of the Ambassador's death. Alongside stood his son, and next to him his tutor, Herr Huttner. The proclamation continued: 'The impressions made upon Chinese minds, in consequence of the irregularities committed by Englishmen at Canton, are unfavourable even to the degree of considering them the worst among Europeans.' The same words were being delivered to all hands on board the *Hindostan*, anchored across the bay: 'These impressions are communicated to that tribunal in the capital which reports to and advises the Emperor upon all concerns with foreign countries.'

James Dinwiddie, forty-seven, Scots 'Machinest' and self-made autodidact, was employed not only to erect and demonstrate those presents that leant heavily on the Enlightenment's penchant for natural philosophy, but also to construct, fill and ascend in a balloon, operate a diving bell and give lectures. He possessed a missionary zeal to imprint on the supposed scientific *tabula rasa* of China the rationality of the clockwork universes in his care. If his fragile charges – planetarium, orreries, globes and much else – all survived the sea journey and the subsequent jolting of offloading and road travel, he had no doubt whatsoever that Chinese amazement at the Cartesian confrontation of the Confucian would make a major contribution to the certain success of the Embassy.

His colleague, William Alexander, the twenty-six-year-old draughtsman to the Embassy, excitedly anticipated the visual promise of things to come. Although not the senior artist, his drawings were to bring the Embassy alive for posterity. Outward-bound, he had already drawn and painted some 270 sketches, and he cannot have failed to look forward to the opportunities to be offered to his talent by China. In spite of the importance of the announcement from the quarter-deck, his attention could not help wandering towards the shoreline, the pagoda of Dengzhou and the junks sailing around the flotilla, his eye taking in the myriad details of faces, clothes, posture, landscape, flags, shield bosses, arms and those who bore them.

The oration continued, stressing that the Chinese authorities would support the humblest Chinese in any differences with a stranger, and citing the recent case of the gunner on an English vessel in Canton who, in firing a salute, had accidentally killed a Chinese. The authorities had insisted that the gunner be handed over for execution by strangulation. Aeneas Anderson, valet de chambre, a man sensitive to nuance, shuddered. But worse was to come: 'If offence should be offered to a Chinese, or a misdemeanour of any kind be committed, which may be punishable by their laws, the Ambassador will not deem himself bound to interfere for the purpose of endeavouring to ward off or mitigate their severity.' Anderson shuddered again, not only because he feared the draconian punishment of Chinese law, but because he sensed that he, a gentleman's servant, was being placed under British martial law, whose field punishments were equally severe. Yet more fundamental liberties were to be denied: 'None of the mechanics or servants are to leave the ship without leave from His Excellency or Commanding Officer. No boxes or packages are to be removed from the ship or . . . from the place where they shall be brought on shore without permission of the Ambassador.'

John Barrow, the Comptroller, who bore responsibility for the numerous packages that made up the presents and stores, sensing something of an Anglo-Chinese thieves' kitchen around him, nodded. At that moment, the proclamation reached its central point:

> None of the suite, guard, mechanics or servants should presume to offer for sale or propose to purchase in the way of traffic the smallest article of merchandise of any kind under any pretence whatsoever . . . The necessity of avoiding the least appearance of traffic . . . was such as to deter the East India Company from shipping any goods for sale in the Hindostan . . . if any transaction for the purpose of gain should be discovered . . . amongst any attending or conveying an Ambassador . . . the report would soon swell into a general system of trading.

This stricture was most unpopular with Captain Mackintosh, Master of the *Hindostan*: it deprived him of his right to conduct private trade, a perquisite allowed to commanders of East-Indiamen. Already, he had held one tense conversation with Macartney on the subject. With a free transit allowance of fifty-six tons of trade goods, he had too much at stake to take this last restriction with equanimity. The proclamation ended with a threat:

> His Excellency is bound to punish the slightest deviation from this regulation; he will have it in his power in regard to the persons in his train or services. The discipline of the Navy will render it easy to Sir Erasmus Gower in respect of those under his immediate command, and the East India Company have fully authorised His Excellency to enforce compliance, with the same regulation among the officers of the Hindostan.

After wielding the big stick, the Ambassador's proclamation ended with an emollient promise to award merit.

Lieutenant Campbell stepped down and ordered the master-at-arms to clear the deck. The threat of martial discipline was not unfamiliar to soldiers and seafarers. And although the Ambassador's train and the civilian artisans felt affronted by the threat of corporal punishment and by being placed under military law, they had no choice but to accept the situation.

That evening, the Governor of Dengzhou chose to visit Macartney, to present his compliments. Immediately, the interpreters were sent for.*

---

* The Embassy had left England with two interpreters on board. One of them, Padre Zhou, frightened that on arrival in Peking he would be punished for having left China, left the Embassy at Macao. The other, Mr Plumb, remained with the Embassy and served it faithfully throughout.

There were now three of them: two Chinese priests who had been given passage from Macao to Peking, and the official Embassy interpreter, Father Jacobus Li, or 'Mr Plumb'. (The family name Li means 'plum tree' in Chinese, hence the British calling him Mr Plumb.)

To the shrill of bos'ns' pipes and nautical honours, the Governor, the first mandarin of high rank to be met by the Embassy, boarded the *Lion*. All eyes were on the flowing robes, the embroidered breast cloth, the coloured ball, denoting rank, on the hat and the long queue of hair – the symbol of dominance forced on the Han Chinese by their Manchu conquerors. They also noted, with surprise, the obsequiousness of the kneeling bow and the knocking of the forehead on the floor by one of his entourage when he addressed the Governor. 'This did not seem to proceed from any particular haughtiness on the one part or abjectness on the other, but indicated the respective disposition . . . established for inducing habits of subordination,' George Staunton presciently observed. But the sight that met the Chinese must have been no less startling. Here was a black-and-white world of holystoned decks, tarred rigging, coiled rope and furled sails which constituted the military precision of a man-of-war's gun deck. The sailors in their jack tar uniforms, and the Embassy's guard in their powdered wigs, made an aisle to lead the Governor aft to the Ambassador's quarters.

Governor and Ambassador met at the head of the companion-way. Mr Plumb relished his task. So far, there had been little chance to interpret for the Ambassador, but now the Latin equivalents of the Governor's preamble rolled off his tongue. Macartney had little difficulty in following this lingua franca, though the overlay of a Neapolitan accent on Chinese tonality at times strained understanding. First from Chinese into Latin, the words were then converted from Latin into English. Continuing his speech, the Governor imperiously gestured a mandarin forward, who then knelt down and presented to the Ambassador a golden cylinder beribboned in yellow silk. The Governor repeated the gesture, and another cylinder was reverentially presented. Macartney passed these offerings to Staunton, who in turn handed them to Mr Plumb.

Of this meeting there is little record. The Governor was 'thirty-five years of age, courteous, intelligent and inquisitive,' Macartney recorded. He declined the Governor's invitation to go ashore to watch entertainments and plays that would 'correspond in small degree to the splendid reception planned at the Imperial Court'. The golden cylinders turned out to contain scrolls about five feet long, made of orange paper embossed with the Imperial dragon: they were rescripts from Emperor Qianlong addressed to the Ambassador and to Mackintosh of the *Hindostan*:

To Macartney and others of England, country of the red hairs, newly appointed Minister of State. You have been blown by the wind and billows and moored on our shores, suffering from shortage of food and seeking safety and provisions. The

Court extends to all merchant ships of all countries that come to the southern shore from far across the sea, protection of life and well being and permission to provision themselves. Conscious of your circumstances of shortage, the Heavenly Court has made a special order of three thousand pecks of grain for your journey's needs and trading purposes and, moreover, bestows on the Ambassador a pair of ivory tusks and five loads of black pepper as a token of our good faith.

First contact had been made.

21st July The Governor of Dengzhou far exceeded the spirit of the Imperial rescript. At noon, food in abundance was sent out to the ships. John Barrow took note as each package and each protesting animal was winched on board: four bullocks, eight sheep, eight goats, five measures of white rice, five measures of red rice, two hundred pounds of flour and several baskets of fruit and vegetables.

Sir Erasmus Gower, hearing the noise, was delighted that fresh food, including antiscorbutic additions to the diet, was now on board. The symptoms of scurvy – swollen gums and painfully inflamed joints – and the acute dysentery contracted in Batavia by many of his crew made it essential to land the Embassy as soon as possible, and then find an anchorage for the *Lion* where he could get the sick ashore and fumigate the vessel; he was also worried that the weather might deteriorate. He did not think he would find a safe anchorage in the Gulf of Beizhili: Zhoushan, from which they had sailed a month ago, would be the best place to set up a hospital for the sick members of the crew. In turn, permission needed to be sought from the Chinese before he could land there and bring everyone ashore, for this was forbidden at any port other than Canton.

Meanwhile, immediately after reading the proclamation, Lieutenant Campbell had been dispatched with Huttner in the *Jackall* to explore the navigation towards Tientsin. A new Chinese pilot, about seventy years of age, now came on board the *Lion*. He assured Captain Gower that the Gulf was always safe for weather in the months of July, August and September and that the boats for carrying the baggage and the presents were now ready at Dagu at the mouth of the Hai River leading to Tientsin. 'The boats are large and convenient, and so constructed that there is no danger to our packages being wetted or damaged,' he added.

That evening Lord Macartney and his suite were joined by the East India Company brig, the *Endeavour*, ordered by the Company Commissioners stationed at Macao to sail up the coast and seek the Embassy. Carrying the mail (now six months old) from Britain, the *Endeavour* was to accompany them to Tientsin and return with their latest dispatches. Next morning, at first light, the enlarged flotilla sailed from Dengzhou for Dagu.

Wednesday 31st July Comings and goings! The *Jackall* returned safely from Tientsin. Huttner reported that all was ready there to receive the Embassy. He also reported that he had been closely cross-questioned about the composition of the Embassy and, above all, about the presents they had brought with them. Great expectations had been raised. The Chinese at Tientsin believed the packages in the hold of the *Hindostan* to be of immense value.

Macartney was worried about this question of presents. He knew that the East India Company had assembled the most prestigious array possible, but just as he had had to forbid private trade, so too he wanted to ensure that any gifts brought along as a private venture by his suite or any of the ships' officers would not outshine the official ones. He argued that if any such privately owned goods were sold to a Chinese merchant who subsequently sent them to the Hoppo, the Collector of Customs, as a bribe to be passed on to the Emperor as a gift, they would diminish the impact of the official offerings. Mr Browne, one of the senior East India Company Commissioners, was therefore persuaded, when visited by Sir George Staunton at Macao, to give up the Herschel telescope that he had exported for trade, and Captain Mackintosh of the *Hindostan* was coaxed into selling to the Embassy, at cost price, the sixteen-inch burning lens made by William Parker which had been brought along as a speculative trading venture.

Nor was this all. Junior mandarins ashore wanted to purchase some of the sword blades and watches that the travellers had with them. In spite of Macartney making it clear that the Embassy was not there to trade, something had to be done in the interest of goodwill. There were some small presents still parcelled in the hold of the *Hindostan*, so Macartney made arrangements to acquire these items from the officers of that ship, who had brought them in the hope of trade.

At midday, seven junks came alongside. Two mandarins of high rank were in attendance. This is how Staunton described their arrival:

> These mandarins, it seems, had never before been on salt water. They had never seen a ship of the Lion's construction, bulk or loftiness. They were at a loss as to how to ascend her sides, but chairs were quickly fastened to tackles by which they were lifted up, while they felt a mixture of dread and admiration at this easy, rapid but apparently perilous conveyance.

These two mandarins, one civil and one military, were to accompany the party throughout their long journey. They would become loyal friends to Lord Macartney. Their names, as transliterated by the Embassy, were Cho-ta-gin (Qiao Renjie) and Van-ta-gin (Wang Wenxiong).

Since they are to assume major importance, a word on their background is in order. Qiao was born in the province of Shanxi. After passing the Imperial examinations at the provincial level, he became a district magistrate.

At the time of the Embassy's arrival he held a senior post in the provincial government at Tientsin. Wang was born in Guizhou, entered the Army and rose through the ranks. He fought in Burma and Yunnan, and was wounded in 1775. Subsequently promoted, when Macartney met him he was Commander of the garrison at Tongzhou, the town where the Embassy would ultimately disembark for Peking.

The two Chinese stepped from the bos'n's chairs, resplendent in full regalia. (William Alexander was to paint them later.) Wang carried a bow and a full quiver. On his bonnet he wore a badge of rank, a red button, and a peacock feather given to him by the Emperor for his courage in battle; Qiao wore a blue button. Each belonged to one of the top four classes of mandarin. Staunton tells us that Wang and Qiao 'were forcibly struck with the orderly as well as martial appearance upon the Lion's deck, the size and elegance of the great cabin fitted up for the Ambassador into which they were introduced, as well as the multiplied conveniences throughout the ship.' They greeted Macartney, presented the Emperor's congratulations on the completion of a safe journey, and informed him that their task was to conduct the Embassy to the Imperial Court. (A third, senior, conducting officer, a Tartar called Zhengrui who was the Salt Administrator at Tientsin, being frightened of the sea had not accompanied his junior colleagues. To their cost, the Embassy were to meet him on arrival at Tientsin.)

Now, on the deck of the *Lion*, a farmyard cacophony marked the arrival of more food. This delivery was five times as large as the previous one, John Barrow agitatedly told the Ambassador: twenty bullocks, 120 sheep, 120 hogs, 100 fowls, 100 ducks, 160 bags of flour, fourteen boxes of Tartar bread, ten chests of tea and one thousand each of water and musk melons and squash. So far above the Embassy's needs was this second provisioning that the greater part had to be reloaded on to the junks and returned.

In the state cabin, the Ambassador had much to discuss with Wang and Qiao. It was agreed that the unloading of presents would begin the next day. When asked if the letter he was bearing from King to Emperor had been translated into Chinese, Macartney decided it would be prudent to maintain his reserve until they arrived in the capital. So he replied that the original, together with the translation, was locked in a golden box to be delivered by him directly into the Emperor's hand. The mandarins were equally solicitous about the presents, demanding formally that a full list be made for transmission to Peking. On the British side there was a feeling that an ordinary catalogue would not communicate the originality, the quality or the worth of the gifts. Moreover, they might be misunderstood through clumsy translation; or, worse still, these carefully selected gifts might be confused with the kind of clockwork toys and 'sing-songs' (mechanical automata) that were 'more glittering than useful'. It was decided that the name of each artefact would be broken down into syllables corresponding with a Chinese character and embellished 'in an oriental style', in the hope that such description would reveal their true worth.

'His Britannic Majesty has been careful to select only such articles as might denote the progress of science and of the arts of Europe,' went the preamble to the catalogue, ending with the cautious qualification that 'the intent and spirit of the accompanying presents, not the presents themselves, are chiefly of value between sovereigns'. All this, of course, was first translated into Latin before being retranslated into Chinese. Then came the catalogue itself. The planetarium (Pu-la-ni-ta-li-weng) demonstrated

> the utmost effort in astronomical science and mechanic art ever made in Europe. It shows with great exactness the several motions of the earth . . . likewise the moon, the sun and the planets which surround it; the particular system of the planet Jupiter which has four moons . . . Also the planet Saturn together with the eclipses, conjunctions and oppositions of heavenly bodies . . . This machine is calculated for a thousand years.

The Herschel (He-zhi-er) telescope was 'for observing distant and minute bodies in the heavens . . . not by looking directly at the object but by perceiving sideways the reflection of such objects upon mirrors . . . as invented by a great astronomer Newton and improved by an excellent astronomer called Herschel . . . both deserve their names should reach to his Imperial Majesty.' Continuing in this vein, the document went on to list celestial and terrestrial globes, quadrants, watches and clocks, a barometer, an air-pump, brass cannon, muskets, sword blades, pistols, a model of the largest British man-of-war (110 guns), Wedgwood porcelain and Derbyshire vases and figures, glass lustres for candelabra (for use in palaces), Parker's big lens, an orrery by Fraser, woollen and cotton goods, paintings of the British aristocracy and their houses, portraits of King George and Queen Charlotte, and two phaetons.

While Huttner and the two missionaries worked on the translation in one part of the ship, the mandarins were offered the full hospitality of the Ambassador's quarters. The Chinese have always loved banquets, and although the handling of knives and forks caused problems, Macartney's journal noted it as 'a difficulty that disappeared as for the first time they tasted of rum, gin, arrack, shrub, raspberry and cherry brandy'. Like Englishmen, Wang and Qiao shook hands as they left, stopping on the quarter-deck to admire the guard of marines drawn up in their honour and to listen to the music provided by the band. 'They departed,' said Macartney, 'much pleased by our manner of entertaining them!'

Friday 2nd August revealed a sea filled with the sails of junks clustering around the *Lion* and the *Hindostan*. Twin-masted and square-sailed, twenty-five sea-going vessels each of some two hundred tons burthen were provided by the mandarins to take the Embassy's baggage and presents over the sand-bar to Dagu, for transfer to the barges that would convey them up the Hai River and the Grand Canal to Tongzhou.

In spite of the pilot's promise, a spectacular thunderstorm three nights earlier had made them worry that the good weather was about to break. A bad bottom and an exposed shoreline rendered a permanent anchorage dangerous, so Macartney made new orders for the ships as the unloading went on.

The original plan had been for the *Hindostan* to sail to Canton, there to take on a cargo for Britain. However, since she had once again to sail past Zhoushan on the way it was desirable she should call in there. As Zhoushan was a port of call closed to British shipping, it might be possible to pick up a cargo of tea and silks from the neighbouring provinces on more advantageous terms than those available in Canton. So Macartney told Mackintosh that he could accompany the Embassy to Peking. But instead of the expected expression of gratitude, Mackintosh, to Macartney's annoyance, raised yet again the question of his 'right' to trade privately. Not only had he brought his full free-freight allowance of fifty-six tons of trade goods, he had also brought his own personal carriage. 'He may come to Peking if he pleases, but merely from curiosity not from trade,' Macartney noted. 'Expressed my answer at his putting the chariot on board the junk and told him it must go back . . . he has behaved very ill in this matter!'

The disposal of the *Lion* during the Embassy's stay in China presented another problem. They knew of no harbour sufficiently secure for her to winter in the Gulf of Beizhili. In any case, the very thought of wintering in a Chinese port gave concern. What would happen if the crew misbehaved on shore? How would this affect the Embassy? Might not any such misbehaviour give the Chinese a reason for seeking the Embassy's premature departure? Since Macartney's instructions for after the Peking mission were to try to open trade with Japan, it was decided to send the *Lion* on a reconnaissance to that country. However, this could not begin until the crew had recovered from the combined effects of scurvy and dysentery from which they were still suffering. Hence Sir Erasmus Gower would first take the *Lion* back to Zhoushan to prepare for the exploratory voyage in the hope of departing before the start of the typhoon season.

Dispositions made, Macartney prepared to go ashore at Dagu on the following day. He was pleased with the way things had gone so far, and particularly with the manner in which the presents had been handled. He marvelled at the strength, ability and resource of the Chinese sailors. He noted: 'All the Chinese we have seen have their heads close shaven, except on the crown where the hair is left untouched by the razor for about a couple of inches in diameter and is suffered to grow to a very great length, plaited in a tress a yard long and being considered as a very becoming ornament.' He was, of course, describing the queue. The dominance of which the queue was a symbol – a continual source of friction between Chinese and Manchu – was to keep surfacing throughout the Embassy's dealings in China – as Macartney was about to discover.

5th August On this day, the Embassy vacated the ships that had been their home for nearly a year. At 8am Erasmus Gower gave the command to 'man the yards'. On both the *Lion* and the *Hindostan* all hands, dressed for the occasion in number one uniform, climbed the rigging and spread out along the spars. At 9 o'clock a nineteen-gun salute was fired, and the sound of cheers drifted with the gun smoke across the spring tide. The Ambassador and his suite, in the brigs *Clarence, Jackall* and *Endeavour*, led a long convoy of twenty junks towards the sand-bar at the mouth of the Hai River. It was a six-hour journey. The low-lying land on which Dagu was built did not become visible, except for a few tall buildings, until they came within two miles of the shore.

Crossing the muddy water of the bar posed no problem. Then, beyond the clear water ahead of them, the Chinese military could be seen lined up in salute along the bank, whilst the junks dropped anchor in anticipation that the Ambassador would want to go ashore. Macartney carefully examined the uninviting prospect of salt marsh and reed – Staunton's botanical knowledge provides the name, *Arundo phragmites* – and, declining the offer of a banquet, he decided to continue up river to join the ambassadorial barge which there awaited him.

The convoy sailed on, continually tacking and warping to avoid frequent shoals and sand-bars. At 4 o'clock they reached their destination: the fleet of barges that would take them on the last leg of their journey to Peking.

In his journal, for the sake of his future readers Macartney compared what he saw with England: 'The river here appeared to be as broad as the Thames at Gravesend. Great numbers of houses on each side, built of mud and thatched, a good deal resembling the cottages near Christchurch in Hampshire.' Reasonable comparison stopped short at the next sentence: 'But inhabited by such swarms of people as far exceeded my most extravagant ideas even of Chinese population.' The Embassy was taken aback by the size of the crowds, who not only lined the bank but, in order to get a better view, stood up to their waists in the water. 'Men well-looking, well-limbed, robust and muscular . . . Women who tripped along with such agility as induced us to imagine their feet had not been crippled in the usual manner of the Chinese . . . children numerous, happy and almost stark naked.'

Quite overwhelmed by their reception, Macartney resorted to quoting Shakespeare:

> O wonder!
> How many goodly creatures are there here!
> How beauteous mankind is! O brave new world
> That has such people in't!

Well might he quote from the *Tempest*: Caliban was waiting on the shore.

2

Obeisance and Precedence: Presents or Tribute?

From Dagu to Tientsin, up the serpentine bends of the Hai River, was eighty miles. The Ambassador's barge was most spaciously fitted out. Divided into antechamber, saloon and bedroom, his quarters took up most of the vessel. In the saloon, Macartney relaxed on the pile of cushions – 'a square sopha as is found in the houses of every chief mandarin', according to Staunton – reflecting on the events of the last few days and how they would affect the immediate future. He sensed that the first moves could be critical. A lifetime in diplomacy had taught him the importance of preparation, presence and protocol, of behaviour matching if not amplifying the dignity of office. If the Viceroy of Tientsin was waiting on shore, what then was expected of him? Who took precedence over whom?

As the sun moved round in the cabin, Macartney permitted himself a wry reflection: that the Chinese were probably having the same thoughts. Everything pointed to foreknowledge and preparation: the Imperial rescripts containing Qianlong's restrained welcome, the conducting mandarins, the copious food, the watching multitudes. What had been going on in Chinese minds?

Court documents made available 140 years after the event partially tell the story. First, a letter dated 27th April 1792 from Francis Baring, the Chairman of the East India Company, to the Viceroy of the province of Canton, tells us:

> Having heard that it had been expected his subjects settled in Canton in the Chinese empire should have sent a deputation to the Court of Peking in order to congratulate the Emperor on his entering into the eightieth year of his age, and that such deputation had not been immediately despatched, His Majesty [George III] expressed great displeasure thereat.

The letter stated that in the hope of improving

> the connection, intercourse and good correspondence between the Courts of London and Peking and extending the commerce between their respective subjects, he has resolved to send . . . Lord Macartney . . . as his Ambassador Extraordinary and Plenipotentiary to the Emperor of China . . .
>
> The Ambassador with his attendants will very soon set out on his voyage, and having several presents for the Emperor of China from the King of Great Britain which, from their size, nice mechanism and value could not be conveyed through the interior of the country with so great a distance as from Canton to Peking without the risk of much damage and injury, will proceed directly and without delay in one of His Majesty's ships properly accompanied to the Port of Tientsin . . . We request, therefore, that you will please convey this information to the Court of Peking.

This letter was handed to the Viceroy on 18th October, nearly a month after the Embassy had set sail, by three East India Company Commissioners appointed to prepare the ground for the Embassy after they, in turn, had duly made contact with the Hoppo and followed the prescribed route through the Chinese bureaucracy. This communication, neatly calculated, created many problems for that bureaucracy. Thus, on 15th November the Viceroy of Canton and the Hoppo memorialized the Emperor. First, they noted the reception of the delegation, then stated its purpose:

> Since the year before last Your Majesty happily reached your eightieth year and both inside and outside China there was great rejoicing, and from every frontier barbarian kings and chieftains flocked to the capital so that, in fact throughout the ages, there never has been such a great occasion, now the King of England has sent an envoy sailing across the oceans on a distant voyage to offer congratulation on the Imperial birthday . . . only, whenever any barbarians happen to present tribute they always forward from the port of the province at which they are customarily allowed to enter a copy of the state message and the list of tribute . . . to the Governor General [Viceroy of Canton] . . . The English have all along been coming to Canton to trade, yet now they want to go to the port of Tientsin. Also, no copy of the state message or list of tribute has been provided . . . the petition was merely sent in the name of that country's Chief Controller of Trade, Folangxisi Bailing [Francis Baring] . . . Your servants have enquired what the articles consist of and when the ship left. According to what the barbarian delegation said when they set out on their journey, the tribute ships had not yet left . . . they were still being prepared . . . many of the presents are heavy and if they were to go by the water and overland route from Canton it would be a long journey and they are afraid lest they should be damaged.
>
> If we notify the king to order them to go to Canton and there await an edict and then act in accordance with it, the ocean is vast and no one knows how long it will take to transmit. Moreover, they say they are going to the port of Tientsin and they are unable to send to find out any details.

The document had been endorsed, in the Imperial vermilion ink: 'Immediately there will be an Imperial Edict.'

On 24th July 1793 a Court letter was sent to the Viceroy of Beizhili (the province in which Peking is situated) and to Zhengrui, the Salt Administrator at Tientsin and senior conducting mandarin deputed to escort the Embassy.

When dealing with barbarians one ought to strike the mean between being too lavish or too frugal . . . The practice of the provinces is either to err in doing too much or not enough. This time, when the English Tribute Envoy arrives, although the entertainments as a whole should not be more elaborate than those set by precedent, yet since the Tribute Envoy will have sailed from far across the sea, and it will be the first time of visiting our illustrious country, he should not be classed with Burma or Annam and other places which come to pay tribute every year.

On 3rd August, three days before Macartney set foot in China, a draft document from the Grand Council* was submitted to the Emperor for his consideration.

We have now drafted an Edict to the country of England which we now submit. As soon as it has been sent down it should be translated into Manchu and Western characters [i.e., Latin] and again submitted [to the Grand Council]. It should then be reverently copied out and as soon as the Tribute Envoy sets out to return to his country, it should be given him in accordance with precedent.

Drafted by some unknown master in classical Chinese, this edict was to dominate the routine administrative dealings between the British Embassy and their Chinese hosts. There is no telling what Macartney would have done had he been aware of its existence, for in its cold authoritarian courtesy it rejected all of the Embassy's proposals.

The problems of protocol that had so exercised the Ambassador sorted themselves out. The conducting mandarin, Wang, announced that two palanquins and a troop of cavalry awaited them, and so on Tuesday 6th August at 8am Macartney, Staunton and young Staunton, in full diplomatic finery and accompanied by their interpreter, crossed the bridge between the barge and shore at Dagu and climbed into the waiting palanquins. Pennants waving, the escorting troops, each with a bow and quiver slung across his shoulder, accompanied them to the Temple of the Sea God where the Viceroy of Beizhili awaited them. 'He was tottering with age, but not less dignified than he was venerable', observed Staunton. Macartney was captivated: 'It is impossible to describe the ease, politeness and dignity of the Viceroy. He is a fine old man of seventy-eight years of age, of low stature, with small sparkling

* The Grand Council, established in 1729, acted as filter between the top layer of bureaucracy and the Emperor. There were five or six Grand Councillors. A tight-knit body, it worked in secrecy, dealing with some fifty memorials a day. Having read a memorial, the Emperor would decide the course of action. After discussion with the Councillors, the Imperial decision would be made known either as a separate edict or as an endorsement to the memorial, in vermilion ink. (Cranmer-Byng, *An Embassy to China 1793-1794*, p. 28.)

eyes, a benign aspect and a long silver beard, the whole of his appearance calm, venerable and dignified.'

The conversation at the audience followed what Macartney was to learn to recognize as the pattern of formalized civility. First, over cups of tea, came the endless compliments, from Chinese to Latin and from Latin to Chinese. They were complimented on their ships and on the splendour of the Embassy, and told of the anticipation of the presents, and of the rumours of their number and their magnificence. They answered inquiries about the length of the voyage and their health. In the middle of these proceedings, Macartney's attention wandered to his surroundings: the magnificence of the buildings of Dagu 'much resembled those in my book of Chinese drawings'; the brilliance and variety of the decoration 'on a nearer inspection I found . . . to be of porcelain and tiles of various mould and colours'. But his reverie was abruptly curtailed: 'It is the Emperor's wish that they visit him at Jehol in Tartary [where the Court always resided at this season] as soon as possible.' Thus compliment elided into business, or so it seemed.

Macartney informed the Viceroy that there were ninety-five persons in the train of the Embassy: together with the presents in the baggage, this meant they would need spacious quarters in Peking. Since it was necessary to go to Jehol, the bulkier presents would have to be left behind because it would be impossible to transport them over the distance without damaging or even destroying them. Moreover, the *Lion* and the *Hindostan* both needed safe anchorage. There were some six hundred men aboard the vessels, and much sickness among the *Lion*'s crew. Her Captain needed a letter of authorization to enlist the co-operation of the coastal authorities in allowing them to anchor at either Miao dao or Zhoushan, for 'the advancing season required his speedy departure from the gulf of Pe-tche-lee [Beizhili]'.

The Viceroy was graciousness itself. Imagining that the long voyage must have exhausted the ships' stores, he offered to provide them with a year's provisions immediately. Macartney hoped this did not presage his wish for the Embassy's early departure. He stressed his wish to ensure the success of his mission by all means within his power, and invoked the advice of the Viceroy on the protocol and ceremonial to be observed at Court. There is no record of any reply to this request. Perhaps none was forthcoming – after all, the Viceroy knew what was in store.

The Chinese having first made sure that they gave thanks for a safe journey in Chinese fashion, they left the temple of the Sea God and returned to their barges. Here they discovered that the Viceroy had provided a 'magnificent and plentiful' celebratory banquet to mark the occasion.

The journey resumed. By sunset, the salt-pans of the Hai estuary were drifting past Macartney's saloon windows. (He noted that his was the only barge to have windows of glass, whereas the others had to make do with paper.) He went out on deck. The twenty-five junks carrying the Embassy and its baggage followed astern. Progress was very slow: the river wound interminably round ox-bow bends, and a favourable wind on one stretch became adverse on another. As they passed the mud huts of the villages, dotted along the banks, the people turned out to greet them, the children running along to keep up with the flotilla. Night and day, the junks would signal to each other and to the shore by beating brass gongs. Alongside each village stood great pyramids of sacks, the harvest of the salt-pans. Barrow, the Comptroller, who liked to demonstrate his propensity for figures, did a complicated calculation to show that some six hundred million pounds of salt were in store there – enough for thirty million people for one year, and enough to provide the Imperial exchequer with a healthy tax revenue.

At dusk, the lanterns of a nearby village lit up the waterway. Pretty though the sight was, it was no time to be on deck: the mosquitoes, buzzing and biting in their thousands, drove Macartney back into the saloon. Thus the Embassy settled down for their first night on the Hai River, to get what sleep they could against the beating of the gongs and the biting of the insects.

11th August Arrival at Tientsin: it had taken four and a half days to cover eighty miles. They tied up at a quay in the middle of the town before the Viceroy of Beizhili's pavilion, opposite which had been erected a theatre where, for several hours without intermission, a company of actors put on a variety of pantomime and drama performances in their honour.

The city seemed *en fête*. For nearly a mile, both sides of the river were lined with troops. Flags, standards and pennants fluttered in the strong breeze, accompanied by the warlike clangour of various musical instruments. At noon, the Ambassador and his suite disembarked. Once again, the Viceroy of Beizhili received them, having travelled overland (half the distance of the winding river) for the reception. But there was now a stranger in the Viceroy's entourage – Zhengrui, the Tartar legate and senior conducting mandarin who took precedence over Wang and Qiao, and who was destined to play a sinister part in the progress of the Embassy. His career had been varied: he was currently the Salt Administrator at Tientsin (as we noted earlier), and had been Superintendent of the Imperial silk factory at Suzhou before that.

The prevailing mood now changed. The friendly tone of the last meeting had, without ostensible change of attitude, cooled. Along with the members of his suite, Macartney was led to a darkened recess at the back of the pavilion. 'The Majesty of the Emperor resides here,' he was informed, 'and to that Majesty a respectful obeisance should be paid by a profound inclination of the body.' Nothing like this had been raised before – the Viceroy had not proposed the kowtow at their previous meetings. It was the first inkling of the effect that the presence of the Tartar legate could have. The Europeans watched the Chinese obeisance: three times kneeling, and nine times knocking the head on the floor. Taken aback by the humiliating nature of this ceremony, Macartney removed his hat and made a formal bow, which was instantly imitated by his suite. They hoped that this would satisfy the immediate demands of protocol, at least until they had had time to digest the meaning of the performance. Then the conversation began to follow the pattern that Macartney had already noted at his first audience with the Viceroy.

First, the compliments: a repeat of the previous two days' performance – gracious comments on the arduous voyage, the size of the Embassy, the value of the presents and the hopes for the outcome of the mission. Then came the particulars, 'during which,' wrote Macartney in his journal, 'I easily discovered a perverse and unfriendly disposition in the Legate towards all our concerns, and which struck me the more forcibly when compared with the urbanity and graciousness of his superior'. The travel plans were laid before them. They were to go up to Tongzhou, some twelve miles from Peking – a seven-day voyage, arriving on 18th August. From there they were to travel by land to Peking. The unloading and transshipping arrangements meant that they would not reach Peking until the 26th. Once there, Macartney proposed ten days to 'repose themselves, to settle the family, to separate the presents and prepare for the six to eight day journey to Zhe-hol [Jehol] in Tartary'. The planetarium, the globes, the great lens, the lustres and the clocks would be left behind at Peking, to avoid damage. Also left behind in Peking would be certain members of the Ambassador's suite – exactly who was yet to be announced.

Macartney sensed general agreement to these plans. Only the Tartar legate demurred. Choosing this point in the proceedings to drop his diplomatic mask and assume the air of importance appropriate to a Tartar overlord and senior mandarin, he now informed the gathering that the Emperor would like to see all the presents delivered to Jehol at the same time.

Appalled by the apparent ignorance and obduracy of the legate, after restating the situation several times, the Ambassador once again explained the delicacy of the nature and the mechanism of some of the presents. But Zhengrui insisted – an insistence that Macartney suspected might constitute an attempt either to avoid losing face or to persuade the assembled company that the presents could indeed be taken overland without damage, thus obviating the necessity of the 'illegal' avoidance of Canton and the use of Tientsin as port of entry. For once, Macartney was grateful for the laboriousness of translation, which gave him time to think. Having considered the contretemps, he delivered the following reply:

> Certainly, the Emperor is omnipotent in China and might dispose of everything in it as he pleases. However, the articles we propose should be left in Peking would almost certainly be totally spoiled if managed according to his notion. Would Zhengrui, therefore, take all the presents entirely into his own hands, thus removing from the Embassy the responsibility for presenting anything in an imperfect or damaged state!

Fortunately, at this moment the Viceroy interceded and chose to disagree with the legate, who had to acquiesce in the original arrangements. But, recalled Macartney later, 'I could not avoid feeling great disquiet and apprehension from this untoward disposition.' They then left through the triumphal arches of the Viceroy's pavilion, with the martial music fading in their ears until only the sound of the horses' hooves of their escorts could be heard. On their return to the junks, for the second time in five days they found a magnificent banquet laid out for them.

Macartney's journal recording the incident in the pavilion assumes that his dislike of Zhengrui was cordially returned. We have evidence that it was. For his part, Macartney felt, the Tartar legate wanted maliciously to thwart the plans of the Embassy. On the other hand, Zhengrui was a bureaucratic mediocrity, frightened for his career because his every move was being watched by the Imperial Court. He was, after all, the senior of the three conducting mandarins appointed to serve the needs of the Embassy and to make daily reports of progress, behaviour and such other intelligence as could be gleaned. Had Macartney seen the exchange of correspondence on the Chinese side, he would have had a better understanding of the 'untoward disposition' displayed by Zhengrui. The legate had, for instance, written to the great Gelao Heshen, Grand Secretary and Chief Minister at the Imperial Court, complaining that Macartney and Staunton considered themselves of high rank and 'worthy to meet others on an equal footing'. It would, therefore, be improper for Zhengrui to visit them first. So it was that he had ordered Wang and Qiao to go on board the *Lion* to obtain the letter from King George to the Emperor and the list of presents.

Heshen was a favourite of the Emperor's. A Tartar of unknown origin, his presence and comeliness while he had been serving in the guard some twenty years earlier had attracted the Emperor's attention. He had proved himself a nimble diplomat and adroit courtier, holding many important posts successively and concurrently. From these he had extracted massive squeeze. Since those seeking preference had to bribe him, he had become the richest man in China. Now, he was the most powerful man after the Emperor himself. His house was magnificent – though, strangely, his own apartments were frugal.

Zhengrui's memorial to Heshen had been shown to Emperor Qianlong; the Grand Secretary's note reflects the Imperial displeasure:

What [Zhengrui] did overstepped the mark. Previously we sent down an Imperial Edict on the method of receiving men from afar. If we treat them with too much ceremony then the etiquette will be improper. But we have never instructed the Salt Administrator to place himself in an exalted position and haggle with men from afar over precedence. However, when Zhengrui received the former edict, because Macartney wanted to be on an equal footing as regards etiquette, Zhengrui would not demean himself by going to the ship. This really is overdoing it . . . ! If the Viceroy is also particular about this point, the matter will become even more ridiculous. The habit of provincial officials is either to do too much or not enough.

Furthermore, these envoys have sailed the sea from afar before reaching Tientsin, so we ought to show them particular consideration. Surely we should not bargain with them over the ceremony for meeting one another . . . If the Salt Administrator is such a stickler and is unable to understand our wishes, it may be difficult for us to instruct you.

The letter continues with a comment on the Viceroy's and Zhengrui's having sought agreement not to give an additional banquet at Tientsin: 'This is not a very important matter. Let the Viceroy and Zhengrui simply obey the edict and give them a banquet.'

The discomfiture of the Tartar must have pleased the Viceroy, a Han Chinese – a pleasure reflected in the two magnificent repasts that had so impressed the Embassy. But the Chinese had carefully watched the behaviour of the Embassy at the banquets, since the question of ceremonial was by no means settled.

On 14th August, Heshen sent another letter to the Viceroy: ' . . . In their memorials the Viceroy* and Zhengrui both report at the time of the banquet on 11th August, the envoy and others removed their hats and knocked their heads.' Sceptically, Heshen continued:

Formerly according to the Viceroy's memorials, at his first meeting on 6th August when he reverentially proclaimed that gracious edict, the Envoy removed his hat and stood in a deferential attitude. In this memorial, why does the Viceroy report that at the banquet the Envoy removed his hat and knocked his head? We have always heard that Western men use cloth to bind their legs and that it is inconvenient for kneeling and kowtowing! This shows that among the customs of that country they are not acquainted with the custom of knocking the head. Perhaps the customs they have are only removing the hat, bowing the body and nodding the head, and the Viceroy and others failed to make this clear and as a result, it may be that they reported it as 'knocking the head'.

In plain words, in order to ingratiate himself at Court and in the hope and belief that the Embassy would ultimately prove pliable in the matter of the kowtow, Zhengrui had misinformed Heshen, who rightly doubted the veracity of his informants. Heshen went on to say that if they had really knocked their heads, then that was the end of the matter; but if not, then Zhengrui was given strict instructions as to what he should say to the Ambassador.

He was to tell him that the various vassal states, when bringing tribute, all perform the three bows and the nine knockings of the forehead, and that even princes perform this ceremony. He was to suggest, moreover, that if his clothing prevented due observation of the ceremony, then the bindings could be loosened temporarily. Failure to kowtow would prove the Ambassador

---

* It was common practice in China for the writer of a letter to refer to the recipient in the third person.

remiss in his duty – for, naturally, having been sent by his King to the Celestial Empire, he should obey the customary regulations. Indeed, failure to do so would mean that he had not carried out his King's loyal intentions. Furthermore, the Envoy would become a laughing stock among the various vassal states, and it was unlikely that the minister at Court responsible for conducting the ceremony would sanction such untoward behaviour.

Zhengrui was so anxious that his letter to Macartney, containing all this advice, be quickly dispatched, that he gave instructions that it be sent at the fastest possible rate of six hundred *li* (two hundred miles) a day.

But it was not only Zhengrui and the Grand Secretary who were exercised on this issue. On the day Heshen sent the letter to the Viceroy, he received one from the Emperor himself who, an old hand at judging the accuracy of his officials' reports, shared his Chief Minister's doubts.

> According to Zhengrui, the tribute Envoy and others were entirely reverential . . . we are afraid nevertheless that Zhengrui may be covering up for them. Let an edict be sent that Zhengrui should notice whether the Envoy is really reverential . . . or whether he cannot avoid giving himself airs and graces . . . Memorialise . . . so that we may decide how to receive him on arrival. Do not screen him.

At 7am on 12th August, the gongs signalled for the convoy to weigh anchor and leave Tientsin. Slowly the fleet of twenty-five junks got under way. In the first five were Zhengrui and his suite. Then came Lord Macartney's barge, followed by the one carrying Sir George Staunton and his son. Seven vessels in all carried the suite of the Ambassador. The last one was shared by Dr Scott, surgeon to the Embassy; the 'Machinest', Dr Dinwiddie; and Mr Hickey, the painter. They had been on deck since dawn. The combination of noise, mosquitoes and indigestion occasioned by the feast of the previous evening had given them an uneasy night. William Alexander was to recall later that, in addition to their daily rations, the six people on his vessel had been sent by their Chinese hosts twenty pounds of beef, two roasted pigs and other joints of pork, ten boiled and roasted fowls, one hundred rolls of steamed bread, rice, a gallon of wine, six pounds of tea, sugar and sugar candy, and a basket of fruit including something new to European taste – the lichee. The superabundance of Chinese hospitality had been such that it had been deemed appropriate to share it with the Chinese crewmen, much to their delight.

In the early light they found a river crowded with junks of all sizes. The day before they had counted six hundred vessels passing their convoy on the up or downstream and as many moored on the banks. On either side stretched Tientsin, whose extent, said Macartney, 'cannot be less than Millbank to Limehouse', and whose population of seven hundred thousand made it one of the largest cities in the Chinese Empire. Alexander observed:

> The throng of inhabitants that poured from their houses to see the Englishmen was beyond belief. Curiosity induced thousands to stand deep in the water . . . The

crowd was so close that the large hats usually worn in China and which answer the double purpose of defence from the sun and rain could not be used for want of room, so that the show of shining heads had a most novel appearance.

Aeneas Anderson recounted that, on their departure, one junk and the adjacent wharf were so overcrowded that they collapsed under the pressure of people – forty or so fell into the river, some being drowned and some saved by the ropes that were flung to them.

Gongs were being beaten to signal the twists and turns of the river. Gradually, Tientsin's houses merged into a countryside of intensive agriculture. Progress was slow and the British were given permission to disembark and walk along the bank. The botanists among them identified sorghum, *Panicum italicum* (small yellow millet), a new kind of *Phaseolus* or kidney bean, tea, several varieties of rice, cucumbers, water melons, apples, pears, plums and peaches, but very few trees except for large willows. Others enjoyed walking, and taking in the strange sights of a strange land – but not for long. Suspicious of their intentions, the Tartar legate had them recalled to their boats, where for a while they sat sharing tea and observations. These they were to distil into their journals. They noted that the Chinese drank only boiled water, and the mandarins had a liking for ice; and they remarked on the use of alum for ridding water of sediment. They observed that the Chinese drank wine hot, that they chewed areca nut, and smoked a little opium and much tobacco. They speculated on the unattainable – on Chinese women with their bound feet. They agreed that never had they seen a country so populous, or agricultural land so meticulously tended.

Macartney was tired and listless. Like many of his suite he had been awake since 4am – mosquitoes and a two-hour thunderstorm with spectacular lightning had prevented sleep. He found himself reflecting on a strange happening of the previous evening. Somehow evading the guards, and at considerable risk to himself, a young Chinese Christian convert had secretly brought two letters from a Mr Grammont, a missionary in Peking, seeking a post within the Embassy. One of the letters cautioned Macartney against a Portuguese missionary, one Bernardo d'Almeida, antagonistic to the British purpose, who was likely to be appointed interpreter to the Emperor at Jehol. Macartney immediately asked the conducting mandarins, who were in ignorance of the letters, to seek permission to be allowed to select one of the European missionaries in the Emperor's service (and with whose native language the Embassy was acquainted) to advise them on Court custom and to inform them generally about the country. They agreed to do this, but Macartney thought the ways of the country as serpentine as the river they were travelling on.

By noon, they were some thirty-three miles from their destination of

Tongzhou and the end of the tidal reach of the Hai River. From here onwards, each junk in the fleet would rely on ten to fifteen trackers yoked to a rope to haul it upstream. Over five hundred men were employed at a time, with a further five hundred alternately relieving them. As they heaved in unison, they sang a rhythmical work-song. Huttner, young Staunton's tutor, asked the interpreter Mr Plumb to translate the words whilst he notated the music; then he cast the words in verse:

> The silver waters gently flow
> Amidst thy winding banks, Pei-ho.*
> The stately junks are moved along
> While boatmen with their lofty poles
> And cheerful toils soon clear the shoals;
> Resounding to their jocund song:
> Higho, highau, higho, highau;
> Highodee, highau, highau, highau!

Aeneas Anderson, irritated by the dirge-like quality of the song, commented: 'The regularity . . . was essential to the draught of the vessel and could only be maintained by a sort of chime . . . the words had no more meaning than the bawling tones employed by our own seamen.'

The following day, 13th August, was hot, the thermometer reading eighty degrees Fahrenheit. As a result, on delivery, some of the food had already gone off. Chinese justice exacted swift retribution for this laxity. Those responsible were deprived of their rank and their servants were bambooed. The Embassy tried to intercede through Wang and Qiao, but to no avail. To the British, with their own ideas of rights and justice, such action seemed a little summary. 'But although we were heard with great attention and received very flattering answers, we easily perceived that no indulgence or relaxation of discipline was to be expected,' commented Macartney.

On the 15th, the travellers' spirits were raised by the sight of mountains in the distance. After the alluvial plain of the Hai River, the prospect of Tartary lifted their morale. Sensing the end of the journey, Zhengrui, Wang and Qiao made their daily call on the Ambassador. The mandarins' talk of arrival matched the mood of the moment. But if anything, they were more formal than usual, Zhengrui informing Macartney of the Emperor's pleasure and saying that Qianlong was inclined to allow the arrangements for travel and accommodation to go ahead as proposed. Two residences had been placed at the Embassy's disposal, one in the city of Peking and the other in the country about six miles from the city and near the Emperor's summer palace of the Yuanmingyuan. The Ambassador was invited to choose which he would like best, but he was also given to understand that because of its gardens the

* An eighteenth-century name for the Hai River.

Emperor thought the residence nearest the Yuanmingyuan the one that would be preferred.

With the chance of permanent British representation in mind, Macartney inquired what would happen after they had been presented to the Emperor at Jehol. Zhengrui replied that immediately after the ceremonies they would return to Peking, and the Emperor would follow shortly thereafter. Zhengrui also suggested that since the stay in Jehol would be very short, the field pieces and howitzers should not be taken there, since no opportunity would arise to demonstrate these particular presents.

To Macartney's surprise, the legate's attitude to him now became almost charming, and he inquired, with a palpable effort at artlessness, about the form taken by Court ceremonies in England. How was due reverence displayed? Was the posture of the body truly in keeping with the degree of deference required? Macartney quickly saw the direction the man's mind was taking, and admired the 'degree of art, address and insinuation' shown by all three mandarins. Now Zhengrui asked about the mode of dress at these ceremonies. And, apparently under his direction, Wang and Qiao pretended to be taken aback by the tightness of the court breeches, the knee buckles and garters: these were not only uncomfortable in hot weather, but also restricted movement. They implied that loose-fitting garments as worn in China allowed the courtier to make the necessary humble obeisance before his Emperor. And so, the mandarins concluded, before coming to Jehol the Embassy personnel should perhaps divest themselves of all encumbrances likely to interfere with ceremonial.

Macartney begged them not to be uneasy on this score, as he supposed that, whatever ceremonies were usual for the Chinese to perform, 'the Emperor would prefer my paying him the same obeisance which I [do] to my own Sovereign'. Zhengrui then suggested hopefully that the Chinese and British ceremonies were similar. In China the form was to go down on both knees and make nine prostrations or inclinations of the head to the ground – and this procedure had never been, and never could be, dispensed with. Macartney received this intelligence with calm. British custom was somewhat different, he informed the mandarins diplomatically. He had the most earnest desire to do everything that might be agreeable to the Emperor, but his first duty was to do that which was agreeable to his own King. If, however, they were in earnest in objecting to his following the ceremonial procedure of the English Court, he would deliver his response to them in writing on arrival at Peking.

As the barge followed the bends in the Hai River, so the sun and the shadow moved round the saloon. From outside came the sound of the gong and the shanty of the trackers. And just as the river's course shifted so did the mandarins', from frontal assault to a more oblique approach. Solicitously Zhengrui inquired about the length and danger of the voyage – since they were so far from home, naturally their King would be anxious for their return. The Emperor did not intend hunting this autumn as usual, but to remove the Court very early to Peking so that the Embassy's return might not be delayed. At this Macartney bridled. After all, he had not yet even arrived. Speaking in sonorous Latin with the intention that Mr Plumb should carefully translate both substance and tone of his reply, he pointed out to Zhengrui:

His Imperial Majesty would judge from the King's letter and from his representations what was expected on his return to England, what time was needed for the business to be transacted in China and to describe to his Sovereign the glory and virtues of the Empire, the wisdom of its laws and moral institutes, the fame of which had spread to the most distant regions.

Diplomatic hyperbole had brought Zhengrui to a halt. There was now a pause in the dialogue, while tea was poured for all to give the interpreter some rest. The discussion soon resumed, though, with Zhengrui inquiring of Macartney whether besides presents from the King of England, he had brought presents of his own for the Emperor. This unexpected turn in the conversation displeased Macartney, but concealing his discomposure he replied that 'he brought a chariot which was indeed (as it ought to be) much inferior to those in value sent by the King yet, being of a different form and remarkably elegant of its kind, he hoped the Emperor would accept it from him'. Playing for time in more than one sense, he added that he expected to have some other present to offer at the New Year, thereby conveying that he envisaged staying on beyond that period. For ever since the briefing in London, and even more so since their departure from Tientsin, Macartney had entertained the thought that Chinese customs and policy would not allow the Embassy a long residence – and so he would seize any opportunity to convey to his hosts that he expected the opposite.

There the conference ended. The three mandarins returned to their junks. To make his farewells, Macartney accompanied them on deck. With particular trepidation, he watched the departure of the Tartar legate. He felt, even though Zhengrui attempted to conceal his hostility with extravagant compliments, that he manifested a 'settled prejudice against the Embassy'. No matter how hard Macartney tried to conciliate him, he sensed that his efforts would be in vain. On the other hand, the two Han Chinese, Wang and Qiao, he felt to be sympathetic to the Embassy's cause. They did not disguise that the Emperor favoured Tartars in preference to his Chinese subjects. Nor, though they might appear when in his presence to go along with him, did they hide their own antipathy to the Tartar legate. Being ranked first in the triumvirate of conducting mandarins, Zhengrui had the exclusive privilege of corresponding with the Court on the affairs of the Embassy. Wang and Qiao, Macartney was delighted to discover, supported him in his characterization of the Tartar as 'a sort of crazy morose man', and the Ambassador was flattered by their admiration of 'the complaisance and patient attention of his deportment to him'. But whether it was his apparent piety towards the Emperor or his political acumen that excited their admiration was unclear.

As the mandarins reached their junks, the yellow pennants flying at the mastheads attracted Macartney's attention. They bore Chinese characters, which Mr Plumb interpreted for him thus: 'The English Ambassador bringing tribute to the Emperor of China'. Macartney made no complaint. He would take notice when a proper opportunity presented itself.

16th August By the afternoon, the end of the canal journey was in sight. In the distance they could see the pagoda of Tongzhou, and by 6.30pm had moored in the basin at the end of the Grand Canal. It was about a mile across, crowded with junks, an endless sea of masts and shipping. From here, the Embassy was to journey on land to their twin destinations, first Peking and then Jehol. That night, however, with so much to unload and darkness nearly upon them, they decided to remain on board. Macartney was not too tired to update his journal.

Two entries are noteworthy: one of grave import that could threaten the success of the Embassy, the other an attempt to rationalize and explain the behaviour of their hosts.

One of the conducting mandarins had affirmed that British troops from Bengal had given assistance to the insurgent Gurkhas in Tibet. Macartney knew that he had to rebut this charge decisively, for the distance between Bengal and Tibet was so large as to make such intervention impossible. In further conversation it transpired that 'the Emperor's troops had met with a set-back on the Western borders which . . . they could not account for other than by supposing their enemies had been assisted by Europeans'. Macartney hoped that his firm response would kill the rumour, but the Chinese returned to the matter by inquiring whether the English in Bengal would assist the Emperor to quell the rebellion then going on in those parts. Macartney saw the trap laid for him. Had he replied in the affirmative, the Chinese would have assumed that if Britain were to intervene, then her troops could just as easily be used against them. So once again he stressed the 'distance of our possessions from the scene of action'. No more was heard on this score.

The second entry reflects Macartney's diminishing euphoria. For after eleven days of on-shore contact with the Chinese, reality had begun to dampen the enthusiasm generated by the novelty of people and surroundings. Whilst acknowledging their hosts' munificence in the provision of food and other necessities of life, the Embassy found itself under continual constraint and observation. Macartney wrote:

> The most refined politeness and sly good breeding appeared in the behaviour of all those mandarins with whom we had any connection. Although we found an immediate acquiescence in words with everything we seemed to propose yet, in

fact, some ingenious pretence or plausible objection was usually invented to disappoint us . . . The refusal or evasion, however, was attended with so much professional artifice and compliment that we soon got reconciled and even amused with it.

The Embassy was aware that it was being watched, that everybody and every small detail of behaviour were being observed with an attention well beyond the bounds of natural curiosity. Macartney, although briefed by his reading of other embassies and travels in China, was nevertheless surprised by the degree of suspicion that his mission seemed to be encountering.

For five days they were to lodge in a Buddhist temple in Tongzhou. It was the first time in months that they had stayed in one place and slept on land, and so it was also their first chance of close contact with the Chinese. In their various journals, the members of the Embassy took due note.

In the course of a single day the baggage and presents had been unloaded from the twenty-five vessels and secured under heavy guard in two *pandals* (temporary buildings built of bamboo), each two hundred feet long. Nearby, within the temple caravanserai, they explored the rooms allocated to them, making acquaintance with the *kang*, the raised wooden platform covered with felt and cushions on which they would sleep. They also discovered with surprise the fierce-looking insects of China, as well as the scorpion and the *Scolopendra*, a large centipede.

By this point the Chinese seemed to have relaxed their surveillance a little. Horses were provided for some members of the Embassy to ride about the countryside. Staunton was disdainful of this horseflesh: 'they were strong and bony but the breed does not seem to have been improved by care. Many were spotted as regularly as a leopard . . . The saddle furniture differs as much from the neatness of what is made in England as the cattle themselves from Arabian coursers.'

On the morning of Monday 19th August, Macartney went down to the pandals. Qiao, Wang, Zhengrui and several other mandarins were assembled there to discuss their move to Peking, scheduled for two days' time. Macartney decided to take their minds off the problems of logistics and at the same time to amuse himself with a trial firing of the brass field pieces that were to be given to the Emperor. He was very proud of them – they could fire about seven rounds in one minute, and he calculated that a little display of fire-power might enhance his standing in the eyes of his hosts. Also, the demonstration might make them change their minds about taking the artillery to Jehol with the rest of the presents.

The firing was about to begin. But just then some men were passing about six hundred yards away on the far bank of the Hai River, and with much hallooing and waving of arms, several mandarins signalled to them to get out of the way. However, since Lieutenant Parish was standing within fifteen feet of the muzzle of the guns, they incurred the contempt of their colleagues for their unnecessary caution. From this Dinwiddie, donning the superiority of the dominie and having, in any case, little time for the Chinese, inferred aphoristically, 'The more ignorant men are, the more they are offended by the discovery of their ignorance.' The conducting mandarins watched impassively, leaving Macartney to conclude privately that since nothing like this existed in the whole Chinese Empire they were 'not a little mortified by this display of superiority'.

On the walk back from the pandals, Wang and Qiao informed Macartney that they had received the Emperor's answer to his request for a missionary to be attached to the Embassy: he could choose any of the Europeans in the Imperial service. They added, for good measure, that from the accounts they had heard the Emperor had conceived the highest esteem for the Embassy. This flattering prelude led to their once again pressing the question on which there had been silence for some days – the matter of the kowtow. Macartney remarked that it was a mere trifle, but noted that they took it extremely seriously. To emphasize their point they demonstrated the obeisance in front of him, begging him to try. Macartney declined. In desperation, to demonstrate the kowtow's universal usage amongst the Chinese, they then ordered Mr Plumb the interpreter to perform it. Incensed, he refused and told them that, although Chinese, he could only act as directed by the Ambassador.

Macartney viewed the incident with detached good humour, but could not fail to notice the anxious disappointment displayed by Wang and Qiao. As a diversion, he invited them to stay to a concert given by his German band. Later, he was to note in his journal: 'As to Wang and Qiao, they are wonderfully supple, and though generally considered as most respectable characters, are not very scrupulous with regard to veracity, saying and unsaying without hesitation what seems to answer the purpose of the moment.'

The enjoyment of the concert on that Monday evening was marred by tragedy. At 8pm Henry Eades, one of the mechanics attached to the Embassy, 'a cunning artist in brass and iron', died of dysentery. He had volunteered for the Embassy and, although ill, had refused to be sent home from Madeira. Macartney decided: 'To give the Chinese a favourable impression even of our funeral solemnities, the ceremony will be performed with military honours in the local burial ground.'

Mr Plumb was therefore summoned to acquire a coffin, and the next day, since no clergyman was attached to the Embassy Aeneas Anderson, the Ambassador's valet, conducted the service. There was no doubt that Henry Eades, mechanic, received a better send-off in China than ever he would have had in England. A detachment of Royal Artillery with arms reversed led the funeral procession, followed by the coffin supported by pall-bearers. Two fifes played a funeral dirge, the Ambassador's guard in full uniform followed, and other members of the Embassy brought up the rear of the procession. The proceedings were watched by a large concourse of Chinese. Describing the scene, Alexander noted in his journal: 'When the body was committed to the earth, the parties discharged three volleys over the grave which, according to the customs of the country . . . had no greater depth than was just necessary to cover the coffin.'

So poor Eades was laid to rest with all the pomp at Macartney's command. And he observed with satisfaction that the vast number of spectators seemed a good deal affected by the order and solemnity of the ceremony. No sooner was it over than the baggage began to be moved. A great part of it was dispatched before nightfall, including the bedding.

On the Wednesday morning at 2am the Embassy was roused from an uncomfortable slumber. Two hours later they set out for Peking. Their train was made up of ninety small wagons, forty handcarts or barrows, some two hundred horses and nearly three thousand men serving in different capacities. The Ambassador, Sir George Staunton, his son and Mr Plumb travelled in palanquins, each carried by four men. Others in the Ambassador's suite, and the conducting mandarins, were on horseback. Ahead of the procession the Chinese footsoldiers cleared the way, not hesitating to use sticks and whips to force a passage through the crowds. At the rear, the servants and private soldiers jolted along in rough carriages or wagons.

Macartney and Staunton, who had always been apprehensive about transporting the heavy yet fragile planetarium, had their fears allayed: 'The Chinese seem to be able to lift and remove any weight by multiplying the power; thus they fasten to the side of the load two strong bamboos. If these are not sufficient, they cross them with two others and so proceed . . . applying more bearers till they can carry it and master it with ease.' The road they travelled on impressed them: running down the middle was a pavement, about twenty feet wide, of granite flagstones, and on either side unpaved road of sufficient width to take six carriages abreast.

By 7am they had reached a village, where they stopped for refreshment. Obviously, word of their arrival had preceded them, for they were overwhelmed by crowds of Chinese fascinated by these strangers from the other side of the world. The soldiers with their scarlet jackets and powdered hair, the gentlemen with their tricorne hats, morning jackets and tight trousers, sweating in the heat and dust, were all figures of fun to the local people – so much so that the English sense of superiority was somewhat dented by their evident amusement as well as by the continued use of Chinese, which the travellers could neither understand nor counter. Aeneas Anderson captured the scene in his journal, admitting that they no sooner obtained a sight of us than they universally burst into loud shouts of laughter . . . we did not, at this time, wear the appearance of people who were arrived in this country in order to obtain, by every means of address and prepossession, those commercial privileges and political distinctions which no other nation has the art or power to accomplish.

Thus this motley group entered Peking 'bearing greater resemblance to the sight provided by the removal of paupers to their parishes in England, than the expected dignity of the representative of a great and powerful monarch'.

It took them some two hours to cross the city from the Western to the Northern Gate, which gave them ample opportunity, once they had recovered from their embarrassment, to look around. Their first impressions, considering their lack of sleep and the bruising jolting of the carts, were remarkably vivid. They were surprised at the low fronts of the houses but delighted with the colourful decorations of the shops, and marvelled at the profusion of golden characters describing their function and the frequent galleries on the roofs, which were ornately painted and embellished. The street traders excited their attention with their bamboo poles with 'baskets at each end carrying fish, vegetables, eggs and other familiar articles'. They were intrigued by the itinerant barbers, each carrying a chair, a portable stove and a vessel of water: 'This trade must be profitable in China because every man must be shaved on part of his head where it is impossible for him to shave himself.' For the first time, too, they had the opportunity of observing Chinese women, who 'whiten their faces with cosmetics . . . they also employ vermilion . . . marking the middle of their lips with a stripe of its deepest hue, which, without pretending to reason upon it, certainly heightened the effect on their features.'

It took them a further two hours from the Northern Gate of the city to their destination – the Emperor's summer retreat, the legendary gardens of the Yuanmingyuan. For some members of the Embassy it was to be their final outward destination; for others, a staging post on their way to Jehol in Tartary.

3

Interlude in Peking

Zhengrui, the Tartar legate, had a problem. As noted earlier, to save face he had not reported Macartney's refusal to practise the kowtow. Instead, hoping that Macartney would ultimately acquiesce, he had misled the Grand Council, to whom he had written: 'The English Envoy and others were deeply ashamed at being unversed in the etiquette of the Celestial Empire and have been daily practising it and are now learning how to kneel and kowtow.' Grand Secretary Heshen had not been duped by Zhengrui's assurances. Once again he warned him that 'if [the Envoy] still does not conform fully to the etiquette, you must instruct him point by point. Only when he is versed in the salutation of the kowtow may he be ushered into an Imperial audience.'

Such undercurrents did not mar the beauty of the Yuanmingyuan, the 'perfect and brilliant garden' – the Emperor's summer palace outside Peking. Laid out in the reign of Emperor Kangxi (1662-1722), Qianlong's grandfather, the garden had been enlarged and embellished by Qianlong; the work was virtually completed by 1744, some fifty years before the arrival of Macartney. Such was Qianlong's admiration and love of this carefully landscaped masterpiece that he wrote: 'Every Emperor and ruler must, upon retiring from his official duties and audiences, have a garden in which to stroll, to look round and find rest for his heart.' And he ordered his court painters, Jesuits and Chinese, to make a record of the Yuanmingyuan. The paintings were then sent to Paris, where a series of engravings of the gardens – in their heyday more spectacular than Versailles – spread their fame throughout Europe.

Covering some fifty thousand acres and ten miles in diameter, the gardens included replica landscapes of many topographical features of the Celestial Empire. Here the Embassy were to stay for a short time, but then the main party would go on to Jehol while a small group would stay behind in order to set up the larger presents. John Barrow was in charge of this group, and as the official who was to have the closest acquaintance with the Yuanmingyuan he was in the best position to describe it later:

[To] the garden appearance of those parts near where we lodged . . . hill, dale, diversified with wood and lawn . . . [the Chinese] add the very great advantage of abundance of canals, rivers and large sheets of water whose banks, though artificial, are neither trimmed nor shorn nor sloped like the glacis of a fortification, but have been thrown up with immense labour in an irregular and, as it were, fortuitous manner so as to represent the free hand of nature. Bold, rocky promontories are seen jutting into a lake, and valleys retiring, some choked with wood, others in a state of high cultivation. In particular spots where pleasure houses or places of rest and retirement were erected, the view appeared to have been studied. The trees were not only placed according to their magnitude but the tints of their foliage seem also to have been considered in the composition of the picture . . . Nothing that I saw could be considered an offence to nature.

The Embassy had arrived at the Yuanmingyuan at 2pm on 21st August. It was billeted in a small palace set in its own twelve acres of grounds on the edge of the gardens, near the small town of Haidian. Consisting of several separate pavilions set around small courtyards, the building had its own ornamental garden with a rivulet and groves of trees, and man-made features with rocks rudely heaped on each other, to give a natural appearance. But Macartney viewed it with a practical eye, one set on the long-term implications of each Chinese move. While he noted that the apartments were pleasingly adorned with water-colour landscapes, he also observed that the building was in such disrepair 'that I already see it will be impossible to reside in it comfortably in the winter'. No sooner had he arrived than he determined to move and, summoning his interpreter, he set out in search of the conducting mandarins.

Meanwhile, those following the Ambassador had discovered that they had not been allocated any living quarters. On alighting, they had been kept waiting 'in tiresome suspense', standing in a passage without an interpreter, not knowing what to do. They were very tired, having been buffeted about throughout the journey, and since their bedding had been taken from them at Tongzhou their exhaustion was compounded by the effect of a sleepless night. So they trudged off to find the Ambassador. He, equally tetchy, was found with Mr Plumb, arguing with the mandarins about the insufficient spaciousness of the accommodation. Try as he might, he could not budge them, and for the time being the Embassy had to make the best of a bad job. The Chinese soothed them with the traditional formula reserved for weary travellers, sympathizing with their tiredness and offering cups of tea. They were subsequently to be moved to superior accommodation in a palace in Peking.

During the journey from Tongzhou our British travellers had seen notices that told of a forthcoming eclipse of the sun. On inquiry, they were told that it was the custom of the Imperial government to post such notices, not only to allay the fears of a superstitious population but also to demonstrate that nothing could happen in the Celestial Empire of which the Court was not aware. Dinwiddie, with his scientist's inquisitiveness, was curious about the accuracy of Chinese astronomical calculation. He suspected that precision was not within the capabilities of the Chinese, and that the necessary calculations had been acquired from the Jesuit mathematicians in their employ. He had himself worked out the timing of the eclipse and had handed his prediction to Macartney. So, to check his accuracy, he was determined to observe the eclipse himself.

At 8pm on the day of arrival, still stiff and bone-shaken, he set up the Herschel telescope. The Chinese prediction, he found to his surprise, was accurate. As soon as the occultation began, the inhabitants of nearby Haidian honoured the event with bells, drums and gongs to drive the shadow away from the sun, performing – in Dinwiddie's disparaging words – 'ceremonies which none but the ignorant observe'. As our dominie made his observations, he realized that he would have to be one of those who stayed behind at the Yuanmingyuan to set up the scientific presents. Fierce resentment prompted him to write to the Ambassador:

> My Lord
> The erecting and regulation of the planetarium; the construction, filling and ascending in the balloon; experiments in electricity, air, mechanics and other branches of experimental philosophy; astronomical and other calculations – these I have all along considered as my province in the Embassy . . .
>
> Pardon me, my Lord, in observing that the term machinest, however it may be explained, will convey to a Chinese no other idea than that of mechanic; and that term mechanic but ill accords with one who has dedicated his whole life to mathematics and natural philosophy. Permit me humbly to request Your Excellency will substitute 'mathematician' instead of 'machinest' to the Embassy . . .

No answer to the letter is recorded. But this was not the only inequality of terms on which Dinwiddie was to meet the Jesuit and Chinese members of the Tribunal of Mathematics – of which, more later.

23rd August By the third day, Macartney could be forgiven for basking in optimism. After a few initial setbacks, the Embassy had been munificently treated: he himself had been accorded all honours due to his station, and had been frequently assured of the Emperor's goodwill and respect. His suite, staff and guard were now well housed and overfed by the Imperial exchequer. So he was at last in a position not only to begin to state his business, but to do so in the reasonable hope that, after all, the mission might be successful.

Even Zhengrui, who turned up that day to compliment Macartney on his presence in the capital and on the achievement of this first objective, seemed in a better humour than usual – though this was probably the result of his misleading reports on the conduct of the Embassy, which were allowing him to bask in the temporary favour of the Court. So when Macartney, on being questioned about the suitability of his quarters, replied, 'handsome they may be but somewhat out of repair and inconvenient to Europeans', Zhengrui showed no displeasure. He reminded the Ambassador that two buildings were available, and he would arrange for inspection of the other immediately. He also informed Macartney that a Grand Secretary was on his way from Jehol with a particular brief to look after the affairs of the Embassy. Also, following the Ambassador's request to be allowed to choose a missionary to assist him, arrangements had been made for a group of missionaries to visit the Embassy on the morrow.

Next day at 10am, in company with Zhengrui, ten missionaries duly arrived. Macartney was aware of the importance of this meeting. He knew that they had a privileged position at Court, with access to the chief ministers and to the Emperor. Their religion and their nationalities made him wary. The Portuguese had no love for the British, their rivals in trade, nor indeed had the French. In these circumstances an Italian might be the least dangerous – but, of course, Macartney knew that he was ignorant of the pecking order of loyalties within the missionary circle at Court.

Of one thing, though, he was certain. He was not prepared to accept the missionaries' spokesman, the Portuguese doyen of the Apostolic circle, Bernardo d'Almeida, as the Embassy's interpreter. He had been warned that this man was of a malignant disposition, jealous of all Europeans except those of his own nation, and particularly unfriendly to the English. Bred a Jesuit and upwards of seventy years old, he had resided for many years in China and now belonged to the Tribunal of Mathematics, a body of Jesuit and Chinese men of science responsible to the Emperor for cartography, astronomical prediction and the accuracy of the calendar. He had used his skill in surgery to further his career, for recently he had been treating Heshen, the Grand Secretary, for a rupture. Using his influence with this important patient, he had obtained for himself the position of interpreter to the Embassy.

When Macartney met d'Almeida, it was obvious, to his concealed delight, that the man was unqualified for the office, 'being entirely ignorant of the languages most familiar to us'. More important – his unsuitability was quite evident to the nine other missionaries and the members of the suite attending the meeting. D'Almeida was mortified at his loss of face, and in a stage whisper that all could hear he communicated to an Italian missionary near him his 'very unfavourable sentiments of the Embassy'. Macartney unwisely chose this moment to remind Zhengrui of his wish to move to the city of Peking, for d'Almeida immediately advised the Tartar legate against it, 'pretending it would retard our journey to Jehol, but his objections were overruled, although Zhengrui seemed much disposed to admit them'. The other missionaries were shocked by d'Almeida's petulant interjection. Macartney, however, remained calm. As d'Almeida departed, the Ambassador, ever the diplomat, had the 'grace to regret his ignorance of the Portuguese language as it deprived him of an able assistant and interpreter'. But later, he made a worldly-wise note in his journal: 'It will be right to cultivate and make use of him, if possible, but it would be egregious folly and dupery to confide in or depend on him.'

That afternoon Qiao invited Macartney to explore the Yuanmingyuan to find the most suitable hall for exhibiting the presents. The Ambassador's reaction to the gardens was far more impassioned than Barrow's recollection in tranquillity, quoted earlier. Perhaps because of being a landowner himself, he was dumbstruck: 'The various beauties of the spot, its lakes and rivers, together with its superb edifices which I saw (and yet I saw but a very small part) so strongly impressed my mind at this moment that I feel incapable of describing them.' In the end it was the Great Hall, or Presence Chamber, of the Emperor that they selected. Larger than necessary (150 feet by 60), it had already an English presence: a musical clock made by George Clarke of Leadenhall Street, London, played 'Lilliburlero' and tunes from *The Beggar's Opera*, while the mahogany throne was also made in England. Trade had preceded the flag.

These mementoes of home had decided Macartney. In his mind's eye he saw the globes displayed on each side of the throne, and the lustres hung symmetrically from the ceiling. At the south end would go the clocks by Vulliamy with the barometer and the Derbyshire porcelain vases and figures, and Fraser's orrery. He reassured himself that night by describing it in his journal as 'an assemblage of such ingenuity, utility and beauty as is not to be seen collected in any other apartment, I believe, of the whole world besides'.

On Saturday 24th August, the members of the Embassy began to turn Macartney's vision into reality. Sir George Staunton went to the chosen hall in the Yuanmingyuan, taking with him Barrow the Comptroller, Dinwiddie the Machinest, Thibault the mathematical instrument maker, and Petitpierre the watchmaker. They were told where the exhibits were to be positioned, and that they would remain at the Yuanmingyuan to set up the display while the Embassy went on to Jehol. They, in turn, estimated that it would take them six to seven weeks to do the job.

While at one end of the Great Hall the Europeans conferred among themselves on the allocation of duties, Mr Plumb the interpreter, at the other end, found Chinese workmen with no experience of handling such delicate articles beginning the unpacking. He told them firmly that, until erected and delivered to the Emperor, the presents must be considered to be in the care of the Embassy. Overhearing the altercation, Zhengrui interjected: 'Not so. They are cong-so [*gong shou*, tribute] to the Emperor. Consequently the Embassy has nothing to do with them.' Having heard about the incident of the yellow pennants on the mastheads of the junks at Tongzhou, Sir George

Staunton held his breath. The status of the packages was a vital point. Mr Plumb held his ground, firmly maintaining they were not tribute but presents. The Grand Secretary deputed to look after them in the Yuanmingyuan also disagreed with the Tartar legate. He ruled, thereby ending the conversation, that the packages should be regarded as *song-li* (presents). The phrase was proper enough.

There followed a puzzling incident. Returning to his quarters, Mr Plumb sought audience with the Ambassador. Wang and Qiao had asked him to explain that although the Emperor's allowance for defraying the Embassy's expenses was considerable, it did not cover everything. It was expected that the Ambassador would make up the difference, which would be five hundred dollars a day. To this request Macartney acceded for, having agreed to the sum, he deemed that the Chinese were now at *his* mercy, and unlikely to demand further favour for future services – 'as it is observed of certain beasts of prey that having once smacked human flesh, they never afterwards have relish for another,' noted the Ambassador in his journal.

But the next morning produced a volte-face. Mr Plumb demanded to see Macartney again – this time, to tell him that Wang and Qiao could not think of accepting any presents of money. True, their expenses had been considerable, but Qiao was very rich and well able to bear the outlay on their behalf. Macartney did not know how to account for this sudden change of mind. With hindsight, he was to wonder whether they had become aware of Zhengrui's misleading dispatches to the Emperor. In case of any investigation of *their* conduct of affairs, it would be unwise to place themselves in any position that might be seen as incriminating.

On the following Wednesday, three of the Emperor's grandsons visited the Yuanmingyuan. Progress had been made. The two lustres had been hung, and the globes had been set in their proper places, as well as the orrery and Vulliamy's clocks. The young Chinese professed themselves delighted with the sight, as was the senior mandarin who attended them. He seemed to 'be much struck with the attention manifested by our bringing several spare glasses for the dome of the planetarium, one of the panes of which happened to be cracked and which without such a precaution could not be repaired in China'. Whether the Imperial visit occurred out of mere curiosity was open to question.

The Emperor had been angry at the British suggestion that the instruments were too delicate to be moved once the skilled Embassy craftsmen had set them up and they were working properly. In a Court letter (dated 28th August) circulated within the Grand Council, the unfortunate Zhengrui, transmitter of that suggestion, suffered the Imperial displeasure:

Since Zhengrui has only been in the Salt Administration and the Customs Service in Kiungsi [Jiangxi], Chekiang [Zhejiang], Tientsin and other places and has not held the office of Superintendent of the Canton Customs, his acquaintance with Western clocks and other articles is not extensive and he is inexperienced in such matters. Now that the Tribute Envoy has seen that there are people in the Celestial Empire who are versed in astronomy, geography and clock repairing and are now helping alongside those who are setting up the articles, he can no longer boast that he alone has got the secret. Presumably he has to stop boasting.

By Thursday 29th August the Embassy had been four days in their new residence, a palace of eleven courtyards at Nanchizi in the city of Peking. It was commodious and magnificently furnished. Macartney's apartments even contained a private theatre. The rooms were hung with 'a glistening paper of a pattern both as to colour and beauty far superior to any I have seen in Europe,' noted Aeneas Anderson. Macartney made a mental note to bring some of this paper to England for his wealthy friends. It can still be seen gracing the board room of Coutts Bank in the Strand in London. Costing nearly £100,000 – an enormous sum in those days – the palace had been confiscated from a Collector of Customs in Canton who was now in jail under sentence of death for fraud. The wags of Peking thought it poetic justice that the Embassy should be housed in opulence derived from money extorted from the British and other traders in Canton.

Within the palace, preparations for diplomatic initiatives were getting under way; the possibility of permanent residence after their return from Jehol was always in Lord Macartney's mind. The Embassy's artists, Alexander and Hickey, set up the canopy of state and prepared the royal portraits for hanging. Macartney decided to formalize his domestic dining routine. Aeneas Anderson recorded: 'To support the dignity of his great diplomatic character, His Excellency required that a table should be, in future, furnished for himself and Mr Staunton, distinct from the gentlemen of his suite. This requisition found a ready compliance . . . the upper ranks . . . had a table prepared in one of the courts beneath the shade of a tree.'

Since they had left the Yuanmingyuan, there had been minor diplomatic coming and goings. Zhengrui had once again offered to practise the kowtow in front of Macartney, and once again the offer had been refused. Macartney informed the Tartar legate that he had written a paper on the subject, shortly to be delivered. We have no record of Zhengrui's reaction to this announcement. It was on the same occasion that he handed over a letter bringing news of the *Lion* from Sir Erasmus Gower. As planned, he had built a hospital at Zhoushan for his sick, and set out a boundary over which those on shore leave were forbidden to stray. Macartney prepared an answer, but to his annoyance Zhengrui insisted on knowing the contents both of Gower's letter and of Macartney's reply.

Finally, a decision was made concerning the question of the missionary to be appointed to attend on the Embassy. It was to be a Frenchman, Father Roux, described by the Ambassador as 'a tall, corpulent man of easy manners . . . and great volubility . . . it will not be difficult to learn from him everything he knows.' But it was not to be that easy! The good Father, while willing to translate Macartney's document on the kowtow, was unwilling to have it transmitted in his own calligraphy or that of his secretary. He was only too aware that recently in Canton a man had been put to death for writing a petition in Chinese for the English. So young Staunton, all of twelve years old, who on the outward journey had been learning to speak and write Chinese at Mr Plumb's hand, laboriously did the copying, over several days. The document was addressed to Heshen, Gelao, Chief Minister of the Imperial Court, Grand Secretary:

His Majesty, the King of Great Britain, in sending an Embassy to His Majesty, the Emperor of China, fully intended to give the strongest testimony of particular esteem and veneration for his Imperial Majesty . . . the Ambassador had determined to act in that manner without hesitation or difficulty, on this condition only, of which he flattered himself that his Imperial Majesty would immediately perceive the necessity . . . of preventing the Ambassador from suffering by his devotion to his Imperial Majesty in this instance; for the Ambassador should certainly suffer heavily if his conduct, on this occasion, could be construed as in any way unbecoming to the great and exalted rank which his master, whom he represents, holds among independent sovereigns of the world; that this danger could easily be avoided and the satisfaction be general on all sides, by His Imperial Majesty's order that one of the officers of his Court, equal with the Ambassador in rank, should perform before His Britannic Majesty's picture . . . in his royal robes, the same ceremonies which should be performed before the throne of his Imperial Majesty.

This was regarded by most as a capital suggestion. Father Roux had no doubt that it would be accepted. The Tartar legate, true to form, shook his head. Wang and Qiao immediately offered to perform the prostrations before the picture. However, since they had no authority for the purpose, Macartney civilly declined their proposal.

By Friday 30th August the selection of presents to be taken to Jehol was complete, and the Tartar legate had been given notice that the Embassy would be ready to move on the following Monday. In the intervening two days, Macartney proposed sight-seeing in Peking. Ever since arriving in China, except for a few hours in Tongzhou, the Embassy staff had been virtually prisoners of the palaces in which they had lodged. Having travelled half the world, they wanted to see with their own eyes and confirm the hearsay of the travellers' tales that had reached them over the last year. To no avail – politely but firmly, he was requested to suppress his curiosity till after his return from Tartary. It was thought improper that an Ambassador should appear in public in Peking before he had been presented to the Emperor.

The legate once again raised the matter of Macartney's personal presents intended for the Emperor, indicating that the phaeton he had brought was unsuitable unless the driver's box be removed. 'How can a driver be seated higher than the Emperor?' he asked. 'How can you have a coach without a driver?' replied Macartney. Then, making it clear that the demonstration of fire-power at Tongzhou had been unimpressive, Zhengrui reiterated that he did not want the artillery pieces taken to Jehol. For good measure, he wanted to see the small barrels of gunpowder removed from the Embassy's quarters into his safekeeping. Was it fire, or insurrection, or both that the Tartar legate feared?

Suspicion bred suspicion. Their confinement, with its ritualized claustrophobia, the wariness with which each side monitored the other, the knowledge that the missionaries owed their life and their living to the Emperor – all this made Staunton anxious about the possibility of indiscreet communication between members of the Embassy and those he regarded as Court spies. He therefore forbade his suite the use of Latin. Not only did he want to prevent the spread of illicitly gathered information, but he also wanted to make sure that the Scottish Calvinist and rationalist Dinwiddie did not upset the missionaries by too freely airing his opinions.

On Sunday 1st September, the dispositions for Jehol were finally decided upon. Guards, musicians and servants were told that each would be given a suit of state livery; they were to take no luggage other than their bedding and indispensable necessities. The Ambassador's suite were allowed the scarlet and gold uniform of the Embassy as well as an informal outfit and such articles as were necessary for comfort and for the formality of the occasion. The trunks of the servants' and musicians' livery were of green cloth laced with gold but, whether of diplomatic or theatrical origin, they were clearly never intended for actual service; for sewn to the linings were labels with the names of former wearers, and since these labels were the actual visiting cards of the late French Ambassador to England, it was presumed they were made up for some gala occasion or fete. To add insult to injury, the men discovered that their garments were ill matched, and that there were not enough to make complete suits. 'Two couriers were each issued with beaver hats, but not a hat was issued to accompany these curious liveries . . . which the servants were ordered not to put on until the day, as they were to add so much éclat to the entry of the Embassy into Zhe-hol [Jehol]!' commented an ironic valet de chambre.

To the fascination of the Chinese onlookers, an old post-chaise was now unpacked. Macartney proposed travelling to Jehol in its well sprung comfort. A volunteer corporal of infantry, who had once been a post-boy, was made postilion, and a light horseman was ordered to assist him. Mr Plumb completed the travel arrangements for the rest of the suite by sorting out those who wished to travel on horseback from those who wished to travel by cart.

1 (above) *Lord Macartney of Lissanoure, the first British ambassador to China, who had served in the West Indies, at the Court of Catherine the Great, and as Governor and President of Fort St George, Madras. From a portrait by Thomas Hickey, Painter to the Embassy, of whom it was said: 'He executed nothing whatever while on the Embassy, but in conversation he was a shrewd, clever man.'*

2 (above) *The Emperor Qianlong, whom Lord Macartney met three times during his mission. From a drawing by William Alexander, Draughtsman to the Embassy, based on sketches made by various members of the Embassy at the time of their presentation to the Emperor on 14th September 1793, three days before his eighty-third birthday celebrations.*

3 (above and below) *On 20th July 1793 the British Embassy anchored off Dengzhou in Shandong province. That evening, the Governor of the town visited Lord Macartney on board the* Lion, *bringing with him two rescripts from the Emperor, one addressed to the Ambassador* (above) *and the other to Captain Mackintosh of the* Hindostan. *Each scroll was about five feet long, of orange paper embossed with the Imperial dragon.*

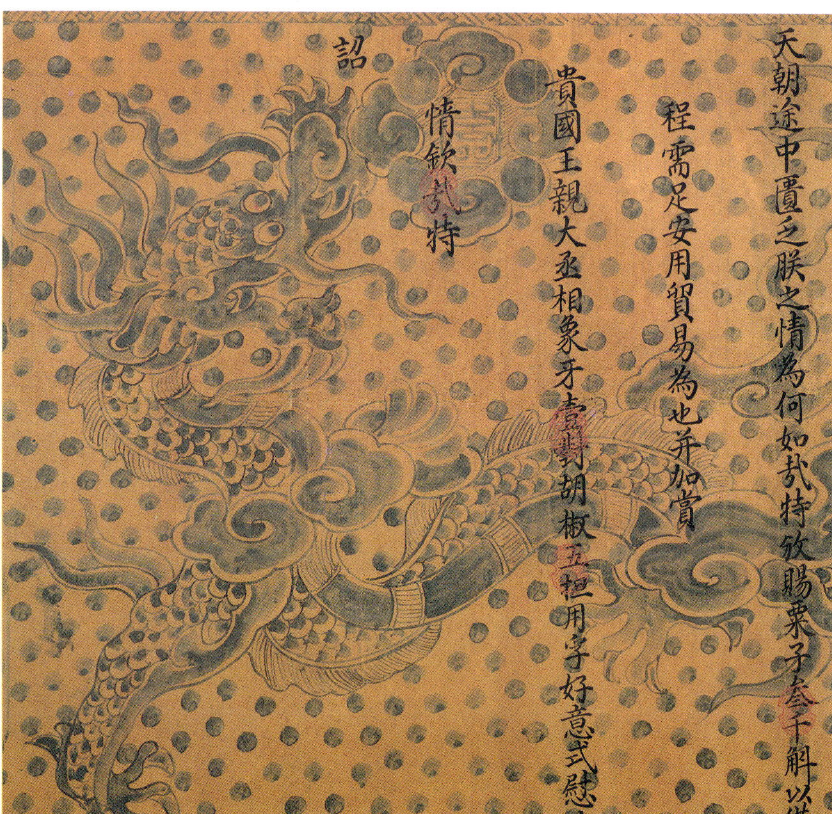

4 (above) *Wang (called Van-ta-gin by the Embassy), military commander at Tongzhou and one of the two mandarins responsible to the Manchu Zhengrui for conducting the Embassy to the Imperial Court.*

5 (right) *Qiao (Cho-ta-gin), administrator at Tientsin and the other mandarin who accompanied the British travellers throughout their journey. Both became great favourites with Macartney and his staff. From William Alexander's* The Costume of China.

A Chinese who was appointed Servant to the Vessel in
which I travelled — WA
140

8 (above) *The Western Gate, through which the Embassy left the city. The scale of the walls that surrounded Peking greatly impressed them. From a sketch by Alexander.*

9 (overleaf) *The Emperor approaches his ceremonial tent in the Garden of Ten Thousand Trees at Jehol, for the presentation of the British Ambassador and his suite, 14th September 1793. 'His Excellency was inhabited in a richly embroidered suit of velvet adorned with the diamond badge and Star of the Order of the Bath.'*

6 (top left) *'A Chinese who was appointed servant cook to the vessel in which I travelled' – Alexander's caption to his sketch. Note the queue, a symbol of the dominance of the Manchu conquerors over the Han Chinese.*

7 (bottom left) *An itinerant tinsmith at work in Peking – one of the many street traders who attracted the attention of the British when they arrived in the capital on 21st August 1793.*

10 (above) *After a tantalizing glimpse on 4th September, the next day the travellers reached the Great Wall at Gubeikou. Awestruck by this feat of engineering, many of them later described it to Alexander, who based the original drawing for this engraving on their account.*

11 (below) *The Potala, a copy of the temple of the Dalai Lama in Lhasa, built at Jehol by Qianlong to flatter the Tibetan Buddhist leader. Parish drew up a plan, from which Alexander made the drawing on which this engraving is based.*

12 (above) *The presentation ceremony inside the Emperor's tent, sketched by Parish. 1 Lieutenant-Colonel Benson; 2 Lieutenant Crewe; 3 Lord Macartney; 4 a Chinese – probably Mr Plumb; 5 Lieutenant Parish; 6 William Mackintosh, Captain of the* Hindostan*; 7 Sir George Staunton; 8 Dr Gillan; 9 Mr Barrow; 10 Mr Winder, an under-secretary; 11 Master George Staunton; 12 Herr Huttner.*

13 (below) *The Great Hall at the Yuanmingyuan, where the Embassy's presents were displayed. From a drawing by Alexander.*

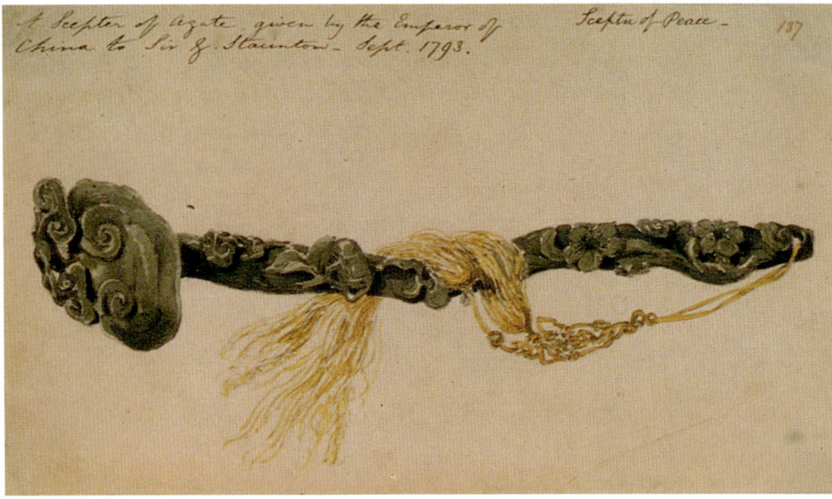

14 (above) *The jade* ruyi, *or goodwill sceptre, presented to Staunton by the Emperor, and the yellow silk purse containing areca nuts which young Staunton received.*

15 (top right) *Peasants with fighting quails. On his daily journeys to the Yuanmingyuan, Alexander sketched the Chinese at work and at play. Many of his drawings appeared in his book* The Costume of China.

16 (bottom right) *Gamblers arguing – another of the nine hundred sketches that Alexander made during the trip.*

奉
天承運
皇帝勅諭嘆咭唎國王知悉國王遠在重洋傾心嚮化特遣使恭齎表章航海來庭叩祝萬壽並備進方物用將忱悃朕披閱表文詞意肫懇具
見國王恭順之誠深為嘉許所有齎到表貢之正副使臣念其奉使遠涉推恩加禮已令大臣帶領瞻覲錫予筵宴疊加賞賚用示懷柔其已
回珠山之管船官役人等六百餘名雖未來京朕亦優加賞賜俾得普沾恩惠一視同仁至國王表內懇請派一爾國之人居住天朝照管爾
國買賣一節此則與天朝體制不合斷不可行向來西洋各國有願來天朝當差之人原准其來京但既來之後即遵用天朝服色安置堂內
永遠不准復回本國此係天朝定制想國王亦所知悉今國王欲求派一爾國之人住居京城既不能如來京當差之西洋人在京居住不歸
本國又不可聽其往來常通信息實為無益之事且天朝所管地方至為廣遠凡外藩使臣到京譯館供給行止出入俱有一定體制從無聽
其自便之例今爾國若留人在京言語不通服飾殊制無地可以安置若必似來京當差之西洋人令其一例改易服飾天朝亦從不肯強人
以所難設天朝欲差人常住爾國亦豈爾國所能遵行況西洋諸國甚多非止爾一國若俱似國王懇請派人留京豈能一一聽許是此事斷
難行亦豈能因國王一時之請以致更張天朝百餘年法度若云國王為照料買賣起見則爾國在澳門貿易非止一日原無不加以恩視即
如從前博爾都噶爾雅意達哩亞等國屢經遣使來朝亦曾以照料貿易為請天朝鑒其悃忱優加體恤凡遇該國等貿易之事無不照料備
周前歲廣東商人吳昭平有拖欠洋船價值銀兩之事即飭令該管總督由官庫內先行動支帑項代為清還並將拖欠商人重治其罪想此
事爾國亦聞知矣又何必派人留京為此越例斷不可行之請況留人在京距澳門貿易處所幾及萬里伊亦何能照料耶若云仰慕天朝欲
其觀習教化則天朝自有天朝禮法與爾國各不相同爾國所留之人即能學習爾國自有風俗制度亦斷不能效法中國即學會亦屬無用
天朝撫有四海惟勵精圖治辦理政務奇珍異寶並不貴重國王此次齎進各物念其誠心遠獻特諭該管衙門收納其實天朝德威遠被萬
里來王種種貴重之物梯航畢集無所不有爾之正使等皆所親見然從不貴奇巧並無更需爾國製辦物件是國王所請派人留京一事於
天朝體制既屬不合而於爾國亦殊覺無益特此詳晰開示遣令貢使等安穩回國國王惟當善體朕意益勵款誠永矢恭順以保乂爾有邦
共享太平之福除正副使以下各官及通事兵役人等正賞加賞各物件另單賞給外茲因爾國使臣歸國特頒勅諭並錫賚國王文綺珍物
具如常儀加賜綵緞羅綺文玩器具諸珍另列清單王其祗受悉朕眷懷特此敕諭

乾隆五十八年九月初三日

18 (above) *On occasions of public rejoicing such as the New Year or the Emperor's birthday, plays were performed in the streets. The Ambassador and his suite saw many such presentations. The character depicted here was said by one of the interpreters to be an enraged military officer. From* The Costume of China.

17 (left) *The edict from Qianlong to George III (in Manchu, Latin and Mandarin Chinese), which dashed Macartney's last hopes of salvaging his Embassy. This infamous diplomatic snub rejecting the King's requests – which was to harden Britain's attitude to China well into the next century – was drafted before the Embassy even set foot in China.*

19 (top right) *'Before we took our leave a Mandarin of the fifth order ... was called forward, who immediately kneeled down, and continued in that posture till [the second edict] and list of presents were fastened on his back by broad yellow ribbons tied round both his shoulders ... and thus accoutred [he] rode before us the whole way to Tong-tchoo [Tongzhou].' Drawing by Alexander.*

20 (below) *Six types of vessel, varying in size and shape according to the depth of the water and the speed of the current, carried the Embassy down the Grand Canal. The baggage junk below was used on the outward journey. Sketch by Alexander.*

The men about to be left behind were disappointed. They were divided into two groups. Dr Dinwiddie, Mr Barrow, the watchmakers and scientific instrument makers were to live at the Yuanmingyuan to ensure that the presents were in working order and ready to be shown to the Emperor on his return from Jehol. The other party consisted of one of Macartney's secretaries, Mr Maxwell, and three servants, who were 'to settle the household of the Ambassador so that on his return it should, in every respect, be suited to the character and dignity of his mission'. In addition, Dr Scott was left behind to look after the soldiers and servants suffering from dysentery. Idle Hickey and industrious Alexander were to finish what little remained to be done on the mounting of the two portraits of their Britannic Majesties. Alexander, with a vivid sense of the loss to posterity caused by his staying behind in Peking, protested strongly at his omission, aware that the only draughtsman's skills remaining to the Embassy on their journey would be those of Lieutenant Henry Parish, commander of artillery. But his complaints were to no avail.

The day before departure Macartney spent receiving visitors. He had instructed the band to give a nightly concert which had proved to be a great attraction. The chief mandarin of the Emperor's orchestra, a regular patron of the concerts, had painters copy the instruments. Wrote Macartney: 'The Chinese, notwithstanding their vanity and conceit, are not above being taught.'

On this last day in Peking, the morale of the Embassy was lifted by the visitors' evident interest in the goods brought from England. The portraits of King George and Queen Charlotte by Sir Joshua Reynolds excited such attention that access to them had to be regulated. Interest was also shown in smaller articles, both presents and personal effects, such as dressing-tables, shaving mirrors and pocket instruments. The flexible sword blades from Birmingham created special excitement. Wang, the conducting mandarin, was given two, 'and was more pleased than if he had been offered a present of a hundred times the value'.

Macartney's hopes in the ultimate success of the mission were raised yet again. Like many visitors before and after him, he was seized with a vision of the infinite markets of China. Buoyed up with this vision and encouraged by greetings from the Emperor brought by a Grand Secretary, who came in the evening to wish them a safe journey, they retired to bed to prepare for an early departure.

4

The March into Tartary

They were to travel a hundred and twenty-five miles along the Imperial Way, from Peking to Jehol. Made of compacted sand and clay, that great highway was 'as clean as the floor of a saloon, swept with so much attention that nobody notices the least dust on it'. So that the Emperor would always enjoy a dust-free journey, there were frequent reservoirs providing water for sprinkling on the road. 'Nowhere in the world,' said Huttner, 'is there a more beautiful road than this one, running over mountains following the contours of escarpments and bridging rivers.' Macartney and young Staunton bowled along in their neat English post-chaise drawn by four little Tartar horses not eleven hands high – 'the first piece of Long Acre machinery that ever rattled up the road to Jehol,' boasted Macartney.

Behind him were his cavalry guard and the Embassy members who were travelling on horseback or in carts. The rear was brought up by those on foot, led by Sir George Staunton, who suffered from a touch of gout and had opted for a palanquin as the smoothest means of progression. The whole cavalcade consisted of some seventy persons, backed up by baggage animals and two hundred Chinese porters who covered the daily twenty-five or so miles. As the Embassy advanced towards Jehol, no longer confined by the walls of their palace or by guards at the gate, a sense of newly found freedom overcame them. The ordinary became the extraordinary: they were impressed by the trim countryside – even by the flat alluvial plain, the background to the beginning of their journey. 'The neat husbandry of the country, the industry of the people and the air of business that appears in their faces, the goodness of the road and the circumstances of travelling in a post-chaise, almost made me imagine myself in England,' rhapsodized Macartney.

The plant life fascinated them. Haxton and Stronach, the two botanists, as well as Staunton and Macartney, collected and catalogued specimens. They noted, en route, the uses to which various plants were put, in the hope that commercial advantage might be gained from them. They witnessed the manufacture of oil from the seeds of sesame, hemp, cotton and turnip, and from the kernels of apricots. And they were impressed by the manufacture of cloth from nettle fibres and of paper from the skins of different vegetables, from hemp fibre and from rice straw. What surprised them most was the extent of tobacco cultivation and its widespread use by the Chinese: 'Girls of not more than ten years old or younger, coming from houses near the road out of curiosity to see strangers pass, were observed to have long pipes in their mouths.' Tobacco was also taken in powdered form; mandarins were seen to carry with them small ornamental phials to hold snuff.

On each night of the journey, the Embassy stayed in one of the elegant palaces built as stop-overs for the Emperor on his journeyings to Jehol. They were all beautifully appointed, in landscaped grounds. As at the Yuanmingyuan, Macartney the landowner waxed lyrical in his admiration: 'A Chinese gardener is a painter of nature, consulting which he contrives, without rule or science, to unite simplicity and beauty.'

They set off at 5am each day, having packed by the light of flickering tallow candles. By this time the porters would have gone ahead, followed by the baggage animals – horses, mules, donkeys and a dromedary. There was only one of these beasts in the Embassy train, carrying coal for cooking; but dromedaries were frequently to be seen coming down the road, saddle bags slung across their humps, laden with furs for Peking and returning with charcoal and other produce.

One typical day, they advanced by twenty miles. Macartney in his post-chaise covered the first eight miles in less than two hours, and the remaining twelve in two and a half. As the mountains of Tartary advanced towards them, in spite of their following the contours the road was getting steeper. Suddenly, about ten miles away they saw what appeared to be a snake coiling its way across the hills. It was their first glimpse of the Great Wall of China.

That evening, discord intruded upon Macartney's contemplation of a 'beautiful weeping willow hanging over a sweet pastoral stream on one side of the road': he learned that the letter he had given to the Tartar legate for Sir Erasmus Gower had not been sent. Its contents, Zhengrui informed him, were not of sufficient worth to justify the use of an Imperial messenger. Macartney, who had read the letter to him in order to put his mind at rest, could not disagree with his judgement, but wondered what lay behind this unfriendly gesture. Zhengrui, meanwhile, informed the Ambassador that on the morrow he would go ahead to prepare for their arrival in Jehol.

There was another possible explanation for Zhengrui's action. He had received an Imperial reprimand for memorializing that he considered it improper for the barbarian ships to return to England in advance of the Ambassador and his suite. A Court letter emanating from the Grand Council and dated 20th August bluntly said:

What he memorialised was extremely silly. This really shows how unlucky the Salt Administrator is to be so muddle-headed. Because the people on that country's ships are unaccustomed to the climate, the Envoy wants to send them home in advance and, naturally, ought to let them please themselves. How could Zhengrui advise them and suggest it would be improper for the ships to return home in advance?

Worse was to come. The following day, sent at the express rate of two hundred miles a day, another Imperial rebuke arrived from Grand Secretary Heshen:

Since the tribute Envoy set out from Tientsin, he has been in Zhengrui's sole charge. As a consequence, Zhengrui thought there was no service more important. He actually thought his merit was greater than that of the General responsible for quelling the Gurkha rebellion* . . . he looked upon himself as an Imperial Commissioner, in his own eyes belittling his colleagues. Zhengrui [is] not worthy to receive our favour, he is so muddle-headed and blundering.

While Zhengrui was rushing to Jehol to salvage his career at Court, the Embassy made steady progress. After the tantalizing distant glimpses of the previous day, on 5th September they came to the Great Wall at Gubeikou. Their excitement was intense. They were, after all, some of the first Englishmen to see it, let alone set foot on it. During a short walk after breakfast, they discovered a breach in the wall and through it climbed to the top. This is what they recorded:

The Wall is built of blueish coloured brick, raised on a stone foundation. As measured on the ground on the side next to Tartary it is about twenty-six feet high in the perpendicular . . . It is carried on in a curvilinear direction often over the steepest places and craggiest mountains . . . and measures upward of one thousand five hundred miles in length from its commencement in the Gulf of Pe-tche-lee [Beizhili] to its termination in the Province of Shanxi, west of Peking.

Lieutenant Parish drew a meticulous plan of it and later, from their accounts, Alexander was to paint a highly idealized view. They were overawed: 'It is certainly the most stupendous work of human hands . . . if the outline of all the masonry of all the forts and fortified places in the whole world besides were to be calculated, it would fall considerably short of the Great Wall of China.' Some members of the Embassy were observed by others in the act of collecting bricks from the wall to sell to 'antiquity dealers' back in England.

Macartney speculated on the wall's purpose. Was it a boundary to keep the wild and ferocious beasts of Tartary from the fertile plains of China? Was it to prevent emigration? 'Those who depart from China without licence are inevitably brought back,' he reflected. Certainly, it was no longer of use for

* Heshen refers here to Fukhang'an, former Viceroy of Canton and the General who fought against the Gurkhas in Tibet in 1790-2.

defence, 'for the Emperor has extended his territory so far beyond it that I doubt whether his dominions without the wall are inferior to those within it'. Aeneas Anderson was careful not to let his imagination run away with his judgement. He believed that its reputation depended on imagination 'as to the astonishing circumstances connected with it, and [he] saw it in a comparative view with natural objects infinitely superior'.

The detailed examination of the wall, the sketching, the measuring and the souvenir hunting excited unease, impatience and suspicion. The Chinese themselves were indifferent to this magnificent feat of engineering. Although Wang and Qiao had passed it at least twenty times, not once had they visited it. They were, therefore, astonished at the degree of curiosity being shown by the barbarians. What was their design? The questing curiosity of these eighteenth-century rationalists was totally at variance with the Confucian disinterest of their mentors.

When, a few miles beyond Gubeikou, a Tartar servant of the Embassy stole some cooking vessels, it was firmly emphasized that the wall marked off China from Tartary. Taxed on the matter by Wang and Qiao, the servant answered so impertinently that they ordered him to be bambooed. Insolently, he insisted that no Chinese had jurisdiction over a Tartar outside the Great Wall. So the punishment was repeated, the stolen goods were restored, and he repented his topographical objections. (In this context, it is worth noting that when a Tartar of the Imperial Court paid the Ambassador a courtesy visit, Wang, although of equal rank, could not sit in the same room, 'so great is the respect affected by the Chinese towards the Tartars of the Court'.)

As they approached Jehol, the going became rough and steep. Macartney had to exchange his post-chaise for a palanquin, and the pride of Long Acre had to be ignominiously hauled up the steep inclines.

Everywhere they attracted onlookers. Not only were their persons and clothes scrutinized, but rumour had spread of the miraculous nature of some of their presents. A local mandarin came up to Mr Plumb and diffidently inquired if it would be possible for him and his friends to be shown the astonishing rarities being brought for the Emperor. Plumb asked what rarities he was referring to. The mandarin said that he had heard in Peking and other places that they had a chicken that ate fifty pounds of coal every day and only fed on that. He had also heard that among other presents there were several dwarfs not twelve inches high, but in form and intellect as perfect as grenadiers. There were also supposed to be an elephant as small as a cat and a horse the size of a mouse. Lastly, there was an enchanted pillow on which anybody who laid his head fell instantly asleep, and if he dreamt of any distant place he was transported there without the fatigue of travel. Huttner, who recounted this tale, said that the man was very sad when told he could not see these marvels. What, apparently, gave rise to the rumour was the frequent practice of the ambassadors of small empires of bringing to the Emperor gifts of birds, rare animals and other curiosities of nature. The dromedary laden with coal fed not the hen, but imagination and rumour.

Sunday 8th September As they marched, they climbed, and the weather became cooler. Over these last twelve miles the alpine countryside reminded them of Savoy, as did the preponderance of large goitres on the spectators watching the parade. For most of the year the road they were following was above the snowline, and the Chinese, like the Europeans, attributed the swollen necks to the drinking of snow water.

As they neared Jehol, a spectacular landmark loomed in front of them. High on a hill a pillar of rock called Shuangdashan, some two hundred feet high, heralded the strange features that marked the hilltops of Jehol. So they were now very near to their destination, Macartney realized: the moment had come to 'dress and marshall the procession for my public entry. It was arranged in the following manner, and made a splendid show.'

In his journal, Macartney then listed the order of procession. Preceded by a hundred mandarins on horseback were the Light Dragoons led by Lieutenant-Colonel Benson, the Artillerymen led by Lieutenant Parish, and the Fife and Drum followed by the infantry; then came the servants and musicians in their rich green livery, the gentlemen of the Embassy in their uniforms of scarlet and gold, Lord Macartney in a chariot (on the Emperor's orders he had been required to forgo the post-chaise), Sir George Staunton also in a chariot, and finally a black boy servant in livery and turban.

Anderson, in his journal, contradicted his lordship's assessment:

> It was by no means calculated to impress a favourable idea of the greatness of the British nation on the minds of those who beheld it . . . the military departments made a respectable figure and the gentlemen of the suite could not, for a moment, be supposed to derogate from the diplomatic character in which they were involved, but the rest of the company exhibited a very awkward appearance, some wore round hats, some cocked hats, others straw hats, some were in whole boots, some in half boots and others in shoes with coloured stockings. In short, unless it was in second-hand coats and waistcoats which did not fit them, the inferior parts of the suite did not even enjoy the appearance of shabby uniformity.

In this state and in this careful order the procession moved slowly into Jehol. Soon after ten o'clock it arrived at the palace provided for the accommodation of the British Embassy. Here the military part of the cavalcade formed a line to receive the Ambassador with the usual honours. But it was seen by few and greeted by none. The waiting had begun.

Part Two
At the Court of Qianlong

5

Anticipation in Jehol

THEY MAY NOT HAVE BEEN WELCOMED, but they were observed. From a hilltop pergola, Emperor Qianlong watched the arrival of the multicoloured tatterdemalion file. The taunting whistle of the fife and the rat-tat-tat of the snare drum drifted up from the valley on the thin mountain air. Daily dispatches had reported on the activities of the Embassy – now, for the first time, in the Emperor's sight. Not only had these dispatches revealed the self-promoting manipulations of Zhengrui, they had also confirmed Imperial suspicions of the Tribute Envoy's arrogance.

The Imperial gaze shifted. Below him, in one of the many Gardens of Jehol, the Garden of Ten Thousand Trees, he could see the Tartars' yurts* being erected for the birthday ceremonies. Better, he thought, to receive the Ambassador there than in the Palace. Irreverence would count for less in these surroundings. No precedent would be created, nor would the reception be taken as a sign of weakness by the other embassies at present in Jehol. The fife completed its tune and the cavalcade below marched on to the tap of the drum. The Emperor ruminated on the foreigners. It was not British aggression that caused the greatest worry – although China had not forgotten Weddell's bombardments of the Anung-Hoi forts in the Pearl River approaches to Canton, nor Anson's attacks on those forts, nor the drunken barbarian behaviour of British sailors on shore leave. Aggression could be isolated and contained. Had not a system of containment been devised, and was it not working well in Canton? It was more the independence of thought that Western barbarians brought with them which posed the threat to the delicate stability of relationships that held the Empire together. It was this invisible threat that had to be

* Round tents made of interlaced bamboo covered with thick felt.

contained. Qianlong recalled an old Han dynasty saying: 'The three cardinal virtues of government are – to simulate affection, to express honeyed sentiments and to treat one's inferiors as equals.' The Envoy sought advantages that could not be granted except at the expense of long-term damage to the social fabric. Defensive prevarication, therefore, was the best policy.

Many of the Embassy may well have been surprised that, when honours were accorded to the Ambassador by his own military on their arrival at the palace in Jehol, no mandarin appeared to congratulate them or to show them to their apartments. Contrary to expectation, Heshen, Chief Minister of the Imperial Court, paid no call of welcome. In case he should appear, the guard were held on standby, ready to fall in at a moment's notice. Since they did not know what he looked like, there were false alarms when the soldiers found themselves saluting curious but, as it turned out, insignificant mandarins – a state of affairs that occurred at least a dozen times in the next six hours, and ended, somewhat anticlimactically, with the serving of dinner.

The Tartar legate, who had gone on ahead of the Embassy and was already in Jehol, was their first visitor of stature. He handed back to Macartney his paper on the kowtow, implying (although the contrary was known to be the case) that he had not passed its contents on, and suggesting that the Ambassador personally deliver it to Heshen. For good measure he added that the Minister had hurt his knee and so, being immobile, could not attend Macartney. Would the Ambassador, therefore, call on him? With some civility Macartney demurred. It was hot, he was tired, and the servants had not yet unpacked. If there was urgent business needing attention, he would send his deputy, Sir George Staunton, to attend the Minister in the evening.

Macartney watched Zhengrui take his leave. He was learning to deal with Chinese dissembling. Wang and Qiao had told him earlier that Zhengrui had been degraded by three ranks for misrepresenting the Embassy to the Emperor. Apparently, Qianlong had heard that Macartney had hung his portrait on the wall of his cabin in the *Lion*. When asked if it was a true likeness Zhengrui could not answer, for, as mentioned earlier, contrary to orders, because he was afraid of the sea he had not gone on board the *Lion* as part of the welcoming party. Macartney had also heard that pressure on him to kowtow was to be increased – and there was an implied threat to cut the Embassy's ample food supply in both quantity and quality. Macartney issued an order that, if this were to happen, individual representations were not to be made: the food should be left untouched and he was to be immediately informed.

Within the close confines of Jehol, nothing was secret. The Embassy knew that the Emperor, following his grandstand view of their arrival, had given orders to Heshen to call on Macartney. They felt slighted, with some justice, when he did not. Nonetheless, when the summons arrived for Staunton to attend on Heshen, he set out for the Chief Minister's house, taking with him his son and Mr Plumb.

The scene was impressive. The audience hall was full of palace officials and hangers-on listening to every word that passed. The Chief Minister, flanked by two mandarins of state, sat on a silk-covered platform. A chair was provided for Staunton; protocol demanded that the legate, the two conducting mandarins – Wang and Qiao – and the interpreter stand. Although Heshen spoke with 'dignified reserve', Staunton reported in his journal: 'In his manners and conversation . . . whatever civilities he showed to the English Minister were the condescensions of national as well as personal superiority.'

Heshen began by inquiring after the objective of the British Embassy to China. In answer, he was presented with a letter from King George III to the Emperor, now translated into Chinese. For this he seemed to be grateful. Then Macartney's memorial on the kowtow was presented to him. He did not like what he read. Well briefed by Macartney, Staunton patiently explained the reason for British unwillingness to kowtow: how, in spite of Imperial custom, the Ambassador could not be seen to make obeisance which exceeded that which he would give his own sovereign. However, if a member of the Court appointed by the Emperor were to kowtow to the portrait of King George, in turn Macartney would make the same obeisance in front of the Emperor. Heshen pressed Staunton to reconsider the matter, pointing out that failure of the mission arising from a stubborn unwillingness to comply with the Imperial rules might incur more royal opprobrium than would indulgence in a customary salute.

There the audience ended.

Heshen was angry. Two Court dispatches of 9th and 10th September 1793 reveal Imperial displeasure also:

> Yesterday we commanded the Grand Councillor [Heshen] to summon the Envoy to an interview. The Chief Envoy feigned illness and did not arrive but simply instructed the Assistant Envoy to come, and he presented a document, the wording of which showed ignorance . . . At present instructions have been given for him to practise the ceremonial but he still pretended to be ill and procrastinates. We are extremely displeased at this unwarranted haughtiness and have given instructions to cut down their supplies. Also, it is not necessary to prepare entertainments and operas in the capital.

On the evening of 10th September, the threat became reality. When the Embassy sat down to dinner, instead of the usual abundance of food,

> there was not sufficient quantity of provisions for half the persons who were ready to partake of them . . . We not only felt the probability that we might be starved as well as being imprisoned . . . We also had our feelings as Britons and felt the insult that was offered to the crown and dignity of the first nation in the world.

The meal was left untouched. Macartney was informed. Mr Plumb communicated the cause of the discontent to the Chinese. To everyone's surprise, within five minutes each table was served with a profusion of hot dishes.

On this day, too, as instructed by Heshen, the legate, Wang and Qiao renewed discussion on the kowtow. Macartney detected signs of weakening. They asked him what form of obeisance to the sovereign was used in England, and then, when told that the custom was to go down on one knee and kiss the hand of the monarch, to Macartney's astonishment they asked why this ceremony could not be performed for the Emperor. 'Most readily,' agreed Macartney. The triumvirate took the news back to Heshen. The Embassy awaited their return. Confined to their quarters and wondering how far the Chinese would be prepared to take this threat of reducing rations, they found it a tense wait.

When Zhengrui finally returned, he told them that the English ceremony was acceptable but that the wish of the Court was that the Ambassador kneel on both knees. Macartney stood his ground: he had already given his answer, which was to kneel on one knee when the Chinese prostrated themselves. 'In that case,' parried Zhengrui, 'the ceremony of kissing the Emperor's hand must be omitted.' Macartney's assent gave him the last word. 'As you please,' he said, 'but remember this is your doing and according to your proposal. It is but half the English ceremony and you see I am willing to perform the whole one!'

Thus ended the curious negotiations on the kowtow. In his journal Macartney claimed that the exchange gave him a tolerable insight into the Chinese character. But it was no victory, and proved to be the first of many revelatory shocks.

Wednesday 11th September At 9.30am Zhengrui, Wang and Qiao came to escort Macartney to see Heshen. This was the first time that Macartney had left his lodgings. It was also his first contact with the inner Court, with someone with whom he could negotiate the aims of his mission. He found Heshen 'a handsome, fair man of about forty to forty-five years old, quick and fluent' – totally different from the individual whom Staunton had confronted the previous day. He greeted his visitors most affably.

Heshen was surrounded by four courtiers of rank, the President of the Court of Rites – the kowtow controversy must have necessitated a personal inspection of the offender – Fuchang'an, friend of Heshen, Second Minister and second favourite of the Emperor; the President of the Tribunal of Finance, and an unidentified 'great man in a yellow vest' (this last was a symbol of Imperial favour). Unlike the previous day's audience hall interview, there was no coming and going of onlookers.

The conversation between Chief Minister and Ambassador spanned many topics but at first touched on no issues of mutual concern. Macartney, having recovered from the fatigue of the journey, said he was happy to have an early opportunity of presenting the King's letter to the Emperor – whom, in conveying compliments to Heshen on Qianlong's health, he wished long life. Then Heshen broached the subject of the kowtow. The distance travelled and the value of the presents brought, he said, had impelled them to relax the Chinese customs. Macartney could perform the Court ceremony in the manner of his own country, and deliver the King's letter to the Emperor by his own hand. Outstanding difficulties apparently having been surmounted, and since next Saturday was a great festival at Court, that day was appointed for the presentation of the Ambassador and his suite to the Emperor.

The conversation touched on the voyage. When Macartney mentioned having put in at Tourane Bay in Cochin China, Heshen pointed out that that country bore a tributary relationship and was a dependency of China, and further questioned Macartney about the relationship of other European countries to England. Were not Italy and Portugal near England, and tributary to it? What was the relationship to Russia? It was as though he was unable to conceive of a foreign relationship other than tributary hegemony. Macartney pointed out that at present England was at peace with Russia and, indeed, with all the world. Portugal and Italy were not tributaries, but the King of England had afforded them protection and shown them marks of friendship. Whether Macartney was believed, and whether Heshen from this conversation derived a better understanding of his independent attitude to the kowtow, will never be known.

When they parted, the Chief Minister shook Macartney's hand, assuring him that 'he would be happy to cultivate his acquaintance and hoped for further opportunities of seeing him familiarly at the Yuan Ming Yuan. Meanwhile, the bustle and hurry of business and the festivals of the Emperor's anniversary must necessarily engage the greater part of his time whilst the Court remained at Jehol.'

That afternoon Wang and Qiao visited the Embassy again. They repeated the flattering things that Heshen was supposed to have said of them to the Emperor – who, as a result, was reported to be impatient for Saturday's meeting. Presently Zhengrui appeared, bearing a gift of fruit and sweets from the Chief Minister and repeating the compliments already conveyed. Macartney, although unable to touch on the subject of Anglo-Chinese trade, the purpose of his mission, was fully satisfied with the general tenor of the audience and ordered the presents to be prepared on the morrow.

And so some of the finest specimens of British manufacturing were laid out on trestle tables in front of the Ambassador's apartments, for Chinese eyes to marvel at. (It will be remembered that the main presents – the planetarium, the globes, the lustres, Parker's big lens, the carriages, the field pieces and howitzers – all being too bulky to carry, had been left behind in the Yuanmingyuan just outside Peking.) Here on the tables in Jehol were the two hundred pieces of broadcloth, the Herschel telescope and another large telescope, two air guns, two fowling pieces, one inlaid with gold and the other with silver, two pairs of ornamented saddle pistols, two boxes of Irish linen, two saddles of fine doeskin stitched with silver thread, and two large boxes containing the finest of British carpets. A guard was ordered to be posted over these treasures day and night – but in vain. On the following day Wang, with other mandarins in attendance, removed them to the Emperor's Palace.

On Friday 13th September, Wang and Qiao, paying their daily call, told the Ambassador that the presents were 'much approved, but that it was wished that somebody might be sent to show how the telescopes were to be put up and used'. So Dr Hugh Gillan, physician and natural philosopher, accompanied by Mr Plumb, was duly sent to teach the Court eunuchs the complexities of assembly and operation, how to adjust the day and night glasses and to focus the instruments. In his journal, Macartney reported: 'Notwithstanding their complete ignorance, these gentry pretended to understand, at half a word, all the machinery of these instructions, but Dr. Gillan did not leave them till he thought he had really made them masters of it.'

That day was dominated by preparations for the morrow's climax. The Embassy was to be ready at 3am. The servants were to be dressed in their green and gold livery and to wear white silk or cotton stockings; shoes or boots of any kind were prohibited. As they prepared, laying out the uniforms, polishing the silver and patent leather, pressing the Court dress, practising the music and powdering the wigs, some may have reflected that it was almost a year to the day since they had left Spithead.

6

'SOLOMON IN ALL HIS GLORY'

IMPERIAL AUDIENCES were held at dawn: with the rising of the sun, the Emperor showed himself to his people. The act was symbolic for, like the sun, the light from his central presence was supposed to irradiate his subjects and, indeed, the universe. The universe and the biosphere merged and balanced in him. The maintenance of this cosmological equilibrium determined the behaviour of the elements: Earth, Wood, Air, Fire and Water. If the ceremonial was not correctly observed, not only would natural disaster – earthquake, plague, flood and famine – ensue, but the stability of the reign could be threatened by war or rebellion. This idea of stability between Emperor and subjects, in family relationships, between mankind and nature, dominated Chinese thinking, making change unthinkable if not impossible. An audience with the Emperor, therefore, was in the nature of a communion between microcosm and macrocosm, within a setting of solemn ritual.

Saturday 14th September Today's audience was to be held in a massive yurt some twenty-five yards in diameter set in the Garden of Ten Thousand Trees, not in the nearby Palace. Perhaps Macartney's failure to accede to the full ceremonial had led to a reciprocal diminution of the venue by the Emperor. Although they had been ordered to be ready to proceed to the Gardens of Jehol at 3am, delay had been anticipated. It was as well, for the business of dressing in complicated ceremonial robes by the light of tallow candles had proved difficult. Not until 4am were they ready to depart.

[The Ambassador was] dressed in a suit of spotted mulberry velvet with a diamond badge, a diamond star and the red riband, over which he wore the full habit of the Order of the Bath with the hat and plume of feathers that formed part of it. Sir George Staunton was in full Court dress over which he wore the robe of a Doctor of Law in the English universities, with the black velvet cap and the habit of that degree of scarlet silk, full and flowing.

This fancy dress was Macartney's idea – to show, he said, 'the attention I always paid where a proper opportunity [was] offered to [match] oriental customs and ideas'.

When they set out it was still so dark they could not see one another. The Ambassador and his Vice-Minister rode in palanquins, the rest of the suite on horseback. Aeneas Anderson provides the liveliest description:

> Lieutenant Colonel Benson made an attempt to form a procession to precede the palanquin of the Ambassador. But this manoeuvre was of short duration as the bearers moved too fast for the solemnity of a slow march and, instead of preceding it with grave pace, we were glad to follow it with a quick one. Indeed, whether it was the attraction of our music I know not, but we found ourselves intermingled with a cohort of pigs, asses, and dogs which broke our ranks and put us into irrecoverable confusion. All formality of procession, therefore, was at an end.

They arrived breathless and self-consciously foolish, having taken part 'in an attempt to make a parade that no one could see'.

At 5am Ambassador and Vice-Minister alighted at the gate of the Gardens of Jehol. Sir George and young Staunton bore the Ambassador's train as they walked to the Imperial encampment, where they were conducted to a large tent alongside the Emperor's. There they waited for the sun to rise.

When daylight came to the gardens on the northern side they could see the mountains rising up, some in great masses, others in escarpments culminating in a high peak that dominated the whole countryside, pink in the morning light. On the southern side stood the yurts of the Tartars. In the middle was the Emperor's tent, much larger than the others. Its walls were decorated in yellow and covered in carpets, and the ceilings were painted with garlands and hung with lanterns, while cushions, and tables with refreshments, had been placed on the floor of the covered entrance in which stood the Imperial throne, mounted on a dais.

Since the Emperor's eighty-third birthday was approaching, the Court was particularly distinguished. Some six hundred courtiers were in attendance – Tartar tributary princes and viceroys of China, as well as ministers of the Court and hundreds of lesser mandarins. There were other ambassadors too: the British Embassy identified 'one of dusky hue, dressed in red velvet garnished with gold, as coming from Pegu [Burma]'. The Tartar courtiers crowded round the British, with their 'normal vulgarity' feeling the cloth of their suits and costumes, pointing at them and prodding them. The Han Chinese were more restrained, their inherent courtesy countering Tartar high spirits. And so amidst this jostling crowd, just after dawn, they awaited the sunrise and the arrival of Emperor Qianlong.

It was half an hour after sunrise that a horseman cantering down the road from the direction of the Palace signalled the arrival. The crowd arranged itself in order – a funnel shape leading up to the Emperor's tent. There was silence – but in the distance could be heard music and the sound of drums. A look of anticipation animated the faces of the audience. They were not to be disappointed. First came the Chief Ministers, dressed in Imperial yellow and riding snow-white horses. They dismounted and stood in line a short distance from the Emperor's tent. Close behind, a band and guard of honour headed the Imperial procession. Then came the Emperor, carried on a gilded palanquin by sixteen men and closely followed by Court and government officials.

The procession crossed the ranks of courtiers, who prostrated themselves in the kowtow, forehead touching the ground. The sole exception was the Embassy, who enjoyed the fruits of their negotiations by kneeling on one knee until graciously told by the Emperor to rise. As soon as he had ascended the throne, with his Chief Ministers in obeisance before him, he sent the President of the Court of Rites to conduct Macartney to the place of honour at the bottom of the dais to the left of the throne.

I came to the entrance of the tent and, holding in both my hands a large gold box enriched with diamonds in which was enclosed the King's letter, I walked deliberately up and, ascending the side steps of the throne, delivered it into the Emperor's own hands who, having received it, passed it on to the minister by whom it was placed on the cushion.

Then came the exchange of presents. The Emperor gave three *ruyi*, goodwill sceptres – one in white agate for the King and two in jade for Macartney and Staunton. Macartney gave the Emperor 'a pair of beautiful enamelled watches set with diamonds . . . which, having looked at, he passed to the minister'. Staunton, as Minister Plenipotentiary, gave the Emperor 'two elegant air-guns'. In turn, the Emperor gave presents for all of the suite. The party was then invited to sit on cushions at one of the tables at the Emperor's left hand. The others – princes, ministers and mandarins of the Court – took their places according to precedence. The banquet began.

It was a sumptuous repast: 'The order and regularity in serving and removing the dinner was wonderfully exact and every function of the ceremony performed with such silence and solemnity as in some measure to resemble the celebration of a religious mystery.' Macartney and Staunton were treated as guests of honour, the Emperor sending them food and drink from his own table. For the first time, in spite of the discomforts of sitting on the floor, they had a chance to take stock of their surroundings. They noted the presence of the three other ambassadors from Pegu, as well as six Muslim ambassadors from the Kalmucks of the north-west – 'but their appearance was not very splendid,' wrote Macartney.

Their surroundings, however, were of quite a different order:

The tapestry, the curtains, the carpets, the lanterns, the fringes, the tassels were

> disposed with such harmony, the colours so artfully varied and the light and shades so judiciously managed, that the whole assemblage filled the eye with delight . . . The commanding feature of the ceremony was that calm dignity, that sober pomp of Asiatic greatness, that European refinements have not yet attained.

Discreetly they observed the Emperor, trying the while to fix bearing and visage in their mind's eye. They saw in him ' a very fine old gentleman, still healthy and vigorous, not having the appearance of a man more than sixty, his manner dignified but affable and condescending'. They were to have a further opportunity of observing him more closely, for he sent for them and, offering them a glass of wine, inquired the age of King George – hoping that, like him, he might be hale and hearty at the age of eighty-three. Staunton found the Emperor 'so hale and vigorous that he scarcely appeared to have existed as many years, fifty-seven, as in fact he had governed the Empire'.

Then, when the Emperor asked Heshen if anybody in the Embassy spoke Chinese, he was told that the twelve-year-old Staunton, Page to the Ambassador, had, during the course of the year-long voyage, acquired knowledge of the language. The boy was immediately summoned to the Imperial presence. What transpired between them is not recorded, but it so pleased the Emperor that young Staunton was given the yellow silk purse holding areca nuts which hung from his belt. It was a mark of particular favour.

The audience, banquet and presentation of ambassadors lasted some five hours. At the end the Emperor rose to his feet; and, as the courtiers once more knelt in kowtow, Staunton observed that 'he descended from the throne, marching firm and erect and without the least symptom of infirmity, to the open chair that was waiting for him'.

Thus ended the first meeting between Emperor and Ambassador. Wrote Macartney in his journal: 'Thus have I seen Solomon in all his glory. I use this expression as the scene recalled a puppet show of that name which I recollect to have seen in my childhood and which made so strong an impression that I thought it the highest pitch of human greatness and felicity.' But, as the days passed, it became only too clear who was pulling the strings.

In the succeeding days there were many marks of Imperial favour. It was 11am when the Embassy returned from the Gardens of Jehol, and very soon afterwards presents arrived from the Emperor. They were eagerly unwrapped, to reveal silks – some, intended for the military, woven into patterns with the four-clawed dragon rampant amongst clouds, and others, intended for high-ranking civil mandarins, embroidered with Chinese pheasants. There were also the richest velvets, satins and intricately embroidered purses. In addition, there was porcelain, some of intricate shape and some delicately curved – quite different from that usually exported to England; large balls of tea from the southern province of Yunnan, highly prized by the Chinese but not to English taste; and fruit – grapes from western China, mandarin oranges, pomegranates and lichees from the southern provinces. The presents addressed to the King were set aside, while Macartney distributed the rest to the members of the suite.

Further indications of Imperial favour were to follow. The day after the presentation at Court, on the Emperor's instructions the Ambassador and his suite were invited by Chief Minister Heshen to tour the Gardens of Jehol and their pleasure grounds. So once again the Embassy rose at 3am, and went to the Imperial Gardens. Once again, they mingled with the great officers of state for some three hours, waiting for the Emperor to appear. As on the previous day, he arrived borne by sixteen men in a high, open palanquin. This time, however, he immediately summoned the Ambassador over to him. Macartney recorded: 'He [said that he] was going to his devotions in the Temple of Potala, that as they did not share the same Gods he would not desire His Excellency to accompany him, but that he had ordered his ministers to attend him through his gardens.'

Macartney would have been satisfied with any courtier of rank as his guide, but he found Heshen, Grand Secretary and Chief Minister – next to the Emperor, the most important man in China – waiting to greet and escort him. He was surprised and delighted. It was an auspicious beginning, a prize opportunity to combine pleasure with diplomatic business. After the attentions paid him by the Emperor, and buoyed by generous gifts, he anticipated a fruitful day.

7

At the Yuanmingyuan

The party left behind in Peking was split. Dinwiddie the Machinest, Barrow the Comptroller, Petitpierre the watchmaker and Thibault the mathematical instrument maker were in residence in the Great Hall of the Yuanmingyuan, 'sleeping where none had slept before'. Their job was to have everything ready for the return of the main party from Jehol. Much to their chagrin the two artists, Alexander and Hickey, had been left behind in the palace in the city of Peking that had been allocated to the Embassy. Their job was to finish hanging the pictures of King George and Queen Charlotte, as well as putting the finishing touches to the great canopy of state.

Although the palace covered an area 'the size of Soho Square', they felt it a virtual prison. There were guards on the doors, and nobody was allowed to wander outside. Indeed, when in an attempt to overcome claustrophobia they climbed to the top of a pile of ornamental boulders in order to see what lay beyond the walls, they were firmly and formally rebuked by the mandarin in charge. Yet the cage that held them was indeed a gilded one, not only because of the decorative surroundings but also because of the food supplied: some forty or fifty dishes each day, prepared in Imperial style, rounded off with iced desserts and with all the Chinese wine they could drink. So lavish was the repast that they pleaded for plain cooking.

Only Alexander, in his official capacity of draughtsman, could escape. Occasionally he would journey to the Yuanmingyuan to make drawings of the setting-up of the presents. On these forays he would seize every opportunity to sketch not only the buildings but the scenes from Chinese life, which he was to issue in book form on his return to England. Even on these trips he could not escape the politics of obeisance which haunted the Embassy. He recounts meeting a young mandarin of the Imperial family on the road, of being forced to dismount but then refusing to kneel and kowtow in the mud. No sequel to this act of insubordination is recorded.

These encounters only whetted his appetite, making him the more keenly regret his separation from the main party at Jehol. Not seeing the Great Wall, not painting the presentation to the Emperor from life, having no chance to see and sketch the splendours of the Court – all these were the unkindest strokes of fate to the documentary artist.

Within the Great Hall at the Yuanmingyuan, the assembling of the presents proceeded slowly. Interruptions were many, and interpretation faltering. One interpreter having defected at Macao, and Mr Plumb having accompanied the main party to Jehol, those left at the Yuanmingyuan had no interpreter to help them. So great was the language problem to the Chinese that the Emperor had called in some Portuguese missionaries to assist. However, as mentioned earlier, since the Portuguese were regarded by the Embassy as their political and commercial rivals, Sir George Staunton, fearful lest they discover too much about the British intentions in China, forbade the speaking of Latin – a restriction which led to some ridiculous scenes. 'Tu loquaris Latinum, Domine? [Do you speak Latin?]', inquired one missionary of Dr Gillan, the Embassy physician and philosopher – who, denying his education and upbringing, had to reply that in England learned doctors did not speak Latin. The situation was compounded by Sir George Staunton inadvertently using Latin freely in the missionaries' presence. One letter he sent to Dinwiddie, forbidding him to use Latin, and delivered by the missionaries, bore the words 'Fiat responsio' on its seal.

It was by means of 'ridiculous shuffling' that a Portuguese priest, Father Peter Adeodato, Augustine watchmaker and mechanist assisting Dinwiddie, was 'officially appointed' interpreter. Thus, he could converse 'with the gentlemen in a language which a few days before they could not understand'. Once communication was established with Adeodato and the two other missionaries, Dinwiddie discovered that they belonged to the Tribunal of Mathematics. Their job was to make calculations for the almanac, a task closely followed by the Emperor, who was anxious to know the merits of the various instruments that the British visitors had brought with them. He especially wanted comparison between the Embassy's orrery and one in his possession at Jehol. Dinwiddie, the dominie, was in his element. Having started his career as a teacher, he was more than happy to throw in some of his public lecture material for good measure: 'In this history I shall begin with the most general and then descend to those of smaller extent . . . Of this we have examples in all the bodies of the solar system. Thus, physical astronomy will form the first article of this mechanical history.' The good Fathers listened politely to the flow of Scottish-accented Latin. So much for Staunton's strictures on its use. They may well have wished that they had still been in force.

Dinwiddie, believing that the triumph of Western ideas would be a major contribution to the success of the Embassy, lost no opportunity to display rationality and learning in front of visiting Chinese. There were plenty of them. To Dinwiddie's satisfaction, they showed an ignorance that not only swelled his sense of superiority but also gave him an opportunity to proselytize. Much like children, they asked an endless stream of questions. Where are the five planets on the celestial globe? Why is China so small on the terrestrial globe? Is it deliberately made small by the English? Much like children, they were easily pleased and as soon tired.

The Emperor's grandsons continued to pay daily visits. They giggled and interrupted the work. One brought in a watch by Cummin of London. Capped and jewelled, it badly needed cleaning. When Thibault painstakingly took it apart and cleaned it, the young Chinese aristocrats were delighted. Flattering Dinwiddie, they observed to one of the missionaries: 'The English must be very proud of their knowledge in science, when they make such a parade in bringing so many fine machines to China.'

Dinwiddie's initial contempt for his hosts began to diminish. He was surprised to find the Chinese talent for improvisation as good as, if not better than, that of his own colleagues. And when it was discovered that one of the spherical segments for the Ptolemaic system of the planetarium had been broken, it was not the English who repaired it: 'A Chinaman managed the business with the use of a red hot iron,' reported Dinwiddie – blunting praise with disparagement by adding, 'the edge was not straight but sufficiently so to answer the purpose.' He began to feel occasional self-doubt. He wondered, for instance, about the reliability of the make and about the purpose of the orrery now at Jehol. Gradually, Dinwiddie's change of opinion hardened into Calvinistic certainty. He wondered out loud, within earshot of the Chinese, whether these 'contrivers and makers of such curious and elegant machinery must not be men of understanding and superior persons'.

The Chinese riposted that machines might be curious things, but 'did Europeans understand the art of government as equally polished?' The rationalist in Dinwiddie refused to be sidetracked by either the self-opinion of the Chinese or the received knowledge of a succession of savants who had visited the country and made known their findings. He had seen for himself during his six weeks in China. He believed that the great Empire had usually been described in Confucian terms of 'what ought to be rather than what is'. But filial piety and gentle manners, supposed to exist even in the lowest classes, were simply not apparent in this cursing, hawking, spitting, teeming mass, no different from the wynds of Edinburgh or the alleyways of Southwark. He saw it all in Newtonian terms of irresistible force and immovable object. 'Nothing but conquest by some polished nation will ever render this a great people. Their prejudices are invincible.'

If Dinwiddie believed his eye, so did Alexander – but his saw a different picture. His observations took him behind the façade. These were no heathens

– there was colour in their dress and dignity in their bearing. On the Emperor's birthday he described a visit to the palace in Peking by the attendant mandarins. His eye was caught by their

> court drapes of ceremony consisting of a loose gown, on the breast and back of which is a square of about twelve inches, richly embroidered. In the centre is an imaginary bird, worn by those who are civil magistrates, and a kind of tyger when of the military department. The colour of this exterior dress is generally purple from the neck. They wear a collar of beads of coral, glass, etc., which reaches as low as the middle. Under this there is a rich vest richly embroidered with dragons in gold and in other colours.

He was to capture these robes later in his book, *The Costume of China*. On his daily journey to the Yuanmingyuan he was to depict the walls and gates of the city of Peking and the liveliness of the scene below – a far cry from Dinwiddie the dominie's description, engrossed as it was in military detail and architectural minutiae: 'Yet the brick does not seem old, and I am of the opinion that the walls are not so old as is alleged,' Dinwiddie had concluded. If he had known how the Chinese were going to sum up his endeavours, he would not so eagerly have anticipated demonstrating the air pump, the diving bell, and the aerostatics of ballooning!

8

A Stroll in the Garden with Heshen

SUNDAY 15TH SEPTEMBER 1793 As the Emperor made his way to his devotions, Macartney and his party, accompanied by the Ministers and Grand Secretaries of the Court, retired to a small pavilion in the Imperial gardens. Having risen at 3am and having been compelled by Court etiquette to wait three hours for the Emperor's appearance, they were glad of the collation that welcomed them.

And Macartney was surprised and flattered by the company. There was Heshen, the Chief Minister, and Fuchang'an, the Second Minister. He was accompanied by his brother Fukhang'an, former Viceroy of Canton and now recently appointed to Sichuan. He is referred to in accounts as the 'Thibet General'; he suspected British complicity with his enemies in his recent campaign, and was to display hostility to the Embassy throughout the outing. Finally there was Songyun, Mongol Grand Councillor, recently engaged in negotiation with the Russians. (He was probably included in the party because of Macartney's involvement with the Russian Court earlier in his career.) All of them wore the yellow vest, a mark of their closeness to the throne, and all of them were Tartars. As the introductions were made, Macartney thought thankfully of the fine opportunity, at last presenting itself, to break new ground and broach the preliminaries of his business.

After breakfast, they went for a ride through the gardens. Their great beauty recalled for Macartney the approach to the great house of Luton Hoo in Bedfordshire, owned by his father-in-law, Lord Bute, and landscaped by Capability Brown. Three miles on, they came to a lake alongside which was moored a magnificent yacht and several smaller yachts decked out with flags and streamers. Macartney, who knew the splendour of the artificed landscaping of the great English estates, found himself, as in the Yuanmingyuan, taken aback by the skill of the Chinese landscape gardeners:

Had China been accessible to Mr Brown or Mr Hamilton,* I should have sworn they should have drawn their happiest ideas from the rich sources I have tasted this day; for in the course of a few hours I have enjoyed such vicissitudes of rural delight, as I did not conceive could be felt out of England, being at different moments enhanced by scenes perfectly similar to those I have known there, to the magnificence of Stowe, the soft beauties of Woburn or the fairyland of Painshill.

But try as he might, at no point in the day, whether during the delightful row on the lily-filled lake or while wandering round some fifty palaces filled with Chinese and Western *objets d'art*, could Macartney persuade the Chinese to discuss business.

Since the Chief Minister appeared attentive, he tried a flattering conversational gambit: the creation in such a wild spot of such a paradise as Jehol, he suggested, was a work worthy of the genius of Kangxi. Heshen looked surprised. Back came the reply, through the interpreter's Latin, in the form of a question: How did the Ambassador know this? Who had told him? Macartney applied a little more flattery. Was it to be wondered that the English should be particularly well informed of the history of the Chinese, whose fame extended to the most distant parts of the world? As this sentence passed through the interpreter, Heshen remained impassive. Perhaps it was too much to expect a senior courtier who had built his career on flattery to swallow such flimsy bait; or, more likely, as Macartney suspected, 'at bottom he rather wonders at our curiosity than esteems us for our knowledge. Possibly he may consider it as impertinent towards them and useless to ourselves'.

A bigger cloud was to hang over the next exchange. Trying to appease the manifest antagonism of Fukhang'an, Macartney, affecting to recognize his ability as a warrior, wondered if the General would derive pleasure and entertainment from seeing his guard go through the latest in European drill manoeuvres. This suggestion was dismissed with 'great coldness and a mixture of unreasonable vanity, saying nothing of the kind could be a novelty to him, though I have my doubts whether he ever saw a firelock in his life'.

The situation was not about to improve. When Heshen revealed that he had just received news that the *Lion* and *Hindostan* had safely anchored in Zhoushan, Macartney took the opportunity of proposing that Captain Mackintosh, in whose ship the greater part of the presents had been carried, having made his obeisance to the Emperor, should be permitted to rejoin his ship. But Fukhang'an quickly interjected that it was forbidden by law for foreigners to travel at will through the Chinese Empire. It seemed that neither reason nor flattery could soften this apparent intransigence, nor produce a better atmosphere.

Aware of the folly of pursuing a lost cause on the wrong battleground,

---

* The Hon. Charles Hamilton was a well known landscape architect, famous for his landscaping of the gardens at Painshill in Surrey.

Macartney suggested to Heshen that they might perhaps have a meeting within the next few days. 'I found however that though infinitely gracious and civil in his manner and expression, I could gain no ground from him.' Heshen pleaded pressure of work due to the imminent departure of the Court from Jehol and the forthcoming birthday celebrations. He hoped they would have frequent meetings at the Yuanmingyuan. It was now obvious to Macartney that it had been decided from the beginning that no business would be done at Jehol. Falling back on the final anticlimactic face-saving resource at his disposal, Macartney obtained the Chief Minister's gracious permission to send him a note.

Although by now the coldness of the social climate was to some extent countered by the novelty and elegance of the surroundings, even the beauty of Jehol carried threatening overtones:

> Where any things particularly interesting were to be seen we disembarked, from time to time, to visit them, and I dare say in the course of our voyage we stopped at forty or fifty palaces or pavilions. These are all furnished in the richest manner, with pictures of the Emperor's huntings and progresses; with stupendous vases of jasper and agate; with the finest porcelain and japan, and with every kind of European toys and sing-songs [mechanical automata], with spheres, orreries, clocks and musical automatons of such exquisite workmanship, and in such profusion, that our presents must shrink from the comparison and 'hide their diminished heads'. And yet I am told that the fine things we have seen are far exceeded by others of the same kind in the apartments of the ladies and in the European repository at Yuan Ming Yuan.

So it was that Qianlong trumped Macartney's ace. The Court documents always referred to the arrogance of the British. They had already refused to kowtow. If they chose to use the fragility of scientific instruments as an excuse for sailing up the forbidden waters of the east coast to Tientsin rather than using the overland route, then they were to be shown that the Chinese had knowledge and skills to match any of theirs. They were bringing coals to Newcastle!

16th September When Mr Plumb, the interpreter, called on the Ambassador to tell him that a messenger was on his way from the Chief Minister, Macartney hoped that Heshen had changed his mind overnight. Perhaps there would be a meeting after all. Were they at long last getting down to business? But all the messenger brought with him was a command that the Embassy doctor, Dr Gillan, attend on Heshen. In the hopes that the encounter with Western medicine would reinforce the superiority of Western science, Gillan was dispatched to meet the illustrious patient, whom he found with Chinese doctors and an interpreter in attendance. They were all to be surprised – Heshen and his doctors at the difference between Chinese and European clinical methods, and Gillan at the condition of the patient.

Over the preliminary tea and sweetmeats, Heshen told Gillan that his physicians had decided, after a full examination of his pulses, that his complaints were 'owing to a malignant vapour or spirit which had infused itself into, or was generated in his flesh, which shifted itself from place to place and always excited pain, inflammation and swelling in the part where it fixed itself'. The traditional remedy was to make way for the 'vapour or spirit' to expel itself, by making deep punctures with gold and silver needles – an operation that caused the Chief Minister much pain and suffering and furnished no hint of a permanent cure.

It surprised Heshen that the doctor, having listened to this diagnosis, did not immediately come and take his pulses but instead asked for details of the symptoms – pains in the joints of the back and legs and considerable pain in the lower abdomen. By the time this recital was over Heshen was obviously impatient to have his pulses taken, and summoning the doctor to his side he offered him his right arm on a yellow silk cushion embroidered with gold. To put his patient at ease, the doctor felt the pulses for some time, first the pulse in the right arm and then the left. He then proceeded to deliver a homily to both Heshen and the attendant audience of Chinese physicians, telling them that in Europe we were not accustomed to examine the pulses in various parts of the body, 'that we usually felt it in one place only, because we knew that all pulses corresponded together and communicated with the heart and each other by means of the circulation of the blood'.

The Chief Minister and his doctors were astonished at the novelty of the explanation. With uneasy smiles, the doctors muttered among themselves, causing the interpreter to observe to Gillan that 'they were much embarrassed and disconcerted in their answers to the Grand Secretary.' So, both to clear the air and make his point, Gillan proposed an experiment. Heshen should apply the index finger of his right hand to his left temporal artery and the index finger of his left hand to his right ankle. To his pleasant surprise, in spite of the contortion, he found the beats simultaneous.

Gillan, sensing that his stock was rising, went on to explain that in Western medicine, besides examining the pulse, the physician had to take other circumstances into account. He recorded later: 'And particularly we asked a variety of questions respecting internal sensations and external circumstances, the answers to which enabled us to form a better and more accurate judgement . . . upon full investigation it appeared that the Chief Minister laboured under two distinct complaints.' The first was rheumatism, brought on by the cold and rainy weather in Tartary. And the second was a hernia, which was causing the abdominal pain. It had never given him pain until eight years ago, when it suddenly increased in size whilst Heshen was mounting a tall horse.

His physicians were proposing puncturing this swelling, but Heshen was unwilling to submit to this treatment, fearing damage to his genitalia. Gillan warned him that such treatment could do more than that: it could have terminal consequences. He suggested that Heshen be fitted with a truss.

When the interpreter translated to him my explanation of the nature of his complaint and the method of cure, he seemed quite lost in astonishment. He conversed again with his physicians and at last desired the interpreter to tell me that my ideas and all I had said were so extraordinary that it appeared to them as if it had come from an inhabitant of another planet.

While Dr Gillan was ministering to the Chief Minister, Macartney was grappling with the problems involved in sending him a letter, requesting not only that Mackintosh be allowed to rejoin his ship, but, for good measure, that the private cargo brought out to China by the ships' officers be permitted to be sold and another cargo purchased from the adjoining provinces.

But first there was the problem of court phraseology: at Jehol there was no friendly missionary to make a proper translation of the letter. Fortunately, Mr Plumb found someone to undertake to turn the English into Court address. The actual writing of it was yet another hurdle – no Chinese would do it in case his hand was recognized. So in order to lighten the interpreter's burden, young Staunton, the Page, was pressed into service as calligrapher. The letter took three days to write. Then how to deliver it? The Tartar legate, Zhengrui, was deemed unreliable, having recently been disgraced and demoted, as noted earlier, for misleading the Emperor over the details of his reception of the Embassy on their arrival. So at dawn, dressed in an English uniform, Mr Plumb evaded the guards around the palace and made his way to the Chief Minister's house. He was jostled and obstructed, but he managed to push a way through the crowd that collected around him, handing the message to Heshen's secretary, who promised to deliver it but – and this augured ill for future relations if the British had known how to read the omens – refused to accept a bribe.

Visitors came, all the time, to the palace where the Embassy was billeted. Some came on business, some out of curiosity. So closely was the Embassy guarded that it was difficult, if next to impossible, to leave their lodgings, so in order to make some contact none was turned away. In fact, Macartney welcomed them. Mr Plumb was overworked. Nevertheless, he would hold long conversations from which he was able to glean the historical, geographical and economic background of the country to which they had travelled. And although he was within the Chinese Empire he was well aware that here in High Tartary he was in a different domain, inhabited by a different people.

One young Tartar princeling who paid a courtesy call provided some useful information. He recounted how Qianlong was descended from the Mongol Kublai Khan, grandson of Genghis Khan, who in the thirteenth century had conquered China and set up the Yuan dynasty which ruled the country for a hundred years until dethroned by the Ming dynasty. Subsequently the Mongols retreated into the country of the Manchus, mixed and intermarried. From one of these alliances sprang the Bogdoi Khans, who invaded China in 1640 and had reigned over it ever since. (Since other visitors gave differing accounts, Macartney sounded a note of warning in his journal.) The young man further told him that all the persons with whom they had dined in the Emperor's tent were clan chiefs able to field large bodies of troops in time of war. Their stations, ranks and duties were assigned to them under the grand banners of Tartary; their lands, or fiefs, were hereditary by primogeniture and, though the approval of the Emperor was needed in inheritance cases, he seldom refused it.

The Tartar princes usually married the daughters and nieces of the Imperial family and, by virtue of these alliances, held rank at Court. Every year they were obliged to attend the Emperor's birthday celebrations. They were seldom detained at Court, or employed anywhere in China, in offices that required a literary background, for their education would usually have been directed to military pursuits. Their main weapons were scimitar and bow, the latter being the favourite of the Emperor, who took great delight in being painted loosing arrows at stags, wolves and tigers, but never hunting with a musket. Macartney's informant was surprised when he told him that, as a weapon of war, in Europe the bow had yielded to firearms. As they all did, he received such news from the other side of the planet with a politely embarrassed smile of incredulity.

17th September 1793 On this day, Emperor Qianlong's eighty-third birthday, the Embassy set out for the Court at 3am. Once again they had to run the gauntlet of people and farm animals in the streets of Jehol. Once again they had to wait some two hours for the celebrations to begin, reposing themselves while being served with fruit, warm milk and other refreshments. This time the ceremonies were to take place in the Palace, not in a tent. And this time the Emperor would not reveal himself – rather, his presence was to be symbolized by a series of *coups de théâtre*.

Huttner, philologist as well as tutor to young Staunton, marvelled at the first of these. The centre of the courtyard where the people had assembled was covered with a large red cloth. On each of the four corners stood a man with a large whip at his feet. As soon as the Emperor was on his throne – behind a screen, invisible to the crowd – at a signal, they lifted their whips in unison and cracked them with all their strength to the ground. After three strikes they put their whips down, raising them again some minutes later. They repeated this procedure twice – nine cracks of the whip in all. Huttner sought an explanation, but in vain. He presumed that the ceremony 'dates from the most distant history of the Tartars. The magical number nine inherent in the threefold kowtow, used in venerating the Emperor, with its nine knockings of the head on the floor, would seem to provide some basis for the ceremonies' origins.'

After this overture, the mandarins, ministers and visiting ambassadors moved into a vast hall and thence into an inner building, 'bearing at least the semblance of a temple'. It was furnished with musical instruments, sets of cylindrical bells, triangles suspended in line from ornamental wooden frames, diminishing in size from lowest note to highest. To this was added a choir of eunuchs, whose falsetto sounded like musical glasses heard from a distance. Macartney describes what happened:

> At length the great band both vocal and instrumental struck up with all their powers of harmony and instantly the whole court fell flat on their faces before this invisible Nebuchadnezzar; . . . The music was a sort of birthday ode or state anthem, the burden of which was 'Bow down your heads, all ye dwellers upon earth, bow down your heads before the great Ch'ien-lung [Qianlong], the great Ch'ien-lung.' And then all the dwellers upon China earth there present, except ourselves, bowed down their heads and prostrated themselves upon the ground at every renewal of the chorus . . . indeed in no religion, either ancient or modern, has the divinity ever been addressed, with stronger exterior marks of worship and adoration than were this morning paid to the phantom of his Chinese Majesty.

If the whipcrack at the four corners of the Middle Kingdom symbolized the Emperor's dominance, so the lash carried military discipline throughout the British domain.

Private James Cootie, of the Ambassador's guard, had procured from a Chinese soldier a small quantity of liquor. This was duly reported to the commanding officer, Lieutenant-Colonel Benson. Bearing in mind the Ambassador's proclamation against any form of trading, read out on board ship on 20th July, the officer ordered him to be court martialled. The court, made up of his colleagues with a corporal as president, sentenced him to sixty lashes. Aeneas Anderson, valet de chambre, was horrified at the proceedings:

> In consequence of this sentence, all the British soldiery were drawn up in the outer court of the Palace; and after observing all the forms usual on such occasions, the culprit was tied to one of the pillars on the great portico, and in the presence of a great number of the Chinese, he received the punishment, administered with no common severity. The mandarins, as well as those natives of the inferior classes who were present, expressed their abhorrence at this proceeding, while some of them declared that they could not reconcile this conduct in a people who professed a religion, which they represented to be superior to all others, in enforcing sentiments of benevolence, and blending the duties of justice and of mercy. One of the principal mandarins, who knew a little of the English language, expressed his own sentiments and those of his brethren by saying, 'Englishmen too much cruel, too much bad.'

Had Anderson known the Chinese penal code, he would not have taken this comment at face value.

They were not to see the Emperor at all that day. He remained concealed in the Palace. However, with the feeling of relief that attends the end of a long and hermetic ceremony, they welcomed the invitation from Heshen to complete the tour of Jehol by visiting the Western Garden which, they were informed, made a sharp contrast to the delicate scenery of their previous visit. Their companions were to be the same as two days ago.

The Western Garden lived up to its promise. It overwhelmed Macartney. He wrote in his journal:

> It is one of the finest forest scenes in the world. Wild, woody, mountainous and rocky, abounding with stags and deer of different species . . . woods often clamber over the loftiest pinnacles of the stony hills, or gathering on the skirts of them, descend with rapid sweep, and bury themselves in the deepest valleys. There at proper distances you find palaces, banqueting houses and monasteries adapted to the circumstances and peculiar situations of the place.

Sure of foot, their unshod horses carried them over the mountain trails until at last they came to a hilltop pavilion, 'open on all sides and situated on a summit so elevated as perfectly to command the whole surrounding countryside . . . I saw everything before me as on an illuminated map, palaces, pagodas, towns, villages, farm houses, plain and valley, and certainly so rich, so various, so beautiful, so sublime a prospect my eyes never beheld.' Seeking comparisons, once again his thoughts turned to England, to the home of his brother-in-law:

> If any place can be said in any respect to have similar features to the western park I have seen this day it is Lowther Hall in Westmorland, which from the extent of the prospect, the noble situation, the diversity of surface, the extensive woods, and command of water might be rendered . . . the finest scene in the British Dominions.

In this pavilion, with the view and the dishes spread before them, they dined on *petits pâtés*, salt relishes, savoury dishes with fruits and sweetmeats, milk and iced water. At the end of the meal a number of yellow boxes containing silk and porcelain, presents from the Emperor, were carried in procession before them. They rose and bowed in salute at this Imperial favour.

Then came a puppet show – these were normally performed by eunuchs in ladies' apartments, but as a particular compliment this one had been brought to the hilltop for the entertainment of the Embassy. In their eyes this show bore comparison with those back home in England. They politely applauded the antics of the Punch character, his wife Bandimeer and Scaramouche, and the drama of the knight errant, vanquishing lions and dragons to rescue a princess confined in a castle.

All these distractions, with the clash of cymbals, the beating of the gong and the castrato voices accompanying the marionettes, prevented discussion of serious matters. Macartney recorded:

> I could not help admiring the address with which the Minister [Heshen] parried all

my attempts to speak to him on business this day, and how artfully he evaded every opportunity that offered for any particular conversation with me, endeavouring to engage our attention solely by the objects around us, directing our eyes to the prospects, and explaining the various beauties of the park and buildings.

All that Macartney could accomplish was to remind the Chief Minister of his promise to read the note, at this moment being prepared for him, due to be ready on the morrow.

At three o'clock, Heshen and his immediate entourage took their leave. Grand Councillor Songyun was left to escort them round the twelve Temples of the Wai Ba Miao which adjoined the Western Garden. Eight of these were devoted to the Lamaistic Buddhism of Tibet and Central Asia. Indeed one, the Potala, was a direct copy of the temple of the Dalai Lama in Lhasa. Macartney records it as being home for eight hundred lamas. Lieutenant Parish meticulously measured it and subsequently drew sections and plans, and from these measurements Macartney could state the height of the building as two hundred and fifty feet. Inside the Golden Chapel,

all the monks and lamas were busily engaged in their devotions, dressed in yellow vestments, chanting their liturgy in a kind of recitative . . . In the middle of the chapel is a small space railed off, and elevated by three steps above the floor, which presents three altars richly adorned, and three colossal statues, one of Fo-Hi [Buddha], one of Fo-Hi's wife [Bodhisattva] and the other of some great Tartar divinity, whose name I forget, all of solid gold . . . There are in some of these pagodas [temples], a thousand monstrous statues, all most horribly ugly and so ill-represented, and so unlike anything in heaven or earth, that one would think they might be safely worshipped even by the Jews without incurring the guilt of idolatry. The Emperor, it is affirmed, thinks that he is not only descended in a right line from Fo-Hi himself, but entertains the strong notion that the soul of Fo-Hi is actually translated into his Imperial Body, so that the unbounded magnificence displayed in the erection of these pagodas may be looked on as not quite so disinterested for, according to this hypothesis, there has been nothing spent out of the family.

In his description Macartney overlooked the salient point. Chinese indifference to the British is partly explained by the fact that Qianlong was far more interested in the politics of placating and dominating his Central Asian heartland than in the pinpricks of attempted European expansion along the Chinese coast.

The Embassy's day finished with a climb to the top of the Potala: the roof of the temple, they were assured, was covered with plates of gold. Macartney took this with a pinch of salt. 'It may be so,' he wrote in his journal. 'But so vast is the undertaking and so perfect the execution, that such a monument as the Potala, of grandeur and stability, required not only all the fervour and enthusiasm of the most munificent bigot, but all the exertion and authority of the most powerful and most opulent monarch of the East.'

It was now dusk, some fourteen hours after their expedition had begun.

9

Imperial Pleasures

18th september In their journals, these eighteenth-century Western witnesses reported that the Emperor was in the habit of retiring at 6pm to avoid the night air. It was believed that the large drop in temperature at dusk was the cause of many diseases, some of which were fatal.

So the Ambassador and his suite were summoned once again to take their place at Court at first daylight, for the last of three days of birthday rejoicing. The celebrations took place in an inner court of the Palace, lavishly decorated 'with a profusion of silk, ribands and streamers and illuminated with great splendour and elegance'. The centre of attraction was a specially constructed theatre, with three stages set one above the other symbolizing the three planes of existence – Heaven, Earth and Hell. Sited in the middle of the courtyard, these stages were surrounded by raised and elegantly furnished boxes, with the Emperor commanding a position of honour. Since women were banned by Imperial decree from publicly attending theatricals, they were seated behind a lattice above the boxes, so that they could see the amusements without being seen to enjoy them.

The performance began at eight o'clock. Beforehand, the Emperor sent for Macartney and Sir George Staunton. His message was as surprising as the audience was unexpected. Macartney noted in his journal:

> With great condescension of manner, he told us that we should not be surprised to see a man of his age at the theatre, for that he seldom came thither, except upon a very particular occasion like the present; for that, considering the extent of his dominions and the number of his subjects, he could spare but little time for such amusements.

In his answer, the Ambassador tried to draw him on the subject of the Embassy, but with no success. Instead the Emperor gave him a present for

King George, an elegantly lacquered box, which he averred had been in his family for eight hundred years. Inside were pieces of agate and other stones precious to the Tartars, as well as a book of painting and poetry in the Emperor's own hand. From below stairs scuttle-butt Aeneas Anderson, more hopefully than truthfully, purported to recreate the words addressed by the Emperor to the Ambassador.

> Deliver this casket to the King, your master, with your own hand and tell him, though the present may appear to be small, it is in my estimation the most valuable I can give, or my empire can furnish; for it has been transmitted to me through a long line of my predecessors, and is the last token of affection which I had reserved to bequeath to my son and successor, as a tablet of the virtues of his ancestors, which he had only to peruse, as I should hope, to inspire him with the noble resolution to follow such bright examples.

For his personal use Macartney was given several purses for areca nuts. Staunton and the other members of the Embassy received purses, silk and porcelain. Similar tokens of esteem were distributed amongst the Tartar princes and chief courtiers.

The performances lasted nearly five hours. Everyone was there: mandarins, soldiers and Chief Ministers dressed in ceremonial robes flanked the Emperor. Guards and standard-bearers were ranged behind him. For the Embassy it was an intermittent affair for, as the boxes were interconnected, there was a continuous stream of mandarin visitors, mostly Tartars. Macartney was particularly interested in two callers – Kalmucks of the Torghut tribe, who twenty years before had fled Russian domination to seek the protection of Qianlong. Half the tribe, some ten thousand people, had perished in this heroic migration from the shores of the Caspian Sea to Ili in the Central Asian western approaches of the Chinese Empire. These two Kalmuck visitors were to be shown especial favour on this birthday: they were decorated with 'transparent blue buttons and peacocks' feathers to their caps as an earnest of the Emperor's accepting their submission and allegiance'.

All through the morning, the wailing songs, the percussion and gliding movement of tragedy and comedy alternated on the stages before them. Huttner observed:

> In Chinese Theatre the actors who take the part of ancient Heroes, great warriors or kings, cover their faces in black and white, put on long beards and have wings on each shoulder with different costumes which are all made of silk material of the richest quality. Recalling how much the Chinese are prodigal with percussion and gongs and what they call music, one sees easily what patience it requires to be a spectator at such a spectacle for over three hours.

The climax was a grand pantomime: an allegory which to European eyes seemed to represent the marriage of the Ocean and the Earth. Actors, singly or together, impersonated dragons, elephants, tigers, eagles and ostriches as well as inanimate objects such as oaks and pines. The Ocean was represented on stage by figures of whales, dolphins, porpoises and leviathans, ships, rocks, shells, sponges and corals. For the finale, Earth and Ocean joined together in salute to the Imperial box, the whole tableau culminating in the appearance of an enormous whale which waddled forward, and, taking up his position exactly opposite the Emperor, 'spouted out of his mouth into the pit several tons of water, which to loud applause quickly disappeared through the perforations of the floor'. 'The wretched dramas of the morning', as Macartney was to call them, ended shortly before one o'clock. Chinese opera, with its percussive accompaniment to knockabout action, was alien to the ears of the Ambassador and his staff, brought up on the genteel Court music of eighteenth-century Europe. Nevertheless, at four they were back for the second act of the entertainment, which took place in front of the tent that had been the site of their first audience.

First came dancing, followed by wrestling and acrobatics – of the traditional kind still practised to this day – accompanied by the wild cacophonies of the percussion. Next, there was plate-spinning, starting with three plates spinning on rods attached to the boot of one foot and then on the other, and so on until 'nine dishes were annexed all at once'. Then a man lay on his back and raised his legs, whereupon a heavy jar was placed on his feet and he began to spin it and throw it into the air. One of the spectators put a little boy into the jar, who, after performing several spins, came out and sat on top.

> There were many other things of the same kind [complained Macartney], but I saw none at all comparable to the tumbling, rope-dancing, wire walking, and straw balancing of Sadler's Wells; neither did I observe any feats of equitation in the style of Hughes and Astley's amphitheatres,* although I had always been told the Tartars were remarkably skilful in the instruction and discipline of their horses.

From time to time the Emperor exercised his largesse by sending a variety of refreshments over to the Embassy. They had recently dined, but etiquette demanded gracious consumption. In the end the grandeur of the spectacle, as much as the performances themselves, elicited their grudging respect.

With the fireworks of the grand finale any discomforts they might have been suffering melted away. Even their discharge in daylight – to enable the Emperor to be in the Palace by nightfall – failed to diminish their magnificence. The diversity of the colours attracted both Lord Macartney and Dr Gillan. They agreed there was nothing as varied in Europe. They tried to find out the composition of the mixtures, but the Chinese pyrotechnicians were determined to keep their secrets. Gillan guessed, though, that the vivid

---

* Astley and Hughes were equestrian showmen, the former performing in London and in his amphitheatre in Dublin, the latter at the Royal Circus in London.

red was produced by a mixture of zinc filings, nitre and camphor, while the brilliant white was probably the product of mixing the same filings with gunpowder. But it was the 'novelty, neatness and ingenuity of contrivance', rather than the chemistry, that held their attention.

The most spectacular set piece consisted of the release of numerous lanterns from high up in the sky. A box of some five feet square, along with other, smaller, boxes, was hauled up to a height of sixty feet. Then the bottom suddenly opened, and twenty to thirty lanterns emerged, unfolding and lighting as they fell. This process was repeated, with the smaller boxes doing the same, until some five hundred lanterns lit up the sky: 'an immense network of fire, with divisions and compartments of various forms and dimensions, round and square, hexagons, octagons and lozenges, which shone like the brightest burnished copper and flashed like prismatic lightning with every impulse of the wind,' wrote an enchanted Macartney. The finale of the display was 'a volcano of suns, stars, squibs and bouncers, crackers, rockets and grenades, which involved the gardens for an hour after in a cloud of intolerable smoke'. Such was the discipline of the Court that there was no applause, no gasps of astonishment as at European firework displays. Nobody talked, 'nor even a laugh exploded during the whole display'.

As the smoke began to clear the conducting mandarin Wang, accompanied by the interpreter Mr Plumb, appeared in the ambassadorial box. He had been asked to inform His Excellency that the ceremonies at Jehol had come to an end, that the Emperor had fixed his departure for the Yuanmingyuan for 24th September, and that etiquette demanded the Embassy be in Peking to greet him on his arrival. It was therefore proposed the Embassy leave on the 21st.

Macartney accepted the proposal. He realized that this was the only chance of settling unfinished business. Nothing further was to be accomplished here in Jehol. In fact, he lulled himself into believing, Chinese procrastination and the attentions and hospitality lavished on the Embassy might well imply a wish on the part of their hosts for a long-term relationship. Meanwhile, enough was enough. Exhausted by a succession of early morning reveilles, the Embassy returned to their palace lodgings to make preparations for Saturday's departure.

The Chinese Court records of the time indicate an obsession with the many presents. Not only were the royal presents under discussion, but also those for the Ambassador and his suite, and for each officer, servant, soldier and sailor remaining on the English ships. This generosity was not as magnificent as it appeared, however. A memorial in a Court record states: 'We have checked and found that in the storehouses inside and outside Peking there are many rolls of Korean cloth and other articles [Mohammedan patterned cloth 'from India'].' The idea of recirculating rejected tribute is a measure of the parsimonious contempt with which the Chinese regarded the British gifts, just as the official Chinese Court account of the visit reflects the obverse of Macartney's enthusiasm:

On . . . [14th September] the Emperor took his seat in a great tent in the Jehol gardens. The chief English envoy, Macartney, and the Assistant Envoy, Staunton, had an audience and were feasted along with Princes, Dukes and Ministers in attendance and the Mongolian Princes with their sons and grandsons, Dukes, Imperial Sons-in-Law and tai ji [preceptors of the Imperial Court], as well as the Burmese tribute envoy and others. They were given presents according to rank.

The Emperor composed a poem recording the fact that the King of the red-haired English had sent his envoy Macartney, and others, who had arrived bearing a state message and 'tribute':

> Formerly Portugal presented tribute,
> Now England is paying homage.
> They have out-travelled Shu Hai and Heng-zhang;*
> My ancestors' merit and virtue must have reached their distant shores.
> Though their tribute is commonplace, my heart approves sincerely.
> Curios and the boasted ingenuity of their devices I prize not.
> Though what they bring is meagre, yet,
> In my kindness to men from afar I make generous return,
> Wanting to preserve my good health and power.

* Famous Chinese travellers.

10

RETURN TO PEKING

19TH AND 20TH SEPTEMBER On the evening of the 19th Zhengrui, Wang and Qiao came to see Macartney. With great formality the Tartar legate took from his pocket, and read out, the reply to the letter to Heshen that Macartney had had such difficulty in executing and Mr Plumb in delivering. It gave cold comfort. Captain Mackintosh, having come with Macartney, was to return at the same time. His ship the *Hindostan* might sell at Zhoushan what goods she had brought out, and in return she could load a cargo from which she would be exempted from duty. The two European missionary mathematicians who had been given passage by the Embassy to Tientsin should be allowed to come to Peking, but only providing they first went to Canton and travelled on the designated official route.

In the event, both these promises remained essentially unfulfilled. No cargo was available at Zhoushan, and for the time being the missionaries were made to return to Canton, not arriving at Peking until the following year.

Macartney requested a copy of the letter. Zhengrui refused. The Ambassador was caused further disquiet by the news that a council had been held on the subject of the Embassy. Not only had Fukhang'an, the former Viceroy of Canton who had already shown a marked hostility to the British visitors, been present, but the former Hoppo, Collector of Customs, who had been jailed for corruption, had been summoned from his prison cell and asked for his advice. Try as he might, Macartney could not get an inkling of what had transpired 'at the convention of such a divan!', but he sensed that it augured the worst.

The Friday was spent in preparation for the journey. The Emperor's presents for the King – the silks, porcelain, drawings, lanterns and balls of tea – had to be crated and marked GEORGE III REX. They were sent ahead with the heavy luggage. Wang and Qiao now informed Macartney that, since they would be less encumbered, they would be only six days on the road instead of seven. Had they all been fit, this acceleration would have presented no problems, but the lack of sleep, compounded by the strange diet and poor hygiene facilities, were taking their toll. Dysentery, in varying degrees of severity, had stricken the Embassy.

Saturday 21st September Rain throughout the night. When they set off at 7am the road was so heavy with mud that in nine hours of travel they covered only twelve miles. Since the outward journey, the weather had already begun to change. Tartary's summer was feeling the embrace of the first harbingers of winter; the wind had a cold bite to it, though it was still pleasant in the sun. They trudged past the strange rock pillar, the Jehol landmark that had so impressed them on the outward journey. Today, water streamed from its summit. At four o'clock they arrived at the palace that was to be their first stop-over.

The sick had marched or had been carried. One of them, Jeremy Reid of the Royal Artillery regiment and member of the Ambassador's guard, 'died of a bloody flux' occasioned by a surfeit of fruits, having eaten no less than forty apples at breakfast. Wang and Qiao were shocked. Nobody was allowed to die in an Imperial palace (especially one so close to Jehol), lest the death remind the Emperor of his mortality. So the event had to be concealed by maintaining the pretence that the corpse was still alive. Reid's body was carried to one of the exterior buildings of the palace. The doctor went to see him, as would be usual with a sick patient; the nurse inquired what he needed.

Sunday 22nd September This morning, Reid was placed upon a litter and sent on to the next village to await the arrival of the Embassy, and burial. It was not until he was on the road that it could be revealed that he had just died. As they set out, Wang informed them that the Emperor had unexpectedly left Jehol on his way to Peking. The Ambassador and his train were urged to cover two stages without halting, for the palaces in which they were due to stay were needed for the attendants of the Emperor. They snatched the time to bury Reid at the next village, and then marched eighteen miles without a halt.

The next day, the forced march continued. Up and en route before dawn. Twenty-four miles to the Great Wall at Gubeikou. The breach where they had mounted previously had been blocked by the Chinese, and although another way on to the wall was found, the first thrill of discovery had evaporated. By now many of the party had gone down with dysentery. In desperation, they tried a Chinese remedy – a mixture of cardamom, pepper and ginger taken in hot distilled spirit. This so exacerbated the symptoms that 'they had much difficulty escaping alive to Peking'.

Having spent the night at another Imperial palace, they resumed their journey on the Tuesday at 4am in bright moonlight. It took them nine hours to cover the thirty-five miles to their next destination. On the 25th they marched another twenty-seven miles. Then the next day, Thursday, they set off at 4am for the last stretch of twenty-seven miles, to Peking. They arrived at noon, having covered some 150 miles in five and a half days.

For those who had been left behind in Peking, the return of the Ambassador and his suite was a joyful occasion. They had become more and more isolated, prisoners of the palace in which they were billeted. (The Chinese mistrust of foreigners extended to the missionaries, who at the start of their stay had called on them every day, but had then been forbidden to do so.) With the ending of their isolation came the inspection of their labours. The day after the Embassy's arrival, Macartney went to the Great Hall at the Yuanmingyuan where the presents were on display awaiting the Imperial gaze. If those carried to Jehol were the appetizers, here was the main feast.

At the centre was the planetarium, a masterpiece of astronomical engineering reproducing all the then known planetary movements – the *Weltmaschine*, twenty years in the making, by the German theologian and watchmaker Philip Matthäus Hahn for the Baron Mylius. Subsequently it had been purchased from him by the East India Company for £600, and recased and refurbished by the British watchmaker Vulliamy of London, for £656 13s. Then there was Parker's great lens, used by the natural philosophers of the day as a burning glass. There were the two eighteen-light lustres, purchased for £840, now illuminating the Great Hall with their myriad twinkling candles. There was the Wedgwood pottery – the latest Etruria ware, blue ware and jasperware. There were the globes, muskets and sword blades, microscopes and air pumps, and the chemical and electrical apparatus. There was cloth from Bolton, brass from Birmingham, linen from Ireland. Finally there was the model of the latest and biggest British warship, HMS *Anson*, 110 guns, as well as the pictures of the notables of Britain and their houses. It was a veritable trade fair that lay before Macartney's gaze in the Great Hall of the Yuanmingyuan.

The Ambassador was equally satisfied with the work done in the palace at Nanchizi, the Embassy residence within the city of Peking. In the audience chamber, the portraits of King George and Queen Charlotte had been hung to face the state canopy of flowered crimson satin, richly embroidered with the royal coat of arms and hung with festoons and gold-fringed curtains. There was an air of permanence about the place: this was the residence of the British Embassy in Peking, to be open for business as soon as the word was given. Meanwhile, Dinwiddie was pressing the Ambassador to arrange for the demonstrations of his balloon and diving bell. All in good time, thought Macartney. For his instinct told him, much as he hoped he would be proved wrong, that the hurried pressure of the last few days foreshadowed an early departure for the entire mission. As soon as the Emperor and Heshen returned from Jehol he would try to hold the discussions that had, as if by design, eluded him. His mind desperately sought the answer to the riddle of the Chinese behaviour.

But to no avail – Macartney just could not understand the mixture of courtesy and hospitality and total diplomatic stand-offishness. Surely, after the gracious reception and the favours shown to him and the Embassy, something positive would emerge from their endeavours? Perhaps it was simply that, in the flurry of festivity at Jehol, his Chinese hosts had not had the chance to make a measured assessment, and would wish to meet with him, as Heshen had intimated, in the calmer atmosphere of the palaces of the capital.

As on the outward journey, the rigours of the road had taken their toll on the Ambassador. The lack of sleep, the jolting and now the sudden chill in the weather, had brought on a severe attack of rheumatism and gout. Others were sick too: Huttner had gone down with severe dysentery and many of the guard were severely ill. Macartney retreated to his sickbed to await the call to meet the Emperor, now on his way back from Jehol.

Heshen and the Court had not been slow in deciding what attitude to take to the Embassy. Contrary to Macartney's supposition – as we noted earlier – they had decided on their course of action before he even set foot on Chinese soil. The edict drafted and submitted to the Emperor on 3rd August left no room for doubt. And it had been promulgated in Manchu, Mandarin and Latin on 23rd September, the day on which the Embassy reached Gubeikou on their return journey from Jehol. Written on orange paper flecked with silver, it had been placed in a yellow cylinder and carried in the Emperor's train to Peking. It was not the decision that was important, but the timing of its delivery. Macartney's worst fears were about to be realized.

Friday 27th and Saturday 28th September Wang, Qiao and the Tartar legate pressed Macartney to put the finishing touches to the presents at the Yuanmingyuan. This entailed not only finalizing the arrangement, but instructing the missionaries, into whose charge they were to be given after the Embassy had departed, on the intricacies of the workings of the planetarium, the orreries, the globes, clocks and the rest, so that they could be kept in good working order. It was the haste with which he was urged to do all this that finally persuaded Macartney that he would be unable to realize his ambition of staying in Peking over the New Year.

On the Saturday afternoon, Zhengrui called on the Ambassador. He rose painfully from his sickbed, to be informed by the legate that the Emperor would be arriving in Peking on the Monday and that it was the custom 'for Ambassadors as well as great Mandarins of Court to go to meet him at a palace about twelve miles off'. In view of Macartney's condition it was suggested that, to ease the journey, he spend the Sunday night in his old quarters at the Yuanmingyuan.

From this apparent solicitude for his health Macartney inferred that his presence on the Emperor's return was to be more than a formality. He explained the painfulness of his condition but said that in spite of it he 'would exert himself to the utmost on such an occasion'. After all, he might glean from it some inkling of what was in store.

Sunday 29th September The ambassadorial suite set out for the Yuanmingyuan, on horseback except for one or two who preferred the jolting carriages. All complained about the horses being ill equipped. Alexander was issued with one without stirrups, and the animal chose to lag behind. But then on being given a well (or ill?) meant tap on the rump by one of the Chinese attendants, it bolted, and in doing so threw Alexander and raced on ahead – to the amusement of the spectators, who laughed as Alexander started to walk back to the Embassy's palace. Fortunately he met Mr Plumb setting out in a coach, and was able to share it with him.

Monday 30th September At 3am the Embassy was awakened by the beating of a drum. An hour later they set out on the last few miles, in the direction of Tartary, to pay their homage to the Emperor. The artist Alexander describes the scene:

Along the Imperial route an immense number of workmen laboured with rakes, brooms and hammers to make the highway smooth as a floor. Every ten yards there were lamps suspended under a tripod of sticks, giving light to the labourers as well as marking the bounds of the highway so no-one should intrude upon it . . .

After a five-mile journey there was a pause for tea and cakes at one of the Imperial resting places and then they were led to their station where three tents were prepared for their reception; one for the Ambassador, one for Sir George Staunton and the other for the suite. Before the tents were ranged some five hundred members of the Imperial Guard, with their banners, large silk umbrellas and other trophies, making a brilliant show in the sunrise . . .

As soon as the Emperor and his retinue was seen in the distance, the Ambassador and his suite moved toward the road and were placed within the line of soldiers. Once the Royal procession was in earshot the Chinese band struck up a martial air interrupted as ever by the most discordant percussion . . .

His Imperial Majesty was preceded by a body of horse. His sedan, surrounded by Mandarins and cavalry, was of a rich yellow carried by 8 bearers . . . He looked eminently towards us kneeling on one knee and bowing, and as he passed he sent a message to the Ambassador regretting the Ambassador was not well, and as the cold weather was approaching it would be better for him to return immediately to Peking, rather than make any stay at the Yuan Ming Yuan . . .

Next followed his Chief Minister in a green sedan chair. He gave the Ambassador a very gracious salute . . . The Mandarins employed and connected with the Embassy stood behind us, dressed in their habits of ceremony, while we were kneeling when the Emperor passed by. One of these, thinking my bow was not sufficiently respectful to his monarch, actually put his hand behind my neck and lowered my head almost to the ground. Perhaps my eagerness to see all that was possible of this splendid sight might shorten the inclination of the head on this memorable occasion.

No sooner had the cavalcade passed than Macartney returned to the Yuanmingyuan, where he rested for a while before returning to Peking. He was disappointed: yet again there had been no meaningful communication – not even an attempt to set up a meeting.

As for Qianlong, he went straight to the Yuanmingyuan so as to be ready to view the presents on the morrow.

11

Dismissal

Tuesday 1st October 1793 Macartney was too ill to move from his room. Although his instinct told him that he should be at the Yuanmingyuan, he contented himself by sending Barrow the Comptroller, Alexander and Dinwiddie 'to finish the job'. He was particularly exercised about Parker's great lens, which had so caught the imagination of the Chinese. Indeed, they had already asked Barrow if he could make a duplicate. When told that it was made by the same artist who had made the lustres that they saw above them and that it was unique in the world, they listened incredulously. Only after Dr Gillan had provided the same explanation did they seem to believe it.

When Dinwiddie arrived he discovered that, of their own accord, the mandarins had been trying to assemble the lens on its frame. Not having any plan, they failed to see how things fitted together. Proprietorially, Dinwiddie took charge; and having assembled the apparatus, he proceeded to perform experiments – burning wood and melting coins. The Chinese disparagingly pointed out that they had used crystal lenses for many years in order to light their pipes. To emphasize the point, one mandarin chose to light his pipe at the focus of the lens, as if deriding its usefulness, while a eunuch, putting his finger on the spot, occasioned mirth by the speed with which he withdrew it. 'How can an enemy's town be set on fire by the lens?' they asked. 'How will it act on a cloudy day?'

At this moment, unannounced, the Emperor arrived. 'We turned round the lens house, and while I stood at the mirror had a full view of His Majesty,' wrote Dinwiddie. '. . . He was very near us, and expressed nothing observable in his countenance. He looked at the lenses not more than two minutes and retired. When viewing the air pump he said, "These things are good enough to amuse children!"' The only item that caught his eye and appeared to give him food for thought was the model of HMS *Anson*. Perhaps it was the complexity of the rigging and the thought of the terrible fire-power the man-of-war was capable of that caught his attention – or perhaps his ear caught the name. In 1747, the eleventh year of Qianlong's reign, Captain Anson, later to be First Lord of the Admiralty, had been the first British naval officer to put into a Chinese port. The complexity of the negotiations over revictualling the warship, the seizure off Macao – piratical in Chinese eyes – of the Spanish treasure galleon from Manila, and the contrast of the readily offered British assistance in putting out the fire that threatened to destroy the port of Canton, must all have been reported to the Emperor at the time.

But the indifference with which the presents were received could only have increased Macartney's sense of foreboding. Of the three coaches taken by the Embassy to China, the phaeton was rejected out of hand by the Emperor: the driver and postilion were positioned at a greater height than the Imperial presence. (Zhengrui had warned Macartney, but he had taken no notice.) Two camera obscuras were also rejected, for unknown reasons. More ominously, Heshen refused the proffered Birmingham-made second winter coach. However, those of the Embassy who had stayed behind at the Yuanmingyuan were given by the Emperor ten pieces of silver, each weighing one ounce.

Macartney sensed that the pressure for their departure was rapidly building up. He had just heard from one of the few missionaries allowed to attend on the party at the Yuanmingyuan that the Embassy would be required to depart at the end of forty days – the Chinese were, apparently, pretending that this was the law of the Empire for the stay of an embassy. Deciding to attempt forestalling the inevitable, he wrote immediately to Heshen. He thanked him for allowing Mackintosh's ship to load a cargo at Zhoushan, but pointed out that this would have to be done under the eye of Captain Mackintosh himself. He hoped, therefore, that he would be allowed to rejoin his ship without delay. He further proposed that the Embassy return to Europe by way of Canton, setting out as soon after the New Year as the season would allow.

The answer to the note came promptly. Macartney was requested to call on the Chief Minister at the Yuanmingyuan on the Wednesday morning.

The Chinese Court documents in the Zhang gu cong bian, a collection in the National Archives, reveal that Macartney was being controlled from the Court like a puppet on a string. A document of 22nd September from the Grand Council – in other words, from Heshen – to Zhengrui outlines the arrangements for the Embassy's dismissal.

. . . As regards the tribute Envoys, originally it was intended that after the Imperial Chariot had returned they should be given one feast in the . . . Yuan Ming Yuan. Now we have instructed the Grand Councillors to cancel the banquet . . . after the Envoy has welcomed the Imperial Chariot at the Datong Gate let him return to the city and stay there a few days . . . then let him receive the Imperial decree [that is, the edict of 23rd September] and gifts at the Gate of Supreme Harmony in the Forbidden City. Thus the Envoy's mission to hand over a State message and to bring tribute on behalf of the King of his country will have been accomplished . . .

The tribute envoy will then have no more business to detain him . . . before [the end of the first week in October] he can set out to return home.

Wednesday 2nd October This morning Macartney was quite ill – worse, if anything, than on the previous day. Reading his journal, one gets the impression that the rheumatic condition was amplified by the wearying effect of the impending rejection. He had no means of knowing exactly what was going on at Court, but by now he did have informants who could provide partial facts, rumours and guesses, all of which contributed to the stress under which he laboured.

Although much indisposed, he kept his appointment at the Yuanmingyuan. There with Heshen he found two of those who had accompanied him at the Gardens of Jehol: Fuchang'an, the Second Minister, and his brother Fukhang'an, former Viceroy of Canton and the General who had run the successful campaign against the Gurkhas in Tibet. Given Fukhang'an's suspicion that the British had provided military support to his enemies, Macartney supposed him to be the Embassy's principal antagonist at Court.

The audience began with Heshen handing Macartney three letters from Zhoushan, and demanding to know their contents. One was addressed to Captain Mackintosh from the first mate of the *Hindostan*, and the other two were from Sir Erasmus Gower of the *Lion*. The first said that the *Hindostan* could not sail until her Captain joined her, and the others that the *Lion* was preparing to leave Zhoushan with all speed. To allay Heshen's suspicions, Macartney handed the letters back to him.

Heshen now became the silky courtier. He hoped the *Lion* had not sailed, for he imagined that after so long an absence from home the Ambassador would wish to return to England in her. The Emperor, upon hearing that Macartney was ill and that some of his people had died in China, had observed how much foreigners were liable to suffer from the cold winters of Peking and had expressed apprehension that the Embassy would run great risk of injury to health if it did not set out on the return journey before the first frosts set in. As to the feasts and celebrations of the New Year which the Ambassador would like to attend, they were nothing more than a repeat of the amusements he had witnessed at Jehol.

To this Macartney replied that his tour of duty at the Russian Court had accustomed him to a cold climate. Then he diplomatically reminded Heshen 'of the flattering hope given him when at Zhe-hol [Jehol] that he should have frequent opportunity of seeing him at the Yuanmingyuan'. He wanted to seize the opportunity to explain his Sovereign's instructions and to enter into negotiation on the points contained therein. 'As yet I have barely opened my commission,' he pointed out emphatically.

It was the King's wish, he went on, that he might be allowed to reside for a while, at the King's expense, at the Emperor's Court, for the purpose of cementing a firm friendship between two such powerful monarchs. Furthermore, he had been directed to propose that the Emperor would please send a reciprocal embassy to England, the care of which Macartney undertook to manage. Then, although creaking with pain, Macartney explained with consummate diplomatic skill the favours he had to ask – and in such a manner that they did not appear to be demands, but 'merely to convey a sense of their propriety in themselves, unattended with the slightest inconvenience of any kind whatsoever to China'.

The sixfold proposals for the improvement of trade that should, he felt, seem reasonable and acceptable to the Chinese comprised the detail not contained in the letter from the King to the Emperor but extracted from his instructions. They were:

to allow British Merchants to trade with Chusan [Zhoushan], Ning-po [Ningbo] and Tientsin;
to allow them to warehouse at Peking for the sale of their goods (as the Russians had formerly);
to allow them some detached, unfortified island in the neighbourhood of Chusan, as a magazine for their unsold goods, and as a residence for their people, to take care of them;
to allow a similar privilege near Canton, and some other trifling indulgences;
to abolish the transit dues between Macao and Canton, or at least reduce them to the standards of 1782;
to prohibit the exaction of any duties from the English Merchants, over and above those settled by the Emperor's diploma, a copy of which is required to be given to them (as they have never yet been able to see it) for their unequivocal direction.*

He ended by assuring Heshen that Imperial granting of those favours would be regarded by the King who had sent him as a strong indicator of benevolence and friendship. Moreover, that King's subjects would always endeavour to render themselves deserving of the Emperor's favour and protection.

Fine words indeed! Whether they carried their subtlety and point in the translation, Macartney could not tell. In his answer, Heshen as usual avoided discussion of the matters in hand. Instead, he reverted once again to Macartney's health, assuring him that the Emperor's proposal for his departure arose chiefly from his anxiety about it – otherwise, the prospect of Macartney's staying longer could not but be agreeable to him.

As had happened with so many other meetings, the Ambassador found

---

* The Emperor's diploma was a written list of the customs regulations which, in spite of frequent requests from the merchant community in Canton, had never been shown to them.

himself ambivalent about the outcome of this one. His whole instinct was to draw an unfavourable inference. On the other hand: 'When I rose to take my leave, nothing could be more gracious or more flattering than the expressions which he made use of to me upon the occasion, in so much as my interpreter congratulated me upon the fair prospect of my negotiation and said he expected the happiest issue from it!'

But on his return to his palace lodgings, instinct hardened into certainty. He was met by Wang and Qiao, who told him that 'the Emperor's answer to the King's letter is already prepared and has been sent for translation from Chinese into Latin'. Macartney saw in this an infallible sign of the Court's intention, and a signal for him to take his leave. The conducting mandarins told him, furthermore, that there would be a message from Heshen requesting a meeting at the Emperor's Palace on the morrow, and that – although they were not certain – the Emperor's reply would probably be delivered to him on this occasion. That being the case, they said, it would be wise to ask permission to depart without delay. Delivering this news, Wang and Qiao looked dejected, for besides the loss of the advantage they would have obtained on the success of the Embassy, they now realized they had little hope of advancement and preferment at Court.

There was a second message – from Mr Irwin, one of the East India Company Commissioners at Canton. It was dated 2nd July, and communicated the events in Europe to 10th January last. From this three-month-old intelligence, based on a situation report at least nine months out of date, Macartney saw clearly that a war with France seemed inevitable. He saw too that British ships sailing from China ran the risk of being intercepted by the French. This threat could be met by having the *Lion* convoy the British ships, which usually began their homeward voyage at the end of March. Hence his urgent need to contact Captain Erasmus Gower. He hoped against hope that she had not sailed.

Thursday 3rd October True to the promise made by Wang and Qiao, Zhengrui turned up in the early morning. Although scarcely able to rise, Macartney overcame his rheumatism, gout and depression, to hear the legate's message: Heshen and several other Grand Secretaries were to assemble in the Palace in the Forbidden City. It was hoped that the Ambassador would meet them 'in ceremony' as soon as possible. No doubt partly because of his condition, Macartney could not remember having received a more unwelcome message in his life. None the less, he immediately gave instructions to prepare for the occasion; and then he set out for the Imperial city. 'I need not have been so punctual,' he observed wryly, in his journal. 'We were kept waiting for nearly three hours before the Minister and his coadjutors were in proper order for our reception.'

Finally, they were conducted through many courtyards to the Gate of

Supreme Harmony, which lies between the Meridian Gate and the Hall of Supreme Harmony. It was here, Macartney was told, that the Emperor came to receive the congratulations of the Court on New Year's Day, on Imperial birthdays and on other great ceremonial occasions. At the foot of the great stone stairs leading to the Audience Hall was placed a fine yellow silk armchair, representing the majesty of China and containing the Emperor's letter to the King. Both sides made the usual reverences, the Chinese kowtowing and the British kneeling on one knee. The chair was then carried up the central portion of the stairway carved with the seven-toed Imperial dragon, whilst the Embassy delegation, ordinary mortals, ascended the steps either side of the Imperial path, passing four golden vases and incense burners, into the Hall of Supreme Harmony.

Inside, Macartney beheld a magnificent sight. At the back stood four hundred mandarins in full court dress, and in front of them two long tables. On one of these were placed the presents for His Britannic Majesty, and on the other presents for the Ambassador, his suite and the soldiers and sailors who accompanied him.

Today, Heshen's gracious manner had been dropped. In its place there was 'a degree of constraint and stiffness, that appeared not natural but assumed for the occasion'. Without revealing its contents, he told Macartney that the letter to the King, along with the presents, would be sent to the ambassadorial lodgings with due pomp and ceremony. In turn, Macartney expressed his hope that Heshen would accept the presents that he had offered both to himself and to other Grand Secretaries. 'I soon discovered his real disposition toward us,' Macartney noted, 'by his decisive refusal of some magnificent presents which I had made him, and which I had every reason, from himself, to imagine he had accepted as he had informed me into whose charge they should be delivered. The other Grand Secretaries were equally steady in their refusal and had declined what I had sent.'

Almost fainting with fatigue, Macartney sought the Chief Minister's permission to withdraw. Yet he reminded Heshen, even at this nadir of debility, of the points he had raised with him yesterday, reiterating that he acted under his Sovereign's command to solicit those favours, even if they were not particularly specified in the King's letter. With a disdain allowing no hope of success, Heshen invited Macartney to send him a note, at the same time offering no comment on the note delivered yesterday. With that, the Ambassador withdrew, and left the field to Sir George Staunton.

But there was nothing left to discuss. Instead, they were offered a tour of the Forbidden City – like Jehol, designed to impress and overawe. And as Macartney retreated, perhaps still hoping to salvage something from this diplomatic disaster, Alexander was overwhelmed by what his artist's eye perceived:

We are now conducted to three other magnificent halls of audience, each having thrones with rich state chairs. One [hall] was sumptuous in the highest degree, supported by gilt columns richly embossed with dragons. The floor was covered with the richest worked carpet in which dragons were woven . . . Before two of these buildings, on the pavement in front, stood vases of solid gold about six feet in diameter. These halls were in a line, divided from each other with a court paved with marble. They were richly ornamented, externally as well as within, their broad projecting cornices being gilt and coloured most vividly. One of these buildings was conjectured to be 150ft long. Six of the columns in this hall being embossed with dragons so as to resemble solid gold. The rest of the columns are red, the ceiling is ornamented in square compartments, with green and gold. From an eminence we had a fair view of the whole palace . . . whose yellow glazed tiles glitter in the sun like gold. The walls are roofed with these tiles and painted red.

While his suite was being shown the splendours of the Imperial city, Macartney arrived home. He was quickly followed by sixteen mandarins 'of Rank' and their attendants bearing the Emperor's letter to the King. The presents quickly followed. Macartney gave instructions for them to be inventoried and labelled as before.

He now knew, beyond doubt, that the Court wished the Embassy to be gone. The mission was over. Whether there was ground for hope in the document that the Grand Council had had in its possession since late July and that had only just been sent for translation remained to be seen. In any event, it was abundantly clear that if they did not take the hint to depart, 'it will be imparted in a broader coarser way which would be equally unpleasant to the dignity of the Embassy and the success of its objects'. He had one last chance to make his point to Heshen and achieve some measure of success. Wearily he dictated the note that the Chief Minister had requested of him. After a year's journey and almost four weeks of social dissembling, he thought wryly, here, at the moment of departure, came his one and only opportunity to put forward his country's case.

Meanwhile, below stairs at the Embassy, British permanence was the only prevailing thought. Aeneas Anderson, valet de chambre, had today received the Ambassador's wishes 'for the future order and disposition of the tables for the different departments of the household'. The table for the Ambassador was to be prepared for himself alone, 'with two covers for gentlemen of the suite who would be invited in daily succession to dine with him'. At Sir George Staunton's table would sit the secretary Mr Maxwell, Doctor Gillan, Captain Mackintosh, Mr Barrow and Master Staunton. And Lieutenants Parish and Crewe, Drs Scott and Dinwiddie, and Messrs Hickey and Alexander would be at Lieutenant-Colonel Benson's table. Plans were laid to phase out Chinese food and cook English dishes instead. And while the service of silver plate was unpacked for use, routines were laid down for the social occasions of the coming months.

On his return from the Imperial city, Alexander unpacked his share of the presents. He found eight rolls of cut velvet, satin and silk, each piece containing ten to fifteen yards; two small canisters of jasmine flowers; two flat cakes of tea; one eighty-pound chest of tea of very poor quality; a small box of tobacco, and a few trifles – sandlewood fans and the like.

5th October The missionaries who had translated the Emperor's edict to the King toned down its imperious condescension, but even so, by any standards it constituted a diplomatic snub of the highest order:

In consideration of the fact that your Ambassador and his deputy have come a long way with your memorial and tribute, I have shown them high favour and have allowed them to be introduced into my presence. To manifest my indulgence, I have entertained them at a banquet and made them numerous gifts . . . As to your entreaty to send one of your nationals to be accredited to my Celestial Court and to be in control of your country's trade with China, this request is contrary to all usage of my dynasty and cannot possibly be entertained . . . Your proposed Envoy to my Court could not be placed in a position similar to that of European officials in Peking who are forbidden to leave China, nor could he, on the other hand, be allowed liberty of movement and the privilege of corresponding with his own country . . .

Our Celestial dynasty possesses vast territories, and tribute missions from the dependencies are provided for by the Department of Tributary States, which ministers to their wants and exercises strict control over their movements. It would be quite impossible to leave them to their own devices. Supposing that your Envoy should come to our Court, his language and national dress differ from that of our people, and there would be no place in which to bestow him . . .

If you assert that your reverence for our Celestial dynasty fills you with a desire to acquire our civilisation, our ceremonies and code of laws differ so completely from your own that, even if your Envoy were able to acquire the rudiments of our civilisation, you could not possibly transplant our manners and customs to your alien soil. Therefore, however adept the Envoy might become, nothing could be gained thereby . . .

Swaying the wide world, I have but one aim in view, namely, to maintain a perfect governance and to fulfil the duties of the State: strange and costly objects do not interest me. If I have commanded that the tribute offerings sent by you, O King, are to be accepted, this was solely in consideration for the spirit which prompted you to dispatch them from afar. Our dynasty's majestic virtue has penetrated unto every country under Heaven, and Kings of all nations have offered their costly tribute by land and sea. As your Ambassador can see for himself, we possess all things. I set no value on objects strange or ingenious, and have no use for your country's manufactures. This then is my answer to your request to appoint a representative at my Court, a request contrary to our dynastic usage, which would only result in inconvenience to yourself. I have expounded my wishes in detail and have commanded your tribute Envoys to leave in peace on their homeward journey. It behoves you, O King, to respect my sentiments and to display even greater devotion and loyalty in future, so that, by perpetual submission to our Throne, you may secure peace and prosperity for your country hereafter. Besides making gifts (of which I enclose an inventory) to each member of your Mission, I confer upon you, O King, valuable presents in excess of the number usually bestowed on such occasions, including silks and curios – a list of which is likewise enclosed. Do you reverently receive them and take note of my tender goodwill towards you! A special mandate!*

It is not surprising that this day was one of great regret and recrimination. Having been ill for a week, in great pain, and having just read the translation on his sickbed, Macartney's disappointment was acute. Who was to blame? What had gone wrong? It would have been no relief to him to know that this special edict was referred to in a memorial from Heshen which proved that it had been ready for delivery even while the *Hindostan* was unloading off Tientsin five days before Macartney arrived in China. The hurt comes through the pages of his journal:

Having been selected for this commission to China, the first of its kind from Great Britain, of which considerable expectation had been formed by many, and by none more than myself, I cannot help feeling the disappointment most severely. I cannot lose sight of my first prospects without infinite regret. The consciousness of doing all in a man's power to do in the exercise of public employments is an ultimate consolation against most evils that can happen, but it requires no ordinary strain of philosophy to reconcile him at once to the immediate failure of success in a favourite undertaking.

Father Amiot, a missionary who acted as informant to the Embassy, called on the Ambassador. Unable to see him because of his indisposition, Amiot wrote an emollient letter and handed it to George Staunton. In it he pointed out that the Chinese considered embassies mere birds of passage, here today and gone tomorrow – the last, from Portugal, although well received, had been of less than six weeks' duration . . . Amiot thought that the Embassy would have met with fewer difficulties at its outset if it had arrived before the government had been alarmed by the news of the troubles in Europe, the inhabitants of which were indiscriminately considered to be of a turbulent character. Finally, he offered the wise advice that the ground gained should not be lost, but followed up by an exchange of letters between King and Emperor, which the annual cargo ships might convey.

To alleviate his depression, Macartney plunged into action. He dispatched a note to Heshen, informing him that as soon as he had obtained a written answer to his note containing the sixfold request, he would ask leave of the Emperor to depart and to proceed to Zhoushan, whence it was still possible that Sir Erasmus Gower had not yet sailed. In the case that the *Lion had* sailed, it would be necessary to go to Canton, as the *Hindostan* could not sail from Zhoushan until Captain Mackintosh joined her, and anyway she could accommodate no more than half of the Embassy's baggage train.

That evening, the Tartar legate visited Macartney and told him that the

---

* For the complete text of the edict, see Appendix A, p. 180.

letter had been forwarded to Sir Erasmus Gower. The Emperor had decided that 7th October should be the date for the Embassy's departure – which was, in fact, as soon as possible. For not only was the weather getting worse, but the depth of the rivers depended on the melted snows of the mountains of Tartary. With the onset of winter the water levels were dropping rapidly. Zhengrui's parting shot was that the answer to the six requests contained in his last letter to Heshen would be given on the morning of departure, and that every honour and distinction would be paid to the Embassy on the road.

12

Departure

Now that the matter was settled, even though they had barely two days in which to make their preparations for departure, Macartney felt a sense of relief. He had seen enough of China and the Chinese to recognize that the role of unwelcome guest would be an impossible one to maintain. His only hope now was that the final reply from Heshen would at least fulfil something of the aims of the mission – so long in the planning and so drawn out in the execution. Whatever happened, personal feelings were to be subordinated to the primary aim stated in the written instructions of both Home Secretary Henry Dundas and the Chairman of the East India Company, Francis Baring. On his departure from England, Baring had written to Macartney:

> We are therefore of the opinion that the first and most important object is neither to impair or injure our present situation, thereby checking those prospects which are decidedly in view. The grievances [of our merchants] are no doubt real . . . But when we consider what we suffer under most or all of them and moreover that a representation on the subject is in fact a Charge . . . against persons who may be highly useful or highly prejudicial to the Company on more important occasions, we entertain doubts as to the wisdom or prudence of entering into such details.

The opportunities for trade at Canton were big enough to justify pragmatic rather than principled decisions. Macartney was to get what he could out of the situation, but on no account was he to rock the boat!

Chinese foresight had anticipated all contingencies. As early as 23rd September a Court letter had been sent to the Viceroy of Canton outlining the Emperor's intention to refuse Macartney's requests and warning that, in response, the English might foment trouble in the merchant communities of Canton and Macao. The Court correspondence between 24th and 30th September dealt with the need to get Macartney out of Peking. The Grand Council had written to Zhengrui:

The tribute Envoy is, by nature, very suspicious and fickle. If at this stage we tell him categorically that no-one may be left behind at the Capital, it is to be feared that this will make him all the more suspicious, and on the pretext of illness he will procrastinate or will be unwilling to pack up the tribute articles, or he may find a pretext for not receiving the state message. Any of these things may happen. All Zhengrui should do at this moment is to appear as though nothing has happened . . .

A further letter, dated 2nd October, was written by the Grand Secretaries under direct Imperial instruction and addressed to the Viceroy of Canton and the Hoppo.

. . . Because recently in the English State message there was a request to be allowed to depute a man to remain in the Capital, and because We have not permitted what was requested, We fear that Macartney may be disappointed . . . We now realise that England is the most powerful of the Western Ocean nations. Moreover we have heard that they have been used to plundering the merchant ships of other Western nations on the high seas. Therefore in the regions near the Western Ocean the Barbarians fear their bullying. Now that we are not allowing them to leave a man in the Capital we cannot be sure that the King of that country, when he receives Our Imperial Edict, may not use it as a pretext to stir up trouble because he has not achieved what he wanted . . . We are simply afraid since the English are habitually truculent and since they have so many ships and men there [Canton], the other barbarian merchants may not be able to help being intimidated by them . . . Furthermore, now when the Envoy goes to Canton to return to his country . . . immediately instruct the various regiments and battalions that all the beacons and posts be strictly in order and banners and weapons be polished up so that the barbarians will see the Celestial Empire's impressive military power and will not in the least dare to grow disrespectful. Moreover forbid the barbarian merchants belonging to the foreign firms of other countries to have intercourse with them that might lead to plotting [in Canton] . . . We are much exercised by this.

Within the Embassy lodgings, any sense of security that had lulled them into a hope of permanence vanished instantly. Aeneas Anderson, Macartney's valet, one of those who bore the brunt of the sudden decision, was simultaneously outraged at the way in which his master was being dismissed from Peking and overwhelmed by the work that the dismissal brought with it. He found it contrary to the common rules of political decorum, civility, justice and humanity that an Ambassador of such consequence should be dispatched without ceremony and with no time to make 'common arrangements for the journey', and that he should have been 'refused a respite of only two days to his urgent solicitations'.

Everybody had to pack his own belongings. Porters with cordage, bamboo and string were sent to assist. The work went on day and night. 'This night scene was highly curious,' noted Alexander, 'every Englishman managing his own property, only assisted by the Chinese porters to whom he was endeavouring to explain by dumbshow, with the light only from lanterns, causing a confusion which would have reminded a spectator of the building of

Babel Tower.' Dinwiddie could not sleep for the bustle. 'So peremptory was the order that many things had to be sent unpacked. Before their departure the Chinese servants were observed tearing the silk paper from the walls of the rooms.' Chaos had taken over.

If the soldiers had not been called in to assist in packing the baggage and stores, a much greater part must have been left behind . . . the portraits of their Majesties were taken down, but as the cases in which they had come had been broken down for fixtures in the apartments, a few planks hastily nailed together were now their only protection . . . As for the state canopy, it was not taken down but absolutely torn from the walls and given to some of Lord Macartney's servants, though in the scramble some of the Chinese contrived to come in for a fair share, at the same time also purloining quantities of wine, as well as other stores.

'In short,' Aeneas Anderson observed, 'we entered Peking like paupers, we remained in it like prisoners and we quitted it like vagrants.'

All this, too, in the charnel house atmosphere of the dysentery epidemic, by now affecting the greater part of the Embassy. The suspicion was that it arose 'from the tainted atmosphere produced by the exposed evacuations of diseased persons, the Chinese being strangers to such conveniences as used in England'. No matter what the cause, one of the marines, a man called Newman, died of the disease – the sixth member of the Ambassador's guard to do so. As at Jehol, to prevent the circumstance being known the corpse was conveyed away in the night.

Perhaps to curry favour as well as to lighten their load, Macartney sent his state carriage to Heshen as a present. It was refused. But when its return was requested, so that it could be unslung and packed up, there was no response from the Chinese!

There was some good news, though, amid the panic. Wang and Qiao informed Macartney that Songyun, the former Imperial agent in Russia, would accompany the Embassy to Zhoushan. Macartney was pleased about this. Songyun had been one of those few with whom, because of their common Russian experience, he had found some rapport at Jehol. In fact, no higher appointment could have been made: this forty-one-year-old Mongol had been responsible for the border regions with Russia, and had negotiated the new commercial treaty (of Kiakhta) in 1792 which had ended the cessation of trade caused by the Buriats' invasion of China. He was in favour at Court and, as a member of the Grand Council, would have seen the directive from the Emperor concerning the handling of the Embassy on its departure. Even better was the news that Zhengrui, the constantly officious thorn in their sides, would not be accompanying them. He would go no further than Tientsin.

The journey from Peking to Tongzhou would take five hours. There on the Hai River the barges would be waiting to take them to Tientsin, where they would embark on the fifteen-hundred-mile journey down the canal system to Zhoushan and Canton.

Part Three

The Return Journey: Peking to Canton

Prelude

THERE WAS DISAPPOINTMENT, but no surprise, at the outcome of the Embassy. Macartney's briefing from the East India Company had forewarned him. The six European embassies that had preceded the British had been treated in the same way as the tribute-bearing states from South-East Asia: none had stayed in Peking for more than a few months, with the exception of the Russian embassies of 1693 and 1720, for Imperial Russia and China, by virtue of their common border on the Amur River, supported a mutually beneficial caravan trade. The Manchu emperors, with their interest in the Asian heartland, understood the purpose of these missions and were prepared to offer the Russians limited encouragement.

At the end of his journal, Macartney appended a document listing the days spent in Peking by each embassy. The second Russian embassy, under Ismailoff, had been allowed to stay longest – 114 days. The shortest stay had been the thirty-nine days spent by the Portuguese embassy of 1753. Macartney's mission had lasted forty-seven days, from his arrival in Peking to his departure from the capital on 7th October. And during all this time he had had only one opportunity to air his business!

In the light of this experience, let alone Qianlong's dismissive edict to George III, the prime objectives as listed by Macartney in his last letter to Heshen were over-ambitious. If they failed, then in the interest of trade he was to preserve the status quo ante at all costs. There were, however, three subsidiary aims for which he could strive in the discussions with Songyun that he would have on the journey home.

These were, first, to ameliorate the working conditions imposed on the British in Canton; secondly, to see what British goods might be marketable in China in order to lessen the trade imbalance caused by the British demand for tea; and thirdly, to open a channel of correspondence with friendly –

preferably Italian rather than Portuguese or French – missionaries in Peking, so that the East India Company might transmit proposals and receive intelligence from the Chinese Court. In his journal one sees hints that before leaving Peking Macartney had already set up such a channel of communication. Otherwise, how would he have learned some years after his return to England of the death of one of his conducting mandarins?

To assess what British goods might be generally welcome in China, it was necessary to see what was already available and to study the way of life and geography of that unknown land. The journey from Peking to Canton, a north–south crossing of the continent, gave Macartney such an opportunity. And he had come prepared for the task. As we saw at the outset, the Embassy had amongst its number two botanists, Haxton and Stronach, whose own professional interest was boosted by Sir George Staunton's fascination with plants and plant collecting. Then there was the prolific draughtsman William Alexander, experimental scientist Dinwiddie, natural philosopher Dr Gillan, and Thibault the mathematical instrument maker. The mixed talents of this team were ideal for recording the agricultural and industrial products and processes they would come across as they sailed down the Grand Canal.

Perhaps even more valuable to Macartney was Qianlong's appointment of the Grand Councillor Songyun as conducting official. His role was to be emollient, to soothe Macartney's ruffled feelings. He had on call the resources necessary for displaying the iron hand in the velvet glove, but was to find no need to do so. Instead, he and Wang, in the course of many long conversations, provided Macartney with valuable background information about China and about prevailing attitudes. In addition, these meetings enabled Macartney to plead his case and to explain in detail the Embassy's aims and aspirations relating to trade and conditions in Canton.

Although, in view of the massive setbacks that the mission endured, in his own eyes he may not have achieved much, it is a measure of Macartney's stature that he had the courage to persevere in wresting what he could out of adversity. It is as well that he did, for the Embassy's observations, when formulated, laid the basis of European knowledge about China for the next three decades, dispelling the somewhat rosy view of the Celestial Empire prevalent in the West throughout the eighteenth century.

13

Retracing Footsteps

Monday 7th October 1793 At 1pm, the time set for their departure, the Embassy was still frantically packing. When they did finally set off, it was without regret – indeed, being on the way home they were in good heart. Having suffered from the jolting of the carts on the outward journey, the better to see the countryside, most of the suite elected to ride horseback out of the city. Alexander reflected in his diary: 'We now bade adieu to this wondrous metropolis with the boast of having resided in the largest and rarest city of the world and having seen the sovereign of so large a portion of the civilised earth, such reflections could not entirely be resisted.' Others in the Embassy were enjoying their brief new-found freedom. They gazed at the brightly painted shops with their goods lined up outside: 'We had all along been confined like so many prisoners, never being suffered to see any part of the city or to purchase any of the curiosities it contained, to carry to our friends in Europe.'

Macartney, having been summoned for an audience with Heshen, had left their palace lodgings an hour earlier, intending to make his departure by way of Heshen's pavilion. To his surprise, for the first time in his forty-seven days' residence he was received immediately. There, flanking Heshen in full ceremonial robes, were the Emperor's favourite Fuchang'an and his brother Fukhang'an – who was no friend of the Embassy, as Macartney remembered all too well from his behaviour on earlier occasions. The atmosphere was tense. Other Grand Secretaries were also in attendance, looking 'confoundedly sour', whilst Heshen – 'a smile of affected affability on his countenance' – indicated on a table behind them, beribboned and draped in yellow silk, two large bamboo cylinders, one containing the Emperor's reply to the King in answer to Macartney's six requests, the other containing a list of the Emperor's presents to the King.

Macartney half-suspected a Court intrigue to be the cause of their evident disaffection. More likely, though, it was the Imperial edict conveying the wish to see him off the premises that day. Whatever the cause, he put on his best face and said that he hoped the Imperial answer was favourable to his wishes, as it might contribute in some degree to tempering the regret that it was natural to feel on leaving the place where His Imperial Majesty resided. Heshen seemed taken aback at the courtliness of the address; in reply, 'feeling embarrassed to make a suitable return, [he] quickly changed the subject, enquiring if the Embassy tables had been properly served during their stay and hoping Macartney was pleased with the Emperor's nomination of Sung Yun [Songyun] to conduct them to Chusan [Zhoushan]'.

That was all. The audience was at an end. Macartney expected further reference to the content of the cylinders, but there was none. Instead, a mandarin of the fifth rank stepped forward and, kneeling, had them bound to his back with silk ribbons. Thus accoutred, he rose and immediately mounted his horse, leading the Ambassador and his suite, who had now all assembled outside Heshen's pavilion, on the journey to the east gates of Peking and thence on to Tongzhou.

As they pushed through the crowded streets, Macartney's thoughts were focused on the yellow silk ribbons of the bobbing cylinders in front of him. Unlike Alexander's, his reflections were quite unsentimental. He found himself comparing the crowds in the streets with the London crowds that he had seen on great state occasions. Passing the walls of the *hutongs* – the narrow lanes formed by the boundaries of courtyard houses – he wrongly surmised from the height of the walls and the narrowness of the street that the living quarters of the Chinese in their courtyard houses were cramped and overcrowded. He noted the absence of women and, in his depressed mood, commented that 'what rendered it intolerably offensive is the stench with which it is attended . . . the filth and ordures of the preceding night . . . floating in the air for the greater part of the day'. Again and again his attention was drawn to the horseman carrying the diplomatic cylinders, his only frontal view for the whole of the five-hour journey to Tongzhou.

Had Macartney known what was in the cylinder on the beribboned yellow back, he might have been even less sanguine in his reflections on the passing scene. Heshen could well afford his smile of 'affected affability'. This edict, also addressed to King George, was if anything worse than the preceding one. And this time the missionary translators had no time to soften the message.

> . . . Yesterday your Ambassador petitioned my Ministers to memorialise me regarding your trade with China, but his proposal is not consistent with our dynastic usage and cannot be entertained . . . It may be, O King, that the . . . proposals [Macartney's six-point plan] have been wantonly made by your Ambassador on his own responsibility, or peradventure you yourself are ignorant

of our dynastic regulations and had no intention of transgressing them when you expressed these wild ideas and hopes . . . If, after receipt of this explicit decree, you lightly give ear to the representations of your subordinates and allow your barbarian merchants to proceed to Chekiang [Zhejiang] and Tientsin . . . should your vessels touch the shore, your merchants will assuredly never be permitted to land or to reside there, but will be subject to instant expulsion . . . Do not say that you were not warned in due time! Tremblingly obey and show no negligence! A special mandate!'*

On arrival at Tongzhou, Macartney noted with satisfaction that they were billeted in their old lodgings, the Buddhist temple. Aeneas Anderson was more critical: 'The apartments allotted to us, were nothing more than temporary sheds, hung with straw matting.' However, he did not allow his dissatisfaction to blind him to the welcome fact that the carriage turned down as a gift by Heshen had miraculously appeared on the quayside. It was rapidly dismantled and crated, ready for the long journey back to England.

Dinwiddie inspected the several barges that were to be the homes of the Ambassador and his suite during their journey down the waterways of China. He was to be in the sixth vessel, sharing with Dr Scott, Thomas Hickey, William Alexander and Aeneas Anderson. He judged it to be 'very inferior in accommodation to those which brought the Embassy upstream with such flattering expectation'. And not for the first time on this mission, confusion reigned, as Anderson recorded:

> . . . a new and superior scene of confusion to any we had yet experienced. There was no small difficulty in allotting the junks to those who belonged to them. Nor were there a sufficient number of coolies to transport the different effects on board the vessels. In short, those attentions which were shewn to the Ambassador on his former abode in this city seem to have been forgotten; and the place which was now appropriated to receive the baggage was a small spot, on the side of the river protected only by a screen of matting.

In the midst of this mêlée – Anderson described it as 'the worst day since they arrived in China' – the 'Civil Officer' of Tongzhou, a mandarin, chose to call on Macartney. He rubbed salt in their wounds by remarking how attentive and considerate the Emperor was to fix an early day in the season for their departure: for the river waters were rapidly dropping and could become too shallow to float the barges, and it would be excessively uncomfortable to travel in small boats or overland. Macartney conceded the point, but sardonically noted how quickly Court policy travelled from Peking to Tongzhou.

The next day, 8th October, Macartney inspected the barges – all the others as well as his own. Unlike his valet de chambre he was satisfied with the arrangements, and 'observed with pleasure the same care and attention for our

---

* For the complete text of the edict, see Appendix B, p.183.

accommodation down the river that we had experienced in ascending it'. At six o'clock that evening they set sail from Tongzhou, on what was to be a seventy-two-day journey to the south.

14

Hai River Interlude

9TH AND 10TH OCTOBER The pace changed. The journey from Tongzhou, where the course of the Hai River merges into the Grand Canal on its way to Tientsin, was to be slow and leisurely, as planned, giving the travellers ample opportunity methodically to study and report on the customs, economy, agriculture, industry and society of the regions, both rural and urban, through which they were about to pass. And Macartney had the advantage of the companionship of Grand Councillor Songyun. So here was his chance – and he would have two months at his disposal – to expound on the British position and to rescue something from the tatters of his failed mission, as well as to fathom from a courtier close to the Emperor the complex workings of the Chinese Court and its vast bureaucracy.

The journey did not begin well. There was indeed, already, too little water in the river to maintain navigation, and they spent the first day repeatedly running aground. So the river level was a real issue – not, as Macartney had suspected, a spurious excuse to get rid of them.

The first diplomatic exchange took place on the second day. Through Wang, Songyun let it be known he had received a letter from the Emperor, which he wished to communicate. Macartney went on board the Grand Councillor's barge, where he was received as an old friend. He reminded Songyun of his 'former civilities' at the Potala Temple and the Gardens of Jehol. In turn, Songyun read out the Emperor's letter instructing him to take the Embassy under his particular care 'and render everything agreeable in the course of the voyage. He was to conduct the Embassy to Chusan [Zhoushan] and see them embarked on board their ships; if they were not there he should accompany them to Canton.'

This exchange of pleasantries was marred, though, by Macartney's discovery that the letter he had written to Sir Erasmus Gower, telling him to await the Embassy in Zhoushan, had still not been sent. 'They suspected I know not what and had therefore suppressed it,' he commented in his journal. He immediately explained that, having executed the King's order to land the Embassy in China, Sir Erasmus would certainly proceed with other business unless there was reason to detain him. When Macartney pressed him to have the letter dispatched, Songyun agreed to write to Peking on the subject, and thereupon took his leave.

Half an hour later, Wang and Qiao paid the Ambassador an exchange visit, which extended into the greater part of the evening. Presuming upon their two months' acquaintance, Macartney, for once undiplomatic, asked some direct questions. There were some forty vessels in the convoy, he learned, and a thousand people attached to the expedition. Five thousand *taels** a day, roughly £1700, was the daily cost of the enterprise. Dryly, Macartney observed that though the Emperor might sign big cheques, so much was creamed off that little got through to those who were supposed to be on the receiving end. Qiao agreed, pointing out that of the Imperial flood relief, an annual drain on the exchequer, only 20 per cent ever reached the disaster area. Secure in his national pride, Macartney was to note shortly afterwards: 'The boasted moral institutes of China are not much better observed than those of some other countries and the disciples of Confucius are composed of the same fragile material as the children of Mammon in the Western world.'

Reflections on the Voyage 1: Macartney on Trade with China

THE COST OF THE EMBASSY and the talk of corruption led Macartney's thoughts back to the nub of the mission – trade with China. He recalled the current limitations: since 1757 the only place through which Westerners could trade with China had been Canton. For only five months of the year were they allowed to ply their business, all the while cooped up in the 'factories' on a twenty-one-acre site outside the walls of Canton city. No women were allowed in their enclave, nor were the Westerners allowed outside it – not even for a boat trip on the Pearl River. They were forbidden to learn the Chinese language, and any Chinese caught teaching it to them faced severe punishment. All trading had to be done through the Guild of Merchants, the Cohong, who were exploited by officials, especially the Collector of Customs, the Hoppo. As well as collecting the Emperor's taxes, he exacted squeeze from the Cohong. In spite of the bribes he had to pay to the Imperial Court, the Hoppo was a wealthy man.

* A *tael* was worth 6s 8d in the late eighteenth century.

Thus did the Chinese insulate the barbarian merchants. And there was no means of approaching the Court to seek redress, except through the Cohong, the Hoppo and the Viceroy – none of whom was under any obligation to intercede. However, if they should choose to do so during this voyage, the opportunity for bribery and corruption would be infinite.

It was with some anger, then, that Macartney summarized to himself the terms of trade under which they laboured. Compared with India, where the gentlemen of the East India Company might have an area the size of Britain as their bailiwick, the twenty-one acres of Canton were indeed a hardship posting. Having had the experience of first Peking and then Canton, Macartney was able to write:

> The profits of the Hong Merchants must be very great to enable them to bear the expense of the numerous and magnificent presents which they make to superior Mandarins at Canton, who in their turn send a part of those presents to the Emperor and his Ministers and favourites at Peking. I am led to believe that the Emperor in his own and in his women's apartments possesses to the value of two millions sterling, at the very least, various toys (sing-songs, as they are colloquially named), jewellery, glass, musical automata, instruments of different kinds, clocks, watches etc. all made in London.

What was the total value of the British trade with China which contributed to these kickbacks? Macartney conjectured that in 1793 the value of British exports to China would be some £970,333 sterling, whereas that of British imports from China would be about £1,527,775 at prime cost – say, £3,000,000 when sold in Britain. In making this estimate, Macartney limited himself strictly to the trade generated by the eighteen East India Company ships visiting Canton direct from England in the 1792-3 season. He did not have the figures for the considerable 'private' trade in British goods plied by British ships and by what he called the 'Ostend interlopers' trading under the Genoese, Tuscan, Prussian and other foreign colours. His purpose was to identify items that the Chinese needed and that would serve to correct the balance between import and export – a balance that had to be paid for in silver specie.

British exports were mainly woollen cloth, tin and lead – quite insufficient to pay for the large cargoes of tea that were carried in the East-Indiamen to Britain. So, for the East India Company in London, Macartney drew up a list of articles that might make up the imbalance. It was a diplomat's rather than a trader's list, including as it did semi-precious stones, swords, fowling pieces, nails, coarse linen, whips, necklaces and earrings, spring garters, telescopes, spring glasses and other spectacles, multi-bladed penknives, knives, forks and spoons (one of each in a small case), and saddles made in Chinese fashion. As he wrote, he had to concede that such articles were more suited to private trade than to large-scale export.

However, direct trade with Britain was only half of the East India

Company's trade with China. There was the trade between China and the Company's dependencies in India. India's biggest export was cotton, followed by tin, pepper, sandalwood, elephants' tusks and beeswax. She, in turn, imported from China raw silk, wrought silk, tutenag, sugar, sugar-candy, alum, chinaware, camphor, nankin, quicksilver and turmeric. In 1792 this legal trade came to £693,848. To this sum was added what Macartney called 'the illegal and contraband trade of opium'. In that year, 2,500 chests of opium were privately imported from India into China, adding £250,000 to the balance of trade figures and tilting them in favour of India by £620,971. 'A balance,' noted Macartney, 'that seems likely to increase, for the cotton of Bombay and the opium of Bengal are now become in great measure necessaries in China.'

It was, of course, this trade in opium which was to burgeon tenfold in the next forty-five years and ultimately to undermine the Qing dynasty. Yet so ambivalent was the East India Company about this aspect of its trade, and so fearful lest it damage the legitimate and more profitable lines, that prior to his departure for China the Company instructed Macartney as follows:

> It is necessary you should be on your guard against one stipulation which perhaps will be demanded from you, which is the exclusion of the trade of Opium from the Chinese Dominions as being prohibited by the Laws of the Empire. If this subject should come into discussion, it must be handled with the greatest circumspection. It is beyond doubt that no inconsiderable portion of the Opium raised within the Indian Territories actually finds its way to China; but if it should be made a positive requisition, or an article of any proposed commercial treaty that none of the drug be sent by us to China, you must accede to it rather than risk any essential benefit by contesting for a liberty in this respect, in which case the sale of our opium in Bengal must be left to take its chance in an open market, or to find a consumption in the dispersed and circuitous traffic of the Eastern Seas.

15

The Grand Canal

THE LOW WATER LEVEL ensured that progress remained slow. The trackers who towed the barges had a hard time of it: when one vessel ran aground and stuck fast on the bottom, the superintending officer ordered the whole crew to be flogged – their reward for two days of labour.

To alleviate the boredom, Songyun gave permission for the travellers to walk on the bank, provided they did not lose sight of the barges. However, on taking advantage of the offer, they were bundled back on board by a troop of soldiers. Wang and Qiao exacted exemplary discipline: the soldiers were ordered to be flogged, and the officers were given a mild corrective of forty strokes of the bamboo. The punishment was to be performed in front of the British officers – they, however, declined to be spectators.

Meanwhile, the Ambassador and the Grand Councillor continued their quiet diplomacy. As Heshen and the others had observed in Jehol, Macartney and Songyun seemed to get on well. Certainly Macartney felt an affinity with him. 'His attention and civility continuing so pointed and esteem so unaffectedly expressed, I had less difficulty in engaging him to converse freely upon the subjects which are most interesting to me.' Staunton also took a liking to him: 'He was the only mandarin among those we had a chance to meet who travelled with a library of books.' Every time they met, Songyun opened the conversation with subtle flattery, thereby raising expectations but without yielding any point.

On Saturday 12th October, Macartney, Staunton and Mr Plumb the interpreter paid the Grand Councillor a visit. (Qiao and Wang did not join them, for the presence of someone of senior rank would have compelled them to remain standing for the duration of the interview.) Once again, they were to discuss the question of trading conditions in Canton. Struggling through the double interpretation – Latin to Mandarin and back again – Macartney endeavoured 'to impress with high ideas of the compliment meant to be paid to the Emperor by the King's sending an Embassy from so great a distance, with such distinguished marks of consideration and regard'.

The Emperor had given orders to treat the English and other Europeans at Canton with indulgence and liberality, Songyun replied. Encouraged, Macartney pushed further, and, hoping to put some flesh on the bone of a loose undertaking, he inquired whether it would be possible to reduce the customs duties levied at Canton. Not only, he claimed with justification, were the charges on incoming cargoes very high, but so also were the transport costs and the *likin* (*lijin*, duty) levied by the provinces for the passage of the goods across their territory. Furthermore, whilst the Emperor would always find the merchants well disposed towards his orders and more than willing to comply, they wished to be precisely informed of what those orders were. Hitherto this had not been the case: over the last twelve years several new duties had been levied, without apparent reason. Every year these duties increased, and, if they were not soon regulated, English commerce with China, involving as it did sixty large ships annually (including those from British dependencies), would have to be abandoned. It would be quite unable to bear such a heavy burden.

Songyun heard Macartney and Mr Plumb out with great patience. He confessed that of recent years the duties had indeed been increased, but that this had been on account of the wars in Tonkin and Tibet.* Now that there was peace, these duties would certainly be diminished. Elated at this news, Macartney expressed great pleasure, and

> [begged] leave to request the continuance of his good offices in our affairs. It is much to be regretted that as the First Minister [Heshen] was determined not to give me such opportunities as I sought for conversing upon business with him, he had not appointed Sung Yun [Songyun] to attend to us from the beginning, instead of Zhengrui. Through all [Songyun's] discourse there is such an air of candour, frankness and amity that if I am deceived in him, he must be the most consummate cheat in the world.

Sunday 13th October At 10am the weary trackers hauled the barges clear of the shallows of the Hai River, and the convoy entered the Grand Canal proper.

'Each vessel is towed by six to eight trackers,' noted Alexander, who, fascinated by these ragged men, painted many studies of them as they trudged along the bank, heaving at the tow ropes. And as they heaved in unison they sang that same work-song, with the refrain 'Highau, highau, highau!', that Huttner had noted on the outward journey. This dirge haunted the Embassy

* When the rulers of Annam were deposed by rebels, since the King was in a tributary relationship with the Chinese, in 1792 Qianlong sent an army to support the deposed monarch. Similarly, an army had been dispatched to Tibet in the same year. See p.35.

day and night, except when, going against the current and the wind, they temporarily beached the boats on the bank, or when the trackers, being poorly paid and badly treated, ran away and thus halted progress.

Tientsin welcomed the Embassy's return with all the hospitality of an old friend: 'We were served with a most sumptuous provision for our tables, excellent mutton, pork, venison and poultry of all kinds, fruit in great variety – peaches, plums, apples, pears, grapes, walnuts, chestnuts and several other quite new.' Furthermore, to provide a constant supply of milk the Chinese fitted up a barge to contain the fodder and stabling for two cows. Alexander wryly recorded the arrival of this cornucopia: 'Our soldiers fared so sumptuously as to relapse into their old complaint – the Dysentery. I arrived, ill with the same complaint, to be instructed by my fellow traveller Dr. Scott from partaking of the Mandarins' bounty.'

Macartney could not understand the reasoning behind this generosity:

> How are we to reconcile the contradictions that appear in the conduct of the Chinese government toward us? They receive us with the highest distinction, show us every external mark of favour and regard, send their First Minister himself to attend on us as cicerone for two days through their palaces and gardens; entertain us with their choice amusements and express themselves greatly pleased with so splendid an Embassy, commend our conduct and cajole us with compliments. Yet in less than a couple of months they plainly discover they wish us to be gone, refuse our requests without reserve or complaisance, precipitate our departure and dismiss us dissatisfied; yet no sooner have we taken our leave of them than we find ourselves treated with more studied attentions, more marked distinction and less constraint than before. I must endeavour to unravel this mystery if I can. Perhaps they had given way to impressions which they could not resist but are ashamed to confess; perhaps they begin to find their mistake and wish to make some amends for it.

So as the crowds of curious bystanders lined the banks and the flotilla pushed its way through the mass of craft collecting on the canal to weather the coming winter, Macartney began to reflect on the Chinese people.

Reflections on the Voyage 2: Macartney on Chinese Society

A CHINESE FAMILY is regulated with the same regard to subordination and economy that is observed in the government of a state; the paternal authority, though unlimited, is usually exercised with kindness and indulgence. In China, children are indeed sometimes sold, and infants exposed by the parents, but only in cases of the most hopeless indigence and misery, when they must inevitably perish if kept at home; but where the thread of attachment is not thus snapped asunder by the anguish of the parent, it every day grows stronger and becomes indissoluble for life.

There is nothing more striking in the Chinese character through all ranks than this most respectable union. Affection and duty walk hand in hand and never desire a separation. The fondness of the father is constantly felt and always increasing; the dependence of the son is perfectly understood by him; he never wishes it to be lessened. It is not necessary to coax or to cheat the child into cutting off an entail, or charging his inheritance with a mortgage; it is not necessary to importune the father for an irrevocable settlement. According to Chinese ideas, there is but one interest in a family; any other supposition would be unnatural and wicked. An undutiful child is a monster that China does not produce; the son, even after marriage, continues for the most part to live in the father's house; the labour of the family is thrown into one common stock under the sole management of the parent, and continues in the same union with his younger brother.*

The houses of the better sort exhibit a certain show of grandeur and magnificence, and even of taste and elegance in their decorations, but at the same time discover, at least to our eyes, evident marks of discomfort and inconvenience. There is a want of useful furniture. They have indeed lanterns of gauze and paper and horn and diaphanous gum, most beautifully coloured and disposed, and they have tables, couches and chairs, loosely covered with rich carpeting, with gold and silver damasks, and other silks; but they have no bureaux, commodes, lustres or looking-glasses; they have no sheets on their beds, neither does their bedding itself seem well adapted or agreeable. They don't undress themselves entirely as we do, when they go to rest, but lay themselves down upon alcoved benches, which are spread with a single mat or thin mattresses and adjusted with small pillows and cushions. Their apartments are not well contrived or distributed, according to our ideas of utility and propriety, having seldom any doors that shut with locks or proper fastenings, but in lieu of them screens and curtains, which are removed or drawn back as occasion requires. In the cold weather they are warmed by flues under the floor, for there are neither stoves, nor fire-places in the rooms; but sometimes braziers filled with charcoal are brought in and occasionally renewed.†

The people, even of the first rank, though so fond of dress as to change it usually several times a day, are yet in their persons and customs frowzy and uncleanly. Their outward garment of ceremony is richly embroidered with silks of different colours (those of the highest class of all, with golden dragons), and their common habit is of plain silk or fine broadcloth; but their drawers and their waistcoats (of which they usually wear several according to the season) are not very frequently shifted. They wear neither knit nor woven

---

* A structure which pertains to this day.

† Common in Northern China to the present day.

stockings, but wrap their legs round with a coarse cotton stuff, over which they have constantly drawn a pair of black satin boots without heels, but with soles nearly an inch in thickness. In summer everybody carries a fan in his hand and is flirting it incessantly.

They wear but little linen or calico, and what they do wear is extremely coarse and ill washed, soap being never employed by them. They seldom have recourse to pocket handkerchiefs, but spit about the rooms without mercy, blow their noses in their fingers, wipe them with their sleeves, or upon anything near them. This practice is universal and, what is still more abominable, I one day observed a Tartar of distinction call his servant to hunt in his neck for a louse that was troublesome to him.

At their meals they use no towels, napkins, table-cloths, flat places, glasses, knives nor forks, but help themselves with their fingers, or with their chop-sticks, which are made of wood or ivory about six inches long, round and smooth, and not very cleanly. Their meat is served up ready cut in small bowls, each guest having a separate bowl to himself. Seldom above two sit together at the same table, and never above four. They are all foul feeders and eaters of garlic and strong-scented vegetables, and drink mutually out of the same cup which, though sometimes rinsed, is never washed or wiped clean. They use little vinegar, no olive oil, cyder, ale, beer or grape wine; their chief drink is tea, or liquors distilled or prepared from rice and other vegetables, of different degrees of strength according to their taste, some of which are tolerably agreeable and resemble strong Madeira.

They almost all smoke tobacco and consider it a compliment to offer each other a whiff of their pipes. They also take snuff, mostly Brazil, but only small quantities, not in that beastly profusion which is often practised in England, even by some of our fine ladies.

They have no water-closets nor proper places of retirement; the necessaries are quite public and open, and the ordure is continually removing from them, which occasions a stench in almost every place one approaches.

One great advantage indeed of the Embassy is the opportunity it afforded of showing the Chinese to what a high degree of perfection the English nation had carried all the arts and accomplishments of civilised life; that their manners were calculated for the improvement of social intercourse and liberal commerce; that though great and powerful, they were generous and humane, not fierce and impetuous like the Russians, but entitled to respect and preference of the Chinese above other European nations, whom they had any knowledge of. This favourable impression of us may be confirmed and improved in them by a continuance of our attention and cautious conduct. The restriction and discipline of our seamen at Canton are among the proper regulations for this purpose, not to mention some other arrangements that will naturally be made there, in consequence of the ground we now stand upon.

The common people of China are a strong hardy race, patient, industrious, and much given to traffic and all the arts of gain; cheerful and loquacious under the severest labour, and by no means that sedate, tranquil people they have been represented. In their joint efforts and exertions they work with incessant vociferation, often angrily scold one another, and seem ready to proceed to blows, but scarcely ever come to that extremity. The inevitable severity of the law restrains them, for the loss of a life is always punished by the death of the offender, even though he acted merely in self-defence, and without any malice prepense.

Superstitious and suspicious in their temper, they at first appeared shy and apprehensive of us, being full of prejudices against strangers, of whose cunning and ferocity a thousand ridiculous tales have been propagated, and perhaps industriously encouraged by the government, whose political system seems to be to endeavour to persuade the people that they are themselves already perfect and can therefore learn nothing from others; but it is to little purpose. A nation that does not advance must retrograde, and finally fall back to barbarism and misery.

A Chinese boy who was appointed to wait upon young George Staunton would not for a long time trust himself to sleep in the house with our European servants, being afraid, he said, that they would eat him. The Chinese, however, at all the seaports where we touched were quite free from these foolish notions, and I flatter myself that the Embassy will have effectually removed them in all the provinces which it passed through.

The lower sort most heartily detest the Mandarins and persons in authority, whose arbitrary powers of punishing, oppressing and insulting them they fear, whose injustice they feel, and whose rapacity they must feed. The Mandarins themselves are equally at the mercy of their superiors, the Ministers and Grand Secretaries of the Court, and are punishable by confiscation, and even by death, not only for their own offences, but for what others may do amiss within their department. They are responsible for whatever happens in the place where their authority extends; accident is construed into intention and unavoidable error into wilful neglect. But this is not all, for the penalty is often inflicted on the offender's whole family, as well as on the offender himself.

Although the Emperor, as the father of his people, affects and professes impartiality, and wishes to have it understood that he makes no distinction between Tartars and Chinese, neither Tartars nor Chinese are imposed upon by the pretence. The care taken to preserve the Manchu language among all the Tartars settled in China forms one equivocal line of demarcation, exclusive of the others which I have occasionally taken notice of in these sheets. After a short residence in the country, I found no difficulty in distinguishing a Tartar from a Chinese, although their mode of dress and forms of behaviour are precisely the same, but there was always something (I know not well how to describe it, quod sentio tantum) that indicated the difference in a moment.

It so happened that of our four principal connections, the Grand Secretary Sung Yun [Songyun], the Viceroy Ch'ang-ling* and our constant companions Van-ta-gin [Wang] and Cho-ta-gin [Qiao], two were Tartars and two were Chinese; and although their respective nationalities could not escape us, yet they seemed perfectly united in their friendly and honourable conduct towards us, and made us therefore the more regret our ill fortune in having known so few others that resembled them.

As my knowledge of the female world in China was very limited, I have little to say upon the subject, but it may not be improper to say that little. The women of the lower sort are much weather-beaten, and by no means handsome. Beauty is soon withered by early and frequent parturition, by hard labour and hard fare. They have however a smart air, which arises from their manner of tying up their hair on the crown of their heads, and interspersing it with flowers and other ornaments. In the neighbourhood of Peking I met some ladies of the higher ranks in their carriages, who appeared to have fair complexions and delicate features. They were all painted, as indeed are many of the inferior classes.

There is no law to prohibit intermarriages between Tartars and the Chinese, but they very seldom intermarry. The Manchu and Mongol Tartars chiefly marry together, and scarcely ever with any of the other Tartar tribes. The Manchus often give a large portion with their daughters; the reverse is the case among the Chinese, where the parent usually receives a consideration or handsome present from his son-in-law.

The Tartar ladies have hitherto kept their legs at liberty, and would never submit to the Chinese operation of crippling the feet, though it is said that many of their husbands were desirous of introducing it into their families.

I by no means want to apologise for the Chinese custom of squeezing their women's pettitoes into the shoes of an infant, which I think an infernal distortion. Yet so much are people subject to be warped and blinded by fashion, that every Chinese above the vulgar considers it as a female accomplishment not to be dispensed with. Nay, a reverend apostolic missionary at Peking assured me that in love affairs, the glimpse of a little fairy foot was to a Chinese a most powerful provocative.

The Chinese ladies, like other Asiatics, never alter the costume of their dress, and I suppose the gowns they now wear are much of the same cut as those of their great grandmothers on board of Noah's Ark; but though the habit is the same, they are a little more changeable and coquettish in the choice and disposition of their ornaments.

---

* Changling, the Viceroy of Canton, who was to travel with Macartney on the last stage of his journey to Canton.

16

DIPLOMACY EN ROUTE

16TH TO 23RD OCTOBER After the quick – the dead. Beyond the shipping basin and the suburbs of Tientsin they came across a vast cemetery. As Comptroller John Barrow noted, it was the first common burial ground they had observed:

The Tumuli and different erections marked the mansions of the dead . . . In parts of this massive enclosure there were many coffins lying on the ground, some new, others newly painted but none in a mouldering state awaiting burial at the correct time – until the proper advice had been obtained from the priest or the oracle consulted as to the most propitious place of interment and the most favourable day for performing the obsequies.

Staring morbidly at the graves drifting slowly by, he came to a conclusion favourable, for once, to the Chinese:

On no occasion do the Chinese bury their dead within the precincts of a city or a town, much less within the walls of their temples; but always deposit them at a proper distance from the dwellings of the living, in which respect they have more discretion than the Europeans; who not only allow the interment of dead bodies in the midst of populous cities, but have also thrust them into places of public worship, where crowded congregations are constantly exposed to the nauseous effluvia.

Alexander observed the passing scene without morbidity. His only conclusions are in his sketch-book: studies of trackers; two men transferring water from one irrigation channel to another by means of a rope attached from each to a scoop; soldiers lining the banks to salute the Embassy, their armour of iron, the crowns of their helmets surmounted with a spear from which streamed a tassel of red horsehair: 'This habit with numerous silken strands in array on the wind and glittering in the sun made a splendid show.'

Aeneas Anderson was preoccupied with the problems of catering for his master – not so much with the quantity as with trying to prepare it with the limited facilities at his disposal:

For some days the provisions with which we had been supplied were not only deficient in quantity, but were sent dressed and cold; so that we found it necessary to dress them again, or rather heat them up as well as we could. Mr Plumb, the vehicle of all complaints, was employed to represent the dissatisfaction felt by the different departments of the Embassy . . . This produced an immediate change in supply . . . and we received a large quantity of mutton and beef, with fowls and ducks; to this were added bread, flour, tea, sugar, rice, vegetables of all kinds with soy, oil, candles, charcoal and wood; and while the solid part of the meal with the means of preparing it were amply administered, the elegant addition of fruits of various kinds, and wines and liquors of the country were not forgotten.

Dinwiddie watched the countryside pass by and realized that observation by itself was insufficient. He needed information. He grumbled to himself in his journal:

In all our operations, no plan or system has been adopted; no regular orders given or at least adhered to. Only our interpreter, an ignorant, bigoted priest, without an atom of science, without curiosity or liberality, puts questions frequently different from the intentions of their proposer, either through ignorance or prejudice. We pass through the country like so many dumb persons, having no opportunities of asking or receiving information on the most common subjects.

Meanwhile, diplomatic exchanges between Songyun and Macartney continued. Macartney took every opportunity to press the British position, for he was still smarting from the last letter received at Heshen's hand. On 21st October he discovered that the secretary who drafted that document was employed in the suite of Songyun, and so he taxed Songyun directly, complaining about the fact that the requests made in his note should have been supposed to come from him, on his own initiative, and not from the King (a little diplomatic elision here – they actually came from his East India Company brief). In short, he had been made out by the Emperor to be exceeding his brief. Songyun blandly explained to him:

Chinese urbanity does not allow one sovereign to desire of another what it is possible to be refused. It is therefore concluded that the request has never been made, or if made, that the Ambassador has been guilty of an error in the delivery of his message and to have asked from his own head what had never entered into that of his master. This mode of interpretation, however respectful it may be to the King, is certainly not very flattering to his representative.

Here Macartney concealed his chagrin, reminding himself of the first principle of diplomacy: 'All private and personal consideration must merge in the pursuit of public objects.'

But this was not all. Macartney told Songyun that he had been very surprised to find in the letter that he was thought to have desired to introduce the English religion into China. Once again came the urbane reply: 'The

Grand Councillor and his secretary took it for granted that the English were like other Europeans, who it was well known were industrious and active in propagating their faith.' The Ambassador then pointed out with some vigour that the English never attempted to dispute or disturb the worship or tenets of others, being persuaded that the supreme governor of the universe was equally pleased with the homage of all his creatures when it proceeded from sincere devotion. This was evident from their merchants in Canton and Macao, where there were no accompanying priests or chaplains.

Songyun instantly affirmed that no such thing had been contained in the letter. If it was in the Latin translation, it must have come from the missionaries who translated it!

Obtaining no satisfaction here, Macartney tried another tack, observing:

> The Emperor had chiefly dealt on the request to allow an English Minister to reside constantly in Peking, but he had avoided touching on the other points of his mission, confining himself to a general assurance that the English Merchant should be treated with kindness and favour, and in the second letter he seemed to accuse us of an unfair design to obtain exclusive privileges.

Here Macartney paused. He had already learned the dangers of running ahead of the interpreter. He waited to hear the point being made, then sought a reaction on Songyun's face. There was none, so he anticipated it. 'Tell him,' he said to the interpreter, 'it is true, we admit, but we only asked for ourselves. We by no means desired that this bounty should not be transferred to others.'

The countryside glided by. It was cold and grey with a promise of rain. The constant noise of the gongs and the chant of the trackers could be heard in the cabin. Again, Macartney waited for the interpreter to make the point. 'If only,' he thought, 'I had been given such a chance to explain my mission in Zhe-hol [Jehol] or Peking.'

Since Songyun made no comment, Macartney continued. He stressed the grievances complained of at Canton, so distorted in the Emperor's letter that it was not surprising that they should be disregarded. No matter how much the Chinese might choose to downplay them, these grievances were extremely serious. If they were not speedily remedied, Canton trade would fall into decay – than which nothing could be more prejudicial to China. There was another long pause while the interpreter laboured to get across the nuances of the dialogue, for all the parties realized that this was a crucial exchange. The sunlight slowly swung round in the cabin as the barge was hauled round a curve in the canal.

Songyun replied at length. He begged Macartney to lay aside the uneasiness that he seemed to feel from his perusal of the two letters. They were not meant to convey anything unfavourable or unpleasant to the Embassy or to himself. He reminded the British Ambassador that the laws of China were invariable and the Emperor so strictly observant of them that nothing could ever induce him to infringe them. Upon the slightest appearance of innovation, the Emperor was always on his guard, and had indeed declined to comply with the particular requests made by the Embassy. But that did not imply a disinclination towards Macartney or towards the concerns of his Embassy. He entertained very kind intentions, and the English at Canton would soon be experiencing the beneficial effects of them.

Another pause for interpretation. Macartney and Songyun reached out for a sweetmeat on the table before them.

Enlarging on his theme, Songyun explained that the mechanism of their government was to delegate much to the discretion and recommendation of the Viceroys – whose conduct might not always be unexceptionable – but that as a particular mark of attention a mandarin of high rank called Changling, an ally of the Emperor, had just been appointed Viceroy of Canton. This man was remarkably well disposed to strangers, and the justice and integrity he had lately displayed in his government of Zhejiang Province had marked him out as the fittest person for this new appointment. Orders had been sent to him to make the most minute inquiries at Canton into such grievances as might exist there, and as soon as he had considered them he was to rectify everything that was amiss by the most effective exertion of his authority. This would, of course, take some time. The beneficial consequences could scarcely be felt until the next season, when, upon proper notice of the arrival of the English ships, every reasonable indulgence would be allowed them.

Recognizing here a big step forward from previous positions, Macartney was quick to show his satisfaction. He requested that, in order

> to render [these propositions] completely . . . to my Sovereign, a third letter from the Emperor, confirming the flattering hopes now given, would be very desirable. Sung Yun [Songyun] seemed sensible enough of the value I put upon obtaining a third letter, but said it could make no difference whatsoever as to the public advantages in consideration and that he was afraid, as I had taken leave, a new dispatch would be incompatible with the etiquette of the Court. The assurances which he had given me of the Emperor's favourable attentions were by no means to be taken as effusions of his own friendship, or the compliments of his office, but as the literal words of the Emperor's dispatches to him, and when I came to converse with Ch'ang-ling [Changling], whom I would find at Hang-tchoo [Hangzhou], he could confirm all that he had mentioned in the fullest manner.

Macartney had noticed that scarcely a day went by without Songyun receiving and dispatching letters. He knew that the senior courtiers could use the Imperial postal service, capable of conveying a letter fifteen hundred miles in ten to twelve days. From this frequent exchange of correspondence he deduced that 'it would seem we form no small object of court solicitude'. In this he was right, but for the wrong reasons. The Chinese harboured no goodwill toward the Embassy. As the Court documents have shown, they were engaged in an exercise of potential damage limitation.

They took their exercise along the canal bank, rice fields stretching to the horizon. Aeneas Anderson was fascinated by the irrigation, remarking on the 'stone gutters of channels, finished with great neatness and admirably contrived to carry water to every part of the plantations'. And it was with some admiration that Dinwiddie meticulously described the cultivation and harvesting of the crop – a process that has not changed to this day.

In some fields the young plants of a future crop were just rising above the ground, overspread by a very shallow covering of water; while the crops of the present season had attained maturity and presented a very cheering prospect. Reapers were occasionally busy cutting down fields of the grain which was about two feet high. The blade of a sickle is about five inches long and one and a half broad. The edge of the blade turns downwards like a scythe. Five or six cuts fill the left hand, which is afterward raised and separated from the growing rice, solely by the left hand. It is then laid across the ridge in a smooth even row without any bands, which is an afterwork. When tied into sheaves a bamboo stick is thrust obliquely into the side of one, near the band, and a triangle is formed of three sheaves with the tops down, an excellent contrivance for drying.

Macartney viewed the scene with a landowner's practised eye. It was not so much the crops, the harvest, that attracted his attention, as the question of who owned what, how much rental the peasants paid, how the harvest was divided up and what profit would be gained from it.

Reflections on the Voyage 3: Macartney on Property

As in China the interests of the Emperor are always the first consideration, no property can be secured against his claims. In cases of delinquency, confiscation is inevitable.

A man may dispose of his fortune, real and personal, in the manner most agreeable to himself. By law he may even devise it to the bonzes or other religious fraternities, but of late such bequests are very rare, for the policy of the state, although unwilling positively to prohibit any ancient right, however imprudently exercised, yet renders its abuse as little hurtful as possible, by quartering officers, travellers, couriers and others upon most of the temples that were endowed in mortmain, so that posthumous folly is defeated, and idleness made to contribute to the maintenance of industry.

A testator often leaves his estates to his wife, especially in the case of the minority of his children; but if a man dies without a will, his lands and personalty are equally divided among his sons, reserving a proper dower for the widow, which varies according to the provinces where she chooses to reside. The daughters have nothing but are maintained, till married by their brothers and if there be no brothers, by their next inheriting relations.

There are many great landed estates in China, some even to the amount of £100,000 per annum, accumulated by various means, by legacies, by clandestine trade – that is to say, by trade carried on by inferior agents with the capitals of great men to whom trade is directly forbidden – by usury, by employments, by presents, etc. A widow in Tien-sing [Tientsin], whose husband had been enriched in this manner and who left her his fortune (his four sons being minors), not long since sent a million of taels of silver [£333,333 sterling] as a present to the Emperor towards the expense of the Tibet war.

The legal interest on money is twelve percent, but it is commonly extended to eighteen and sometimes to thirty-six. Usury is punishable by the law but as in most countries is rarely punished. Usury like gaming is a dishonourable mode of getting money, but by a sort of compact between necessity and avarice, between influence and distress, the prosecution of a Jew or a sharper is considered as not very honourable even in those who suffer from them.

In farms (which are usually let for five or seven years, resumable by the landlord or relinquishable by the tenant at the end of those terms) the owner divides the crop with the cultivator. The latter has one half entirely to himself, the former takes the other half and pays out of it the Emperor's tax which is considered to be always the same, whether the season be plentiful or scanty. Five percent is said to be the Emperor's proper share of the valued crop, but the valuation (which is an arbitrary one of the Crown officer) is generally fixed so much higher than the current price of produce, that the landlord's commutation with the Crown is sometimes not less than eight or ten percent instead of five. Though twelve percent be the legal interest, yet land sells for twenty years' purchase in the neighbourhood of Peking.

The only current money in China is a thin brass or copper coin, about the breadth of a shilling, with a hole drilled through it for the purpose of being strung. A thousand of these pieces, which are called sapecas, are esteemed at a Tael or 6s 8d sterling.

A Chinese peasant can maintain himself on fifty sapecas a day. Our boatmen, who draw the yachts in the provinces we [pass] through, generally [are] paid eighty sapecas a day, or one sapeca for each li, each li being equal to three hundred and sixty geometrical paces.

A common weaver, joiner or other tradesman earns little more than a bare subsistence . . . It does not appear that there is always sufficient employment for the people, whose multitude is so great as to exceed the means of subsistence by labour, so that many who are able and willing to work are obliged to depend upon the alms of private charity, or seek for support in the public hospitals; and notwithstanding these resources it is affirmed that in every year vast numbers perish of hunger and cold. The summers are so warm that the common sort go almost naked, and the winter is so rigorous that the mortality is very great from want of clothing and shelter. In the different provinces of the Empire there are often partial famines, and whenever they are attended with very serious or fatal consequences the mandarin of the district is punished, according to Chinese policy, for not having foreseen the calamity and replenished the magazine sufficiently to remedy the accident. From the misery to which a large proportion of the population are thus exposed (the majority is indeed very wretched in all respects) it is not to be wondered that they should lose every sense but that of self-preservation; that they should forget the other ties of nature and sell their children without scruple if they find a chapman, and desert them without pity if they don't. This is the common reproach of strangers to the Chinese, but it should not be made with too much precipitation and severity, for I believe, where the parent has any possible means of supporting his offspring, there is no country where paternal affection is stronger than in China; and it is natural it should be so, because there is no country where filial respect and gratitude are so strong.

17

Promises, Promises

24TH OCTOBER TO 8TH NOVEMBER The waterway meandered. The sun would be ahead and then astern some twenty times in daylight hours. The scenery had changed, too. The flat irrigated rice landscape had turned into fields of cotton dotted with poplar trees. They started to go through sluices, locks made of huge blocks of granite, with no gates – only planks which were lowered to hold back the water. As each boat went through, paying its toll to the Emperor, the planks were raised and the resulting flume propelled the barges helter-skelter on to the next level. Frequently there were accidents, when the boat could not keep to the middle of the lock and was driven hard against the sides by the turbulence of the stream, causing damage, in spite of the fenders of cushions and straw placed along the sides of the lock.

Songyun's visits to Macartney's barge were becoming as predictable as the countryside. Each meeting began with assurances of the Emperor's pleasure at the Grand Councillor's accounts of the Embassy's progress. A testimony of benevolence would then be delivered: today it was a cheese (a rare commodity in China) and some sweetmeats – a gracious repetition of the Emperor's kindness and regard!

The conversation pecked over the points of the previous meeting. Yes, Macartney was assured, it would be an easy matter for the new Viceroy of Canton – a man so reasonable and just he would never countenance the slightest hint of oppression – to set everything to rights. Yes, greater indulgence and favour would be shown to the English than they had ever experienced before. Songyun pressed these points home with such emphasis that Macartney asked himself:

> If the Court of Peking is not really sincere can they possibly expect to feed us along with the promises? Can they be ignorant that a couple of English frigates would be an overmatch for the whole naval force of their Empire, that in half a summer we

could totally destroy all navigation of their coasts and reduce the inhabitants of their maritime provinces, who subsist mainly on fish to absolute famine?

On their part, the Chinese were well aware of the danger of the English, in their disappointment, causing trouble in Canton and Macao. The reputation of the red-haired barbarians had preceded them. All military posts on the Embassy's route were therefore fully manned against all eventualities, parading and saluting to the point of tedium when the Embassy sailed past. Macartney, who by instinct and experience preferred diplomacy to fighting, recognized the same instincts in others. He therefore rated the military display at its true value.

On Saturday 26th October they sailed into the city of Jining. It was the fifth city they passed through, all of them important trading centres, all with their garrisons lining the canal bank. At Jining, Aeneas Anderson reported, the press of junks was so heavy that the Embassy fleet had to come to anchor to give time for a passage to be made.

But the tedium of the long voyage was beginning to tell. The continuous observation of the countryside was palling. On the Tuesday Anderson remarked:

The Voyage of this day furnished no variety unless a great number of flour mills are supposed to vary the scene. The growing wealth of cultivation we had seen every hour as we proceeded on our voyage, and not a spot appeared, which towns and villages did not occupy, but proved the skill of the husbandmen. This morning, however, gave us a prospect of that labour for we passed several extensive fields where peasants were busy with their ploughs drawn by oxen. Of cities, towns, locks and bridges we have seen and said so much that the reader and the writer would be equally fatigued with the daily enumeration of them.

Not so Macartney. His journal reveals a persistent astonishment:

Continuing our course on the canal, which is now supplied from a very extensive lake on our left hand. The bank here between the canal and the lake occasionally varies in breadth being in some places more than half a mile thick, and in others not more than two hundred yards. The prospect of it this morning at sunrise was most delightful, the borders fringed with woods, houses and pagodas on the sloping grounds behind, and the lake itself covered with numberless vessels crossing it in different directions, according to all the various modes of navigation that poles, paddles, oars and sails can supply. On our right are many villages on the bank which is here and there pierced with sluices in order to turn the water for the purpose of agriculture.

And on the following day he noted:

The canal is now conducted over a great morass, which appears without limits on each side, and above which it is raised and embanked by immense mounds of earth very high and very thick. It is a most stupendous work . . . a vast surface of inundation narrowed and forced up by human skill into an artificial channel several yards above its former bed . . . and after a long course falls gently into the Yellow

River or Whang-ho.

Staunton, for his part, was attracted by cormorants fishing on the lake:

On a large lake close to the canal are thousands of small boats and rafts built entirely for this species of fishery. On each boat or raft are ten or a dozen birds, which at a signal from the owner plunge into the water; and it is astonishing to see the size of the fish with which they return, grasped in their bills.

Fish and birdlife excited the interest of all. Alexander did several sketches of birds and fishermen. Huttner noted that the birds had cords round their necks to prevent them swallowing the fish, that they had taken a long time to train, and that as they only ate fish they had a most disagreeable smell!

The diplomacy continued. On the 29th, a mild and pleasant day, Songyun again called on Macartney. After the usual exchange of compliments, he told the Ambassador that he had received a letter informing him that the *Lion* and the smaller vessels had sailed from Zhoushan, leaving only the *Hindostan* to convey the Embassy to Macao. Macartney was very displeased. He coldly told Songyun what he had already made clear in Peking – namely, that since the *Hindostan* was built for trade and not for passengers she was totally incapable of accommodating all of the Embassy. He emphasized that 'from our manners and habits of life we require a good deal of room', and finally, to ram home the point: 'A general sickness is the inevitable concomitant of a crowded ship.'

Blandly, Songyun replied that he would write to the Court, but that he did not doubt that he would receive such orders as would be perfectly agreeable to the Embassy. If they went to Canton through the inland provinces, he suggested, the heavy baggage should go ahead to be loaded on to the *Hindostan* at Zhoushan. Macartney reminded Songyun that this would not have happened if, as requested, his letter to Gower had been forwarded.

Thus from the suspicious nature of the Court which is so disposed to imagine some deep design in almost every proceeding of a European, we are now seriously disappointed. Sir Erasmus Gower, hearing nothing from me, and knowing nothing of the state of things in Europe, is gone to the Eastward and will not return before May. Our valuable China ships must therefore sail home without a convoy, which, should we have a French War, would be attended with very great danger.

The next day the dialogue resumed. Once again Songyun conveyed the Emperor's compliments and his satisfaction that the Embassy had not been sent through mischievous curiosity or ill intentions, but solely to do him honour and solicit commercial privileges and protection. He added that Changling, the new Viceroy of Canton, was fully *au fait* with the Emperor's sentiments and was to allow British merchants free access to him so that they could in person lay before him their complaints, instead of sending them through the channels of the Cohong.

Macartney, who by now must have had his tongue in his cheek, repeated that he was infinitely sensible of the Emperor's goodness and that he would particularly appreciate it if what his Imperial Majesty had said might be conveyed on paper for his Sovereign to see, since, whatever credit he might be disposed to give his Ambassador, King George would pay much more attention to a communication from the Emperor himself. Songyun's reply was tart and to the point: the Emperor had his own method of doing business, he said, and nobody presumed to describe to him a different one; it was his style to give general assurances and not specific promises, and it was not at all unlikely that the former would turn out more to his advantage than the latter.

By Friday 1st November they were about to cross the Yellow River. Since they had passed the last sluices two days previously, the canal had widened and, according to Macartney – allowing himself home thoughts – it was now as broad as the Thames at Putney.

About this time Alexander made a few notes in his diary about his companions in his barge – Dr Hugh Gillan, Dr Dinwiddie, Thomas Hickey and Aeneas Anderson,

> an intelligent man who kept a journal and who was appointed to cook our dinner. His stewed ducks served in an earthenware dish were excellent . . . The supply of provisions is most liberal. The boats with provisions are alongside every morning, orders being sent forward to the towns and villages to provide the several articles. The bread baked in steam is very good, mutton excellent, beef indifferent and the large surplus of ducks and fowl is largely given to the twelve people who navigate the vessel. The vegetables and fruit are good, wine sour and poor is sent in jars as is a strong spirit called Sam-shan, much above proof and distilled from rice.

Occasionally the wine passed down to the crew fomented fights. Alexander observed one man seizing the pigtail of another and slapping him about the face with an open hand. On another occasion five men set upon one. 'The Chinese have no idea of equality in their combats,' he drily noted.

As they approached the Yellow River the current was becoming stronger, and to haul the Ambassador's barge against it they needed twenty-four trackers. The climate reflected the onset of winter: it was now cold enough for ground frost in the early morning. So it was that on the morning of Saturday 2nd November they 'fell down the canal into the Whang-ho or Great Yellow River, which . . . was three miles wide and very muddy. We then struck into another canal [a continuation of the Grand Canal] and proceeded southward toward [that mightiest of rivers the] Yang-tse-kiang-ho [the Yangtze]'.

On 4th November they entered the city of Qingjiang – famed for the beauty of its women, so Alexander was told.

> But this statement must be taken comparatively, for the generality of females we had hitherto seen certainly had no pretensions to beauty. The lower class are seen in crowds stamping along on their little feet, while those of the middle and superior

order are seldom seen except through the gauze blinds of their windows, or when they venture to peep through them, it being ungenteel for ladies of rank to be seen by the populace. Some of them were seen at a distance by telescope. These appeared handsome but possibly they owed much to the assistance of paint which they used liberally, red and white. Their eyebrows are also blackened with a narrow line and they put a red spot like a cherry on the lower lip which altogether gives them a pleasing character of countenance.

After six days' travel, on 7th November near Zhejiang they now entered the Yangtze at a point where the crossing was about a mile and a half wide. They were greeted by a garrison of two thousand troops lining the bank.

All turned out to show themselves as if for review. They consisted of different corps, differently dressed and armed according to their respective services, some with matchlocks, some with bows and arrows, some with halberds, lances, swords and targets. Many of them wore steel helmets, as they are supposed to be, though I suspect they are only of burnished leather or glittering pasteboard. The uniforms which are very showy and of different colours, red, white, blue, buff and yellow, must be very expensive, but after all these troops have a slovenly, unmilitary air and their quilted boots and long petticoats make them look heavy, inactive and effeminate.

Attracted by their fine regimentals, Macartney hinted that he would like one of the helmets as a souvenir, but Wang told him that the uniforms belonged to the Emperor and were kept in the public wardrobe only to be worn on holidays or great occasions like this. No souvenir was forthcoming.

Two miles away on their left were a number of islets dominated by a high conical rock called the Golden Mountain,

built from the water's edge to the top with temples, turrets and belvederes on regular terraces one above the other, intermingled with evergreen trees of various volumes, contracted in so happy a taste and distributed in such a manner to give the whole the air of a fairy edifice suddenly raised on the river by the magic of an enchanter. It has a very striking effect and almost realises the extravagant paintings of China fans and screens, which I am now inclined to think have been done from real views and not the fancy of the artist.

A succession of minor incidents punctuated the journey. The master of Alexander's barge was found guilty of trading privately and evading duties while in the employment of the government. Aeneas Anderson reported: 'The mandarin makes a severe examination into the business and is so convinced of the truth of the charge that the guilty man is taken ashore, stretched on the ground by two soldiers, and in full view beaten with a split bamboo.' Both Alexander and Staunton observed the scene. Alexander painted it. Staunton was to write of it:

The punishment of the bamboo, however degrading it must appear to a European, is ordered upon a very summary hearing upon any individual, not in the rank of mandarin . . . A great proportion of the Chinese are so lowered to their condition, that in those punishments they feel little more than the mere corporal sufferings occasioned upon them.

Towards evening they passed through the city of Suzhou, called by travellers the 'Paradise of China'. Huttner sang its praises:

It is the place where the richest merchants go to relax, the playground of the greatest artists, the wisest philosophers, cleverest actors and acrobats and jugglers of the most amusing kind. It dictates Chinese taste, has the most beautiful women, the smallest feet, the latest fashions, the most cultivated language. It is the meeting point of the most varied types of pleasure, and the most voluptuous licence. It attracts the libertines of the whole of China. The Chinese have a proverb: 'Up there is Paradise, down here Sou-tchoo [Suzhou]!'

But the Embassy sailed through the city, having no time to sample its delights.

The next day Songyun called on Macartney in his barge once again. After the usual pleasantries, he produced a letter from the Court directing him to put the Embassy, as soon as it arrived at Hangzhou, under the care of the new Viceroy of Canton, who would be awaiting them there. The letter also contained instructions for Captain Mackintosh to join the *Hindostan* at Zhoushan. The presents and baggage, as well as part of the guard and the Ambassador's suite, were to go to Zhoushan to be sent on ahead, and Songyun was to accompany this party as far as Ningbo. Captain Mackintosh was to be informed that, if he failed to get a cargo at Zhoushan, he should be allowed to load one at Canton; and as a particular compliment to the Embassy and on account of the *Hindostan*'s connection with it, she should be exempted from paying measurage or other dues.

The barges drifted along the canal, giving ample time for those on board to contemplate the well tilled land on the banks. Comptroller John Barrow observed the diligent cultivation, and was later to record his thoughts in his journal.

Reflections on the Voyage 4: Barrow on Agriculture

UPON THE WHOLE, if I might venture an opinion upon the Chinese as agriculturalists, I should not hesitate to say that, let as much ground be given to one of their peasants as he and his family can work with the spade, and he will turn the piece of ground to more advantage and produce from it more sustenance for the use of man, than any European whatsoever would be able to do; but let fifty or one hundred acres of the best land in China be given to a farmer, at a mean rent, so far from making out of it the value of three rents, on which our farmers usually calculate, he would scarcely be able to support his family, after paying the expense of labour that would be required to work the farm.

Rice, being the staple of China, was abundantly cultivated in all such places as afforded the greatest command of water. The usual average produce of corn-lands is reckoned to be between ten to fifteen for one; and of rice, from twenty-five to thirty; commonly about thirty. Those corn-lands which admit of easy irrigation are usually turned over with the plough immediately after the grain is cut, which in the middle provinces is ready for the sickle early in June, about the same time as the young rice fields stand at the height of eight or ten inches. These being now thinned, the young plants are transplanted into the prepared wheat lands which are flooded . . . Instead of rice one of the millets is sometimes sown as an after crop, this requiring very little water. It is common practice, after taking off a crop of cotton and indigo, in the month of October, to sow wheat, to leave the land again clear in the month of May or June. Such a succession of crops, without ever allowing the land to lie fallow, should seem to require a large quantity of manure . . . They preserve, with great care, all kinds of urine, in which it is an universal practice to steep the ears previous to their being sown . . . Their eagerness to pick up manure led to some ridiculous scenes. Whenever our barges halted and the soldiers and servants found it necessary to step ashore, they were always pursued to their place of retirement by these collectors.

A very erroneous opinion seems to have been entertained in Europe, with regard to the skill of the Chinese in agriculture. Industrious they certainly are, but their labour does not always appear to be bestowed with judgement. The instruments they make use of are incapable of performing the operations of husbandry to the greatest advantage. In the deepest and best soils, their plough seldom cuts to the depth of four inches, so that they sow from year to year upon the same soil, without being able to turn up fresh earth.

The province of Tche-tchiang [Zhejiang], through which we have just come, abounds in lakes; but the produce, except that of a little rice, is very different consisting principally of silk. For feeding the worms that afford this article, all the fertile and beautiful valleys between the mountains as well as the plains are covered with plantations of mulberry-trees. The small houses in which the worms are reared, are placed generally in the centre of each plantation; in order that they may be removed as far as possible from any kind of noise, experience having taught them that a sudden shout or the bark of a dog is destructive of the young worms . . . they are watched night and day.

Besides silk Tche-tchiang produces camphor, tallow from the Croton,* a considerable quantity of tea, oranges and almost all the fruits peculiar to China. I am most astonished at the small returns that must necessarily be made to the cultivators of the tea plant. The preparations of some of the finer kinds are said to require that every leaf should be rolled singly by hand; particularly such as are exported to the European Markets. Besides this, there are many processes, such as steeping, drying, turning and packing after it

---

* A tropical plant of the spurge family.

has been plucked off the shrub leaf by leaf. Nothing can more clearly point out the patient and unremitting labour of the Chinese, than the preparation of this plant for the market. It is a curious circumstance that a body of merchants in England should furnish employment as might be easily made to appear, to more than a million subjects of a nation that affects to despise merchants and throws every obstacle in the way of commercial intercourse.

18

The Parting of the Ways

9TH TO 14TH NOVEMBER Alexander was suffering from a universal ennui that seemed to be affecting them all. His mood was in no way lightened by his cabin companion Dr Gillan's tendency to discourse on Chinese medicine with his colleagues. Furthermore, on the previous day the sight of another cemetery stretching for many miles along the bank had considerably lowered his morale. It was an intimation of mortality that seemed as everlasting as the journey itself: 'The tombs and coffins are thickly interspersed over the fields and of various forms, some like pedestals others resembling decanters.'

A somewhat utilitarian present from one of the attendant mandarins, given that evening to him and his colleagues, did little to lift his spirits. He dutifully recorded his share as eight cups and saucers of rosewood lined with tinfoil, twenty pairs of chopsticks, and fourteen artificial flowers fastened to pins, with which the Chinese ladies ornamented their hair.

Nothing served to raise his morale on the following day, either. It was raining. It rained all day without intermission. He managed to summon enough interest, though, when the Chinese who had gathered to watch the barges on their passage produced umbrellas, to note 'a singular effect, the crowds completely covered with umbrellas, like the testudo of shields used by the Roman soldiers'.

They passed two towns and many villages on the borders of the main silk-producing area of China, the plantations of mulberry trees with their autumn foliage of orange and yellow reminding him of autumn in an English orchard. The rain, however, had made the towpath slippery, 'so that our poor trackers who are completely drenched were continually falling. When this happened they were unfailingly whipped till they recovered themselves again. Some wore shoes made of straw to prevent slipping. Discontented English labourers should see this and be comparatively happy.'

Macartney was summoned, in the rain, to Songyun's presence, only to be shown yet another letter confirming the dispositions. The main party was to go to Canton under Changling's guidance. The baggage, some of the guard, Captain Mackintosh and a few members of the Embassy would go to Zhoushan. Songyun would accompany them as far as Ningbo, but would ensure that they had every facility and that the *Hindostan* would be able to load its cargo at Zhoushan. If the time was too short there, then a cargo would be loaded in Canton. So the die was cast! The Ambassador returned to his barge to make arrangements. He decided that those who would go to Zhoushan would be Lieutenant-Colonel Benson, Dr Dinwiddie and Mr Alexander, plus four servants and two mechanics who were to take care of the stores.

Alexander was hurt. He had not forgotten being left behind in Peking when the main party went to Jehol. For the second time he was to be deprived of a chance to paint for the record. He asked to see Macartney and, taking with him all his sketches, sought leave to remain with the main party. Patronizingly applauding him for his industry, Macartney stood firm. Alexander noted in his diary: 'I cannot reconcile this with painting, with the lost opportunity to exercise my pencil in passing through such an extent of country as from Hang-tchoo [Hangzhou] to Canton.'

The next morning, a Saturday, the flotilla stopped at a village outside the walls of Hangzhou. The new Viceroy of Canton had arrived in his barge to confer with Songyun, and soon came alongside to greet Macartney, who liked what he saw: 'His appearance was much to his advantage. He was perfectly well bred and the whole of his manner candid and gentlemanlike. He confirmed the Emperor's instructions to pay the greatest regard to the English at Canton, who, on every occasion, he said, should have free access to him in person or by letter.' Changling then asked Macartney about his voyage. It was very flattering to the Emperor to have an embassy sent from so great a distance, he said. His Imperial Majesty had charged him to reiterate his satisfaction, and to deliver an additional present for King George consisting of pieces of gold, some purses of his own, and – the most precious gift of all – the 'paper of happiness', inscribed by the Emperor's own hand with the Chinese character Fu (meaning 'good fortune', 'happiness'), the strongest mark of friendship and affection that a Chinese sovereign could bestow on another prince. A similar paper was given to Macartney, as a testimony of the Emperor's approbation of the Embassy and as an earnest of his proposed attention to its objectives.

The Viceroy hoped, he assured them, that in four or five days everything would be ready for them to proceed. However, he was afraid that Captain Mackintosh would not find it easy to get a loading, either at Ningbo or Zhoushan. He explained that the merchants there were not accustomed to trading with the English, and they were probably not provided with such articles at present as Captain Mackintosh might want; moreover, whatever they sold would have to be paid for in ready money. He went on to list other objections, but Macartney, 'observing so many impediments and thinking it better not to urge further a business which we plainly saw they wished to decline', gave up with good grace on the Viceroy's repeating the assurance that the *Hindostan* would be exempt from paying measurage and other duties at Canton.

At noon on 10th November the Embassy entered Hangzhou. It was here that they were to separate, each party taking a different route. The Canton party was to travel part of the way by land, the Zhoushan party to continue by barge. They had only four days in which to sort out the baggage. The whole fleet came to anchor in a part of the city where they were forbidden to go ashore. Furthermore, a body of Chinese soldiers had pitched their tents under a series of triumphal arches in the street opposite the junks, and from this camp they surveyed the Embassy.

Once again the British travellers were frustrated at being confined to quarters in such a populous and flourishing city – the more so because they knew it to be the centre of silk production. Macartney hoped

to be able to learn about the cultivation of silk, but the shyness and jealousy of the Chinese in all matters where they observe us to be curious and inquisitive are inconceivably great. Having asked what kind of mulberries grew here, the red or the white, some informed us the red, others, the white. From whence I conclude they are equally common.

Somehow, though, the persistent Dinwiddie obtained permission to wander the countryside – on a plant-collecting expedition. Macartney having got nowhere with his own inquiries on silk production, he had given the task of industrial espionage to the good dominie doctor. However, it was not silk that captured his attention:

Walked among the rice fields and the plantations of mulberry trees where also a great many tallow trees were cultivated. From the fruit of the latter is distilled an oily substance, which is extensively used by the Chinese in the manufacture of candles. The fruit which contains the tallow is about the size of a sloe, at first green, but black when ripe, in which stage the rind or shell opens leaving a ball, very white on the tree. The process of extracting the tallow is by boiling the bruised balls in water, when the oily matter is skimmed off.

On Monday 11th November Macartney once again found himself thwarted by the Chinese. In the afternoon he received a letter from Sir Erasmus Gower, dated at Zhoushan the 15th October,

which through the singular jealousy and suspicion of the Chinese had been kept from me till now. From this letter I have received news of the Lion's people being very sickly and the surgeon and first mate not being likely to recover. The ship was in such want of medicines, particularly of [quinine] bark and of opium, that it became necessary to have a speedy supply of both and therefore Sir Erasmus was returning to the mouth of the river at Canton, but should proceed again from thence to the northwards without delay.

A letter was immediately dispatched by special courier – thanks to the good offices of the Viceroy – saying that the Embassy was on its way to Canton and requesting Sir Erasmus to remain off Macao till 'either he saw me or heard of me again'.

The 13th of November was a day of last-minute preparations and farewells. The baggage had been transshipped, ready for departure on the following day. Songyun came to say goodbye to Macartney – but not before firing a parting shot in the damage limitation exercise that had been entrusted to him.

Among other things he said to me in a strain of liberality scarcely to be expected in a Tartar or a Chinese, that as all distant countries must necessarily have different laws and customs, we should not be surprised if theirs varied from ours, that we owed each other mutual indulgences and he therefore hoped I should not carry with me to Europe any impressions to the disadvantage or disparagement of China.

Macartney noted his gentlemanly manner, and shrewdly assumed that, since he displayed it in the presence of two of his colleagues, it must have the approval of the Court. He also noticed that, excusing himself in a becoming manner, Songyun declined the present offered to him.

Meanwhile, outside the conference cabin, along the wharf the hustle and bustle of rearrangement continued. In the river astern, boats filled with local Chinese came to peer at the strangers. Alexander noted that most of these were female – and by no means as shy as before. And he could not fail to notice the Embassy's embarrassment when, in full view of their audience, calls of nature obliged them to use the sampans, moored for the purpose, alongside the barges.

That evening Songyun summoned the Zhoushan party to his barge. Through Mr Plumb the interpreter, they were told that because of the shallowness of the water each boat would carry only two passengers and a servant. There was no cabin – only a covering of arched matting to keep off the rain. So dispositions were made: Dinwiddie, Alexander and their servant Antonio in one barge, Lieutenant-Colonel Benson, Captain Mackintosh and a servant in the other. Alexander allows a hint of cupidity to creep into his account: 'Sung Yun [Songyun] on this occasion made us each a present of ten pairs of chopsticks and eight little forks, but nothing to use them on.'

As darkness fell, the attendant mandarin could be seen passing amongst the junks requiring that all baggage be labelled Zhoushan or Canton. No sooner was this task completed, than 'coolies' took them off to the appointed depot. Meanwhile, Macartney ordered ten dollars to be given to the owner of each junk as a reward for the crews. They were ready for the morrow.

It began with ceremony. Macartney received a farewell visit from the Governor of Hangzhou. Having dealt with the formalities, the whole retinue set off for the Qiantang River, a journey of seven miles, where they were to embark in junks of a different burthen. The Ambassador travelled in a palanquin, the rest of the suite in sedan chairs of 'a homely kind' carried, in relays, by two sets of bearers. The procession was led by the guards, commanded by Lieutenants Parish and Crewe, and immediately behind them followed the Ambassador and Sir George Staunton, who, still suffering from the gout, was carried on a litter.

The first four miles of their route took them through the narrow streets of the city of Hangzhou. The side-streets were blocked off by soldiers, to prevent the procession being interrupted by the crowds gathered to see them. Macartney found himself once again viewing the scene with an eye to trade:

> The streets are paved with stone and put one in mind of the courts in London that run parallel with the Strand. Almost every house is a shop. I observed in some of them great quantities of furs, broadcloth and long ells,* mostly imported, I believe on English bottoms to Canton.
>
> The Environs of the Town are very beautiful, embellished by an extensive lake. On one side is a pagoda in ruins. It is octagonally built of fine hewed stone and mouldering away from age . . . It is called the Tower of the Thundering Winds and is supposed to be about two thousand five hundred years old.

At one o'clock they arrived at the river. It was broad and shallow, with a great expanse of sandy beach. Alexander wrote:

> To reach our vessels which lie on shoal water, we had to pass over a long line of wagons covered with split bamboo which formed a convenient causeway. Wagons drawn by buffalo went alongside the vessels that came here to unload, taking their cargoes on shore.
>
> The aspect of the country beyond the beach and around is beyond description beautiful, being enriched with Mandarins' Villas, Pagodas etc. backed by a range of fine formed mountains, with a part of Hang-tchoo [Hangzhou] in the distance. The music, rich silk banners fluttering in the breeze, salutes, triumphal arches with gay silken streamers and the various demonstrations of respect to his Excellency produced altogether a scene so novel it was impossible not to be highly gratified.
>
> The party for Chusan [Zhoushan] took leave of their fellow travellers and immediately embarked on two boats which cruised down the river. We were then carried in sedan chairs about two miles. At 10.00pm we finally embarked our diminished squadron and got under way for Chusan, accompanied by the Great Mandarin Sung Yun.

At this point in the voyage, in view of the many bouts of illness they had suffered and were, indeed, still suffering, Macartney sought the opinion of Dr Gillan on Chinese medicine.

---

* Lengths of cloth.

Reflections on the Voyage 5: Dr Gillan on Medicine

AS THERE ARE NO PUBLIC SCHOOLS or professors of medicine in China, a young man who wishes to become a physician has no other way of acquiring a knowledge of the practice of physic but to engage himself to some practitioner as an apprentice for a certain period of time and on such terms as the master chooses to prescribe. During the time of his apprenticeship the young man has an opportunity of seeing his master practise, of visiting his patients along with him and of acquiring such parts of his knowledge and secrets as he chooses to communicate to him. Physicians seldom make fortunes in China nor can their patients in general afford to pay them high fees. About three pence sterling is the usual fee among the people and fifteen pence sterling among the mandarins. But almost all the great Mandarins and Princes of the Blood have physicians of their own who live always with them and follow them wherever they go. The Emperor has several who always remain at Court. His physicians, like almost all the rest of his attendants to whose charge he commits his principal affairs and especially his domestic concerns, are Eunuchs.

In the distinction, discernment and cure of diseases the Chinese physicians draw their indications chiefly from the state of the pulse, in the knowledge of which they boast the highest skill . . . There is certainly a very close connection established by nature between the state of the pulse and the general affection of the system, with regard to frequency, force, fullness, hardness, softness etc., by which we are enabled to form our judgements respecting the nature and cure of many diseases. But the Chinese carry their pretensions far beyond this. They pretend that the pulse, like a general interpreter of animal life, explains every state and condition of the body and that by means of it alone they can immediately discover the seat, nature and cause of disease without any question of the patient, or those around him, and without being informed of any circumstance respecting him.

Surgery does not exist in China as distinct either in profession or in practice from that of physic. Surgical operations (if such they can be called) are very simple and few in number. In China where anatomy is altogether unpractised and unknown, it is particularly remarkable how ignorant they seem to be of every kind of surgical operation. I neither saw nor heard of any they perform except the following:

1st. Puncturing with gold and silver needles any inflamed or swelled part, to give issue to the malignant vapour or spirit, which according to their theory is the cause of such pain, swelling and inflammation.*

---

* Gillan was mistaken. Acupuncture relies on the implantation of needles into the subcutaneous connective tissue at a great number of points. See Lu Gwei-Djen and Joseph Needham, *Celestial Lancets*.

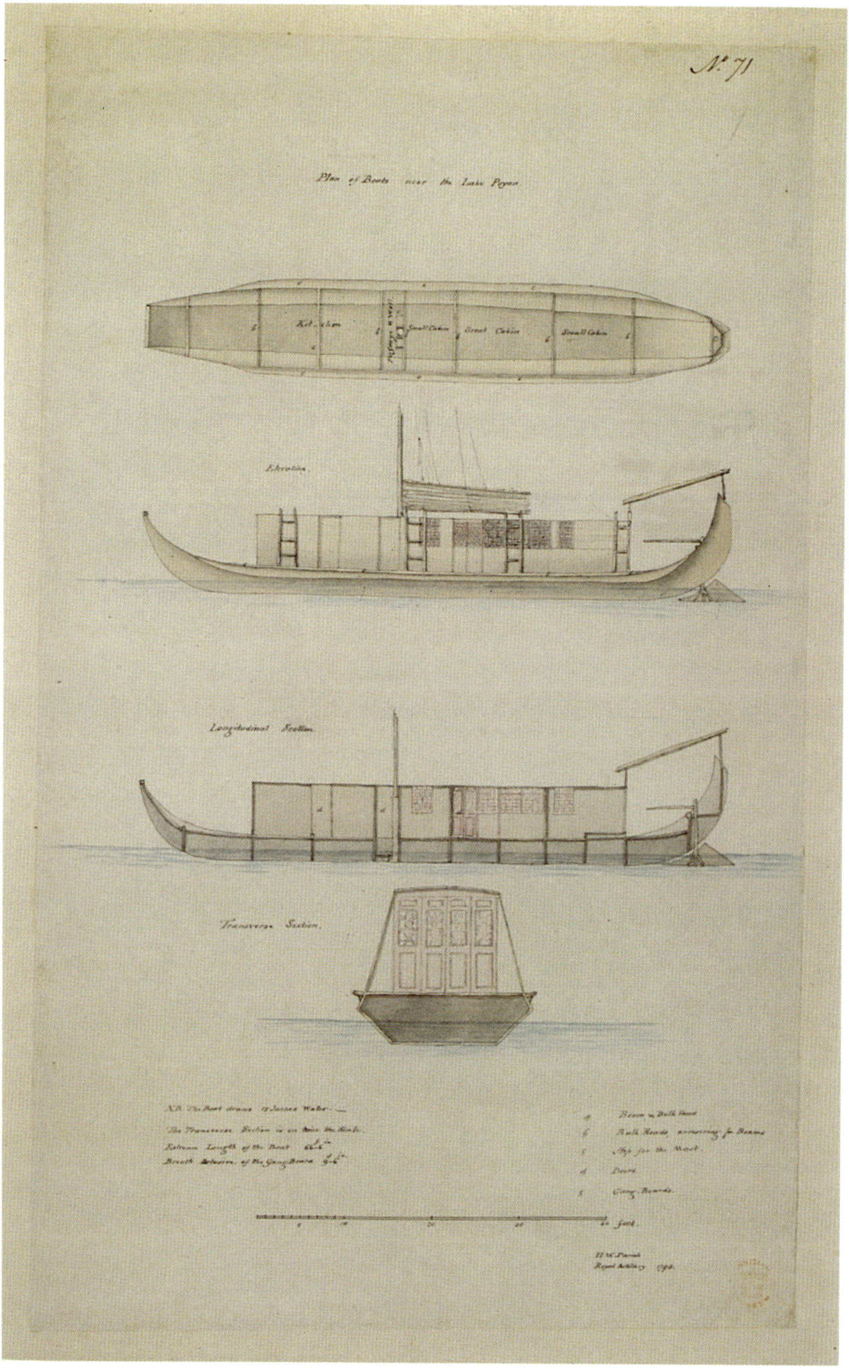

21 (above) *A shallow-draft barge used in the mid-stage of the voyage, around Lake Poyang. This scale drawing was executed by Lieutenant Parish.*

174
Trackers in Rainy Weather

24 *The Embassy had little contact with Chinese women. They were intrigued by the custom of foot-binding, practised on young girls by the Han Chinese (but not by the Manchu). The toes and the heel were squeezed together, deforming the arch and making walking difficult, but in Chinese eyes enhancing feminine attraction. A Chinese lady* (above) *with her son attended by a servant. From* The Costume of China.

22 (top left) *Trackers eating. Alexander was fascinated by the Chinese people. On the Embassy's return journey he devoted many pages of his sketch-book to the trackers, the gangs of labourers, male and female, pressed into service to tow the barges from the bank. From Alexander's* The Costume of China.

23 (bottom left) *Trackers in rainy weather. Sketch by Alexander.*

25 (above) *The Embassy passed many cemeteries, some of them stretching for miles along the banks of the Canal. Alexander captioned this illustration to* The Costume of China*: 'The coffins ... are made of very thick boards plentifully pitched within and varnished without; which makes them durable and prevents them from emitting putrid exhumations, this process being absolutely necessary, where the coffins of the lower class often lie scattered among the tombs, totally covered with earth.'*

26 *As the barges made their way along the Canal, Sir George Staunton observed the Chinese people at work.* Top right: *Men raising water – a common scene, even today.*

27 (bottom right) *A man grinding corn in a crude pestle.*

W. Alexander delin.t J. Pass sculp

28 (above) *Working a chain pump – still used for irrigation in the paddy fields along the Grand Canal, and in fields all over Asia. This and the previous two illustrations (from originals by Alexander) are in Staunton's* An Authentic Account of an Embassy from the King of Great Britain to the Emperor of China.

29 (above) *A family fishing in the Canal. Fish was as much a staple food in China as were arable crops. Illustration by Alexander, in Staunton's* Account of an Embassy.

31 (overleaf) *The Tower of the Thundering Winds on the shores of the Western Lake, near Hangzhou. Staunton writes: 'The lake was full of fish ... Vast crowds of pleasure boats were sailing on it ... One of the pagodas attracted particular attention, four storeys were left standing but the top was in ruins ... It is confidently asserted to have been erected at the time of Confucius.' Illustration (from a sketch by Alexander) from* Account of an Embassy.

30 (below) *The garrison lines the bank on 2nd November 1793. Macartney's journal reads: 'This morning we fell down the Canal into the Whang-ho or Great Yellow River, which ... was about three miles wide and very muddy.' A sketch by Alexander.*

32 (above) *An Embassy barge approaching a bridge near Souzhou. Alexander commented: 'This arch ... occurred very frequently on the route ... from Hang-tchoo [Hangzhou] to Chusan [Zhoushan] ... the temporary ornament over the centre ... was erected in compliment to the Ambassador. The six soldiers from an adjacent military post were ordered to stand on the bridge, by way of salute.' From* The Costume of China.

34 (above) *An infantry soldier, or 'tiger of war'. At every village and town through which the travellers passed, the military saluted – as much to warn as to honour them. Sketch by Alexander in* The Costume of China.

33 (bottom left) *The Embassy were so impressed with the ingenuity of this waterwheel (thirty feet in diameter) that John Barrow was deputed to draw it. Staunton says: 'The only material employed in [its] construction ... except the nave ... and the posts on which it rests, are afforded by the bamboo ... Neither nail, nor pins, nor screws, nor any kind of metal enters into its construction.'*

35 (above) *The Embassy regarded the collection and cataloguing of plants as a primary task, calling for the services of two botanists, John Haxton and David Stronach. The original for this engraving of* Camellia sesanqua *– from a plant picked somewhere between Jehol and Peking – was drawn on the homeward journey. From Staunton's* Account of an Embassy.

36 (opposite, below) *A palanquin carried by four men, sketched by Alexander on the journey to Peking*. Below*: Alexander's sketch of a cart 'in which we entered Peking'.*

37 (above) *Some plants discovered on the mission were named after Staunton:* Escholtzia stauntoni.

38 (above) *A pair of tea caddies made from silver presented by Emperor Qianlong to Captain Mackintosh. The keyholes demonstrate how highly tea was valued in the eighteenth century. The ivory box was specially made in India to contain the caddies.*

39 (above) *Wall-paper brought back from China by Lord Macartney, given to his banker Thomas Coutts, and subsequently installed in the boardroom of the bank's headquarters in the Strand in London, where it can be seen to this day.*

40 (below) *HMS* Lion *sailing down the Canton (Pearl) River towards Macao, on the way home. Alexander's drawing.*

41 (above) *Lord Macartney. 'Drawn by Mr Alexander on the Quarter Deck of the "Lion". His Lordship was in the habit of putting his gloves in the corner of his cocked hat ... and the likeness was considered by Sir John Barrow as very characteristic.'*

2nd. Cutting of Corns and nails. In this they excel and are very expert. I had often heard of them being dexterous chiropodists, and had an opportunity of seeing them perform this operation, so as to be satisfied that they merited the reputation bestowed on them.

3rd. Cleansing the ears. In this too they are very expert.

4th. Applying adhesive plasters to sores, and various parts of the body in case of deep seated pain, and to occasion a revulsion when they apply the plaster at a distance from the part affected. Plasters of this kind too are frequently applied to various parts from motives of religion and superstition. The composition of these is in the hands of the bonzes, who alone pretend to understand and direct the use and situation of them. Many of them pretend to be aphrodisiac and these fetch the greatest price and are most in demand.

5th. Castration. This operation they not only perform upon young children in order to make them Eunuchs for the Emperor, but also upon adults and those past middle age of life. It seems there is some ancient law or custom by which every man who makes himself a eunuch must be provided for by the Emperor. In performing this operation they amputate penis, testes and scrotum, or rasibus as the missionaries call it. The missionaries pretend that the Chinese have a particular art in performing it, and that they manage it with such dexterity that the eunuch is able to walk about after a few days. All their skill, however, has not extinguished the jealousy of the Emperor respecting the possibility of a regeneration of some of the parts. As they alone have care of the Emperor's wives and concubines he causes them to be visited once or twice a year, that no offensive part may have time to become to him an object of jealousy.

The use of General remedies or such as act upon the whole system is unknown to them both in physic and surgery. They never bleed in any case. Amputation they never perform. When accidents requiring it occur it seems they leave the patient to nature and chance. We did not see one person in China who wanted either an arm, leg or any part of a limb.

The prevalent diseases in China in the hot season are inflammatory fevers, coups de soleil, phrenitis, hepatitis and cholera morbus. In the cold season catarrhs, and peripneumonies and among the poor people fluxes, dropsies and typhus fever are the reigning diseases. I heard of no diseases peculiar to China.

The venereal disease in all its forms is common in China. I could not learn anything positive respecting its antiquity from any authentic documents, and had it not been that our Mandarins assured us the general belief in China was that the disease was always known among them even in the remotest periods of their empire, I should have been inclined to have believed it of a more recent date. About Canton where it is most frequent, and where they understand best its nature and cure in consequence of their communication with the Europeans . . . they frequently speak of it under the appellation of the Canton ulcer, a term which would imply its having been first spread through the country from that town, where it had first appeared, and where probably it had been originally introduced by the Europeans trading to that port.

I had an opportunity . . . of seeing the disease in its various stages, in the persons of the four Chief Mandarins who accompanied us to Canton. Van-ta-gin [Wang] and Cho-ta-gin [Qiao] had caught the infection from some ladies of Hang-tchoo [Hangzhou] and about a fortnight after, it appeared in both in the form of chancre and gonorrhea. Van-ta-gin, the Military Mandarin, applied to me and was soon cured of his complaints. His friend Cho-ta-gin, as a civil Mandarin, was more ashamed to acknowledge his situation. He got over his modesty and was perfectly cured in a short time.

The Military Commander at Nan-tchoo [Nanzhou], who came with us from that city to Canton, had been ill of the complaint for many years. He had scabs and eruptions in many parts of his body and as his father had died of a similar disease was extremely apprehensive of his own fate. All the symptoms yielded to frictions with mercurial ointment and he too got a supply for future use.

The new Viceroy Ch'ang-ling was affected in much the same way and treated in a similar manner, with the same success.

From the concurring testimony of these four gentlemen it is certain that the venereal disease is now at least very frequent in China, but that the treatment and cure of it are very ill understood.

19

The Adventures of the Zhoushan Party

14TH NOVEMBER TO 7TH DECEMBER The sense of freedom enjoyed by all of the Zhoushan party was manifest in their diaries. It was not only the absence of the protocol imposed by the Ambassador's presence, but the Chinese were not so suspicious of this twenty-one-person fragment of the Embassy. They relished the freedom to wander, observe and explore.

The voyage proper did not begin until 15th November. For the first twenty-four hours they sailed down river in their small boats, past the walls of two cities, under bridges decked with flags, and with the ever-present guard of soldiers firing three-gun salutes at intervals. On the 16th they left their vessels at 7am and transshipped in sedan chairs to the junks that were to convey them down the Trong-ku-kiang to Ningbo and Zhoushan. On the banks, new boats awaited them – again, of the type covered with arched mats to keep off the rain. Each boat was towed by two or three trackers, assisted by three watermen who sculled the boat with a crooked oar at the stern. The boats carried no masts, so that they could pass easily under the low bridges. Boarding the party was easy; the baggage took longer, but finally they set sail.

The countryside was beautiful, Dinwiddie recorded:

> A broad river full of islands, wound its way through a richly cultivated valley, beyond which, at different distances rose several ranges of bold majestic mountains . . . The varying shadows of the clouds passing along the sides of the fluted mountains; beneath the red tallow trees loaded with ripe fruit, mingled with the deepest evergreen, the fields waving with luxuriant crops of rice and culinary vegetables, villas, and houses scattered around; close to the shore a long line of military decorated with colours and trophies; still nearer, the shipping in the river, with their flags and pennants variegated in the most brilliant colours; all taken together form the noblest scene I ever beheld.

In the middle of the day the convoy came to a new form of lock. Alexander drew it and described it:

We came to a glacis or inclined plane, the water on the upper canal on which we travelled was about five feet above the level of the lower one, which took a direction at right angles, like the roman letter T. The boat is tilted over this slope by capstans, and having a flat bottom, is by this means soon brought to equilibrium and immediately after descends the inclined plane into the lower canal, similar to the launch of a vessel. This is done with much ease even though some of the boats are of several tons burden.

An hour later they came to a glacis with a six-foot drop, and then to one where the fall was seven feet.

Yet we glided down amidst the acclamations of numerous spectators. The declivity being so sudden that we were obliged to stand by cups and other movables, the boatmen taking the precaution of holding a screen of matting to prevent the shipping of water when first reaching the canal. The glacis managed equally well with boats going in the contrary direction.

By six o'clock they had approached two walled cities, the canal running between them. (Having no interpreter – Mr Plumb had, of course, accompanied the Ambassador's party – they could not name them.) On the parapets along the wharf stood the guard of honour. Alexander painted their shields, each embossed with a gorgon's head. Outside the walls and below, triumphal arches fronted the residences of the mandarins. As they sailed under a three-arched bridge, salutes were fired, and thus they entered a tidal yacht basin where twenty sea-going junks, lying among a fleet of trading vessels, awaited their arrival. Each of about six tons' burden, constructed for salt-water and neatly fitted out for passengers, they were navigated by six men and carried a complement of soldiers. For the third time in as many days the travellers once again transshipped. They were now 140 li (27 miles) from Ningbo.

Next day they got under way in their new vessels. The wind being unfavourable, from time to time they had to be towed along the serpentine river – 'the breadth of the Thames between London and Woolwich,' wrote Captain Mackintosh, enjoying this for him unaccustomed inland sailing. 'Nothing could be more pleasing or romantic than meandering through the most fertile valleys, bounded by hills of various form and heights and some stupendous mountains.' Dinwiddie saw the mountains as the source of building material – stone for the triumphal arches, for the bridges and for monuments to local mandarins 'who have served the duties of their offices without blame and with advantage to those under this control'. Alexander observed that these monuments consecrated to the virtuous were built at public expense – and, no doubt, served to set an example to others.

By mid-morning they had reached an alluvial plain at the foot of a mountain, where a large body of soldiers was lined up on parade, in salute to the Grand Councillor Songyun. 'The range of temporary buildings were the richest we had yet seen, the glittering ensigns of silk and satin on which were embroidered dragons of gold. The row of beautiful lanterns suspended from the water's edge and the music, altogether made a show which had a most splendid effect,' commented Alexander.

They were visited at this halt by local mandarins, who wanted – illegally – to trade for watches. Such an offence, if discovered, would have laid both parties open to punishment. Bearing in mind the punishment meted out at Jehol for this very misdemeanour, the British party politely declined the invitation. At the same time extra provisions were brought on board: fruit, wine, confectionery – far more than they could eat. The surplus they gave to the soldiers on their junks and were duly thanked by the corporal in charge, who bowed low in gratitude. 'This man was possessed of most amiable qualities and appeared to be much above his present employment,' remarked Alexander. His diary then assumes a more lyrical tone:

At about 10.00pm the moon being at full, our voyage was most fascinating, the river winding between mountains which enclosed us on each side, the solemn stillness around being disturbed only by the gentle sailing of the vessels. Sometimes an opening between the mountains discovered a distant town, marked by its great feature: a tall pagoda. 'Twas a time for entertaining the idea of 21 Englishmen separated from their companions without an interpreter in the hands of people, certainly highly civilised, but whose notions of justice under some circumstances or accidents would have put us in jeopardy.

At five the next morning the squadron arrived at Ningbo, nosing its way through the sea-going junks with their painted eyes on each side of the bow, the pupil painted black and thrust forward. Once again, on arrival, there was the now familiar sight of lines of soldiers drawn up to greet them. At 8am they went ashore, where Captain Mackintosh, Dr Dinwiddie and Alexander were received by Songyun and taken into a building inside which 'there was a table covered with yellow silk over which hung a picture with four or five figures'. To Alexander, 'the subject appeared to be a madonna presenting an infant to another child and one or two other figures behind, reminding me of our St Joseph with our Saviour and St John'. Today we would probably identify this as the Bodhisattva Guanyin, Goddess of Mercy.

The mandarins waiting to receive them explained that the presents were from the Emperor, and indicated that the customary prostrations should be made. So with hats off, and kneeling on one knee, the British travellers inclined their foreheads to the ground before the picture which seemed to represent the Imperial presence. Of the present, Alexander recorded:

My portion was four pieces of small figures, white silk, four parcels of raw silk, eight pieces of black nankeen, ten small baskets of tea flowers, one package of tea, sixty pounds in weight, and ten small papers of tobacco. The servants had about a fourth of this quantum each. After this ceremony we re-embarked congratulating ourselves at having made out so well without an interpreter.

Two hours later came the time for the brief leave-taking. Songyun introduced them to the two mandarins who would now accompany them to Zhoushan, and gave them a personal present of packages of candy. Captain Mackintosh invited Songyun to accompany him to the *Hindostan*, which would be waiting for him at Zhoushan, and where the Grand Councillor could be royally entertained, but (according to Staunton writing later),

> the most respectable mandarin already somewhat indisposed and fearful of the odour of an English vessel, and anxious likewise to return, quitted the party after giving each of the gentlemen some handsome presents on behalf of the Emperor and shaking Colonel Benson and Captain Mackintosh by the hand in the English manner, as a mark of his cordiality and good wishes for them.

Throughout the next week, bad weather halted progress. They had an uncomfortable time: the rain seeped through the protective overhead matting on to their berths by night, and by day they were surrounded by visitors, some of whom had come on board merely for a closer inspection of the barbarians. Alexander noted:

> Some of the better sort wore glasses at least three inches in diameter. Young boys under five and six years old wore two pigtails or queues with red twists at the end of them, growing from above the ear, with, for good luck, the current coin of the realm, having a square hole in it, stuck into the orifice of the ear. On November 26th at 3.00am the squadron – twelve in all, including baggage-junks – set out for Chusan [Zhoushan] accompanied by the usual salutes from the military. By 11.00am the blue ensign and the pennant of the Hindostan hove in sight.

The noise and smoke of a fifteen-gun salute billowed across the water in welcome.

They were to stay in Zhoushan for four days. Real freedom, at last! Alexander and Dinwiddie were allowed to wander at will on shore. They were fascinated by what they saw. They watched some men playing dominoes, with double dice, a game which they thought was invented in France. They marvelled at the city's fortifications, with a plethora of six-pounder cannon mounted on the walls. They inspected machinery – here Dinwiddie observed that the Chinese were, in some instances, centuries behind the nations of Europe. They looked at a valved smith's bellows which provided a continuous stream of air; a rice mill powered by a bullock (noting – erroneously – to their satisfaction, that they had not seen wind or water mills in China); a shelling machine, a machine for breaking cotton seeds, and a chain pump. Their attention then switched to agricultural machinery – to ploughs, sickles, drags, hedge-hooks – and then to metal mirrors and brass and copper wire.

On 30th November the *Hindostan* set sail, leaving as it went a long train of yellow mud. Alexander recorded:

> At half past eleven a.m. having saluted the Mandarins, weighed and made sail with a light breeze. At ten minutes before twelve, sailing pleasantly at the rate of three knots, the ship struck a rock just off Deer Island, giving a dreadful heel to windward so that we were in danger of shipping water through the gunports at which the guns were out but silent. The consternation was terrible, she hung there for a minute, and then providentially righted herself, in the process losing part of the top of the false keel. At dusk we were clear of the islands and putting out to sea.

They had a stormy passage, with such high seas and strong winds that the foresail was 'shivered to pieces and they continued under bare poles. The ship labouring so in the hard gale that everyone thought of the injury she might have sustained from the rock at Chusan and apprehended the worst.'

On 7th December the *Hindostan* joined the *Lion* at the mouth of the Pearl River near Canton. Captain Mackintosh and his party learned the latest news – of the death of Mr Walker, midshipman; of the *Lion*'s capture and the sale for £2,000 of a French brig; of the execution eleven months previously of the King of France, and of the riots in London caused by the trial of Tom Paine.

They finally arrived at the British factory in Canton five days ahead of the main party.

20

WITH THE AMBASSADOR'S PARTY: HANGZHOU TO THE FIRST PORTAGE

15 NOVEMBER TO 6 DECEMBER The journey from Hangzhou to Canton was to take the main party thirty-four days: first down the Qiantang River, then twenty-four miles of land portage. The next stage would take them down the Gan River; then a further thirty-three miles of land portage to the Bei River (the Pe-kiang-ho), and then the final river stage to Canton. For the travel-weary party already five weeks into their journey, this was to be a relentless voyage, leavened only by the beauty of the countryside through which they passed. They relieved the monotony by mapping the route and minutely describing what they saw. Macartney, still hoping to retrieve *something* from his mission, divided his time between diplomatic contact with Viceroy Changling and writing up his journal.

They were travelling in yet another type of barge, 'sharp built both fore and aft, flat bottomed, about twelve feet broad and seventy feet in length, sailing with cotton sails and drawing very little water'. Ever mindful of status, Sir George Staunton noted: 'One barge, inferior in decoration, was at first prepared for His Excellency; but the Viceroy chose that there should be no discrimination between them, saying that "such a distinction would be more discreditable to him than the Ambassador".'

Before his departure for Ningbo Songyun had agreed, much to their pleasure, that their two friends Wang and Qiao could accompany them to Canton. The Embassy had come to trust and rely on them. And they were to join in innumerable conversations with the Viceroy that were to provide much of Macartney's information about Chinese life and customs.

Their journey began with the routine military parade. Day and night, following their orders from the Court of Peking, at every bridge, village and town the military saluted the illustrious passengers – both as an honour and as a warning of what might happen were they to stray from the straight and narrow – with triumphal arches, flags, lanterns, fireworks and cannonades. Sir George Staunton sought a professional appraisal of military capability from Lieutenant Parish:

The Cavalry carry bows which seem to be the weapon held in highest estimation. They are made of elastic wood, strengthened by horn, connected in the centre, from whence they spring in distinct arches towards the extremities. The string is of silk thread. The strength of the bows varies from sixty to one hundred pounds. The arrows, well turned and feathered, are armed at points with a shank and spear of steel. Both Chinese and Tartars value themselves on their skill in the use of this weapon. They hold it somewhat obliquely in the left hand. The string is placed behind an agate ring upon the right thumb, the first joint of which is bent forward and kept in that position by pressing the middle joint of the forefinger upon it . . . The string is drawn until the left arm is extended and the right hand passes the right ear. The forefinger is then withdrawn from the thumb, which instantly discharges the arrow with considerable force.

Armour consists of an iron helmet in the form of an inverted funnel. The crest, surrounded by a red tassel, stands six or seven inches above the head and terminates in a spear.

The neck is protected by a piece of cloth stuffed, quilted and studded with iron, which hangs forward around the face. On the body is an upper and under dress, also quilted and studded with iron. This has the inconvenience without the advantage of armour.

Officers have their helmets polished and ornamented with gold, with a higher crest than those of the men. Their bodies are covered with purple or blue silk with studs of gold or gilt. Their boots are of black satin.

Another unit of their troops are armed with swords only, whose dress is called Tiger dress. It is of yellow cloth with dark brown stripes, fitted to the shape; the cap, which nearly covers the face, is formed to represent the head of a tiger. They carry a shield of bamboo or rattan hideously painted to represent tigers' or dragons' heads with open mouths and enormous teeth. Much stress is laid on the terrific appearance.

On the evening of 16th November, Macartney called on Viceroy Changling – an occasion, as it transpired, for the exchange of platitudes. Macartney expressed pleasure at the scenery, 'beautiful and romantic, somewhat resembling the scene on the river Conway between Lanrost and the sea'. The Viceroy, slightly non-plussed, made general conversation without touching on the affairs of the Embassy, but 'artfully contrived to intermingle [his comments] with many expressions of compliments to me and professions from himself'.

Sunday 17th November Changling returned Macartney's visit of the previous day. This time the conversation, much to Macartney's delight, turned to the particular. The Viceroy began to talk of the trade carried on between Great Britain and China, seeking information and at the same time asking how he could be of assistance to Macartney when they arrived in Canton. Not content with being told, he asked Macartney to set it down in writing 'so that he might become master of the subject'. Of Changling's response to the question of ameliorating the conditions in Canton for foreign traders, Macartney noted later:

Although he was sensible that some change of conduct would be right both for the sake of justice and the reputation of his country, he confessed that, though his affinity to the Emperor and his rank in the State afforded him strong ground to stand, yet he had measures to keep and delicacies to observe, for he was well aware of the counter-action he must expect at Canton from those who may be interested in the continuance of those grievances the British claimed to suffer. He had heard of the prejudices entertained against the British by some of the great people at Court, particularly his predecessor, Fukhang'an, who would not be much pleased to see him adopt a system the reverse of his own.

There was another thing he candidly mentioned. He knew the refusal by Heshen to the requests of the Embassy and the consequent disappointment. It was therefore to be feared that the English might infer an unfavourable disposition in the Court towards them which really it had not, and to conduct themselves in such a manner as to defeat any indulgence meant to be granted to them and in consequence render him culpable for any representations he might make in their favour.

Changling now paused, seeking Macartney's reaction. It was immediate and eagerly forthcoming. Addressing the Viceroy with equal candour, Macartney told him that from the way in which his requests had been received he had concluded that the Court at Peking was indifferent, if not unfriendly, to Britain; and that he would have represented this in his dispatches home if Songyun had not taken such pains to impress him, as he had declared he had the highest authority to do, with the Emperor's favourable sentiments towards the Embassy and its concerns – and, indeed, if the Viceroy himself had not confirmed this at the first meeting Macartney had had with him in the presence of Songyun. The solemn assurances given by the Viceroy and Songyun, he continued, had not only prevented him from writing home about what he feared to be the Peking Court's true position on the matter, but had induced him to inform his own Court that, notwithstanding what had passed at Peking, so many kind promises and messages had been received from there that it could not be doubted but that very serious attention was being paid to his representations. Thus the matter now stood, and it rested with the Viceroy to determine whether Macartney had deceived his own Court or not. It was from what the Viceroy would do, not what Macartney would write, that they would form a judgement.

The meeting broke up. Both parties were well satisfied, the Viceroy feeling that he had mollified Macartney, who in turn felt that he had neatly turned the diplomatic tables. Sure enough, the customary presents promptly arrived – fans and perfumes for the Ambassador and all the gentlemen of the Embassy. Unlike Songyun, the Viceroy had not been able to avoid the smell of the English ship – perhaps lack of sanitation and bathing facilities prompted these gifts!

Meanwhile Macartney, content, for once, with what appeared to have been a meaningful diplomatic exchange, once again turned his attention to the passing scene. This time his eye was on the future. There were many ways of recovering something tangible from China!

> We have now quitted the mountains and are got into a charming fruitful country. Here trees grow in great abundance on the dry rising grounds. The mulberry flourishes most on loamy flats. I have given directions to have some young tea plants taken up, if possible, also the varnish tree* and tallow tree, with an intention of sending them to Bengal, in hope of their being nursed and brought to maturity, so that one day they may be reckoned among the commercial resources of our own territories. I shall add eggs of silk worm which, I at last, and with great difficulty, have been so fortunate to procure. The Chinese, whether from jealousy or superstition or both, could scarcely be persuaded to part with them.

For the varnish trees, the tallow trees and the silkworm eggs, the outcome was uncertain. The tea plants, however, were dug up and carefully transplanted, according to the instructions the Embassy had received at the start of their journey from Sir Joseph Banks, President of the Royal Society. They were to form the nucleus of the Indian tea industry, which in 1834 was to be actively encouraged by the removal of the East India Company monopoly, which had given that organization 'the whole, sole and exclusive right of trading and trafficking in tea into and from all islands and ports, havens, coasts, cities, towns and places between the Cape of Good Hope and the Straits of Magellan'.

On Tuesday 19th November they began to run into trouble, as Huttner was later to note, rather teutonically, in his book *Voyage à la Chine*:

> The navigation on this river presented a number of difficulties and dangers, not only because in this season the water was extremely low, but also because the bed of the river is studded with rock. Each of the boats almost always was pulled and pushed by twenty men without whose help it would have been impossible to move. The piercing noise which the oars made in touching the rocks, the unexpected shake which threatened the barge, the immoderate and deafening cries of the boatmen and those who pulled them would have made this part of the journey the most tiring of all, if the charms of the countryside through which we travelled had allowed us to think about it.

And here Huttner turned his attention to the fascination of the Chinese landscape:

> The inhabitants of Northern Europe who see the excellent fruits of the South growing without culture and in abundance find these parts of the world picturesque beyond all comparison. At every moment the scene changes . . . the different winding bends of the Tchien-tang-tchiang-ho [Qiantang River] are a constant source of entertainment. On the banks, one saw fields of rice alternating

---

* A tropical tree whose resinous juice is used for lacquering.

with plantations of sugar, orange trees, grapefruit, chestnut trees, tea bushes, camphor and bamboo. Everywhere people were harvesting rice and sugar cane which were taken to water mills built on piles along the river bank.

Such charms were lost on Aeneas Anderson who, having been spoilt by the sumptuous meals they had enjoyed elsewhere in China, complained vociferously that at this point in the voyage the food was of such poor quality that it had to be given away to the trackers!

The diplomacy was soon to resume. Changling still seemed apprehensive – though Macartney could not tell from which quarter the pressure came – that the Embassy might be very dissatisfied at not succeeding in gaining the points solicited. In spite of Macartney's previous assurances, the Viceroy harboured some anxiety that the Ambassador's dispatches home might be the occasion for future trouble or mischief. Macartney repeated his assurance in the same terms as before. Changling, doubting its sincerity, decided to put it to the test. He inquired whether Macartney would authorize him to inform the Emperor that the King, his master, would always continue in friendship with him, and in testimony would write to him and send an Ambassador again if the Emperor was willing to receive him. Macartney recorded his reply:

> Although what I solicited was refused, in every other respect I have no reason to complain, for the Embassy has been very honourably received and entertained, and the Emperor has sent presents to the King as a mark of his friendship in return for those sent by the King to the Emperor. There is no doubt that the King will most probably write to the Emperor to acknowledge receipt of the presents and the marks of distinction conferred on the Embassy. Matters of business, however, stand on different ground. The King's original idea was to have an Ambassador usually resident in China. If I had found my stay in Peking agreeable I should have remained a considerable time, but frequent or temporary Embassies from so great a distance would cause much trouble and expense to both Courts. Possibly another Minister might be sent to China if there was good ground to expect such a measure would be requited by adequate advantages, but my state of health and many other circumstances make it impossible for me to think of undertaking a second Embassy.

'How soon could another Minister come out?' the Viceroy then asked. But he did not propose a repetition of so great and splendid an embassy as the present one. Surprised at this apparent change of tack, Macartney had to tell him it was not in his power to say how soon it could be, the distance from England being so vast and the sea voyage so precarious.

At this the Viceroy made his departure – but only to return again in a few minutes. This time he asked whether Macartney would send a few words of compliment to the Emperor in a letter that was about to be sent off. With pleasure Macartney agreed. He liked this man. 'Every time we see this gentleman he gains upon our good opinion; and I do not despair of the [East India] Company's receiving many advantages by his means . . . It is true,' he summed up, 'he has art and address, and an air of candour to disguise them with, but he has prudence, sagacity and a sense of Character.' That evening saw the end of their voyage from Hangzhou. They had arrived at the first portage.

At 10am on Thursday 21st November they set out on their twenty-four-mile land journey, dining at the half-way house that marked the boundaries of the provinces of Zhejiang and Jiangxi. They were allowed to choose their means of transport, and since the weather was fine they opted to ride. They covered the distance, over terraced hills, in nine hours: 'Wherever the sides of the hill admit of it, they are wrought into terraces. The soil is naturally indifferent, which renders the farmer wonderfully active in his endeavours to fertilize it; the care with which everything convertible into manure is preserved would appear ridiculous elsewhere,' wrote Macartney.

John Barrow noted of another wayside halt:

> Half of the buildings consisted . . . of places of convenience to which passengers might retire to obey the calls of nature; and the doors or rather openings of such erections were always invitingly fronting the street . . . a row of buildings of this kind in so warm a climate is a dreadful nuisance; but the consideration of preserving the kind of manure, which by the Chinese is considered superior for forcing vegetation to all others, has got the better of both decency and prudence.

On this land journey, too, Macartney noted that not only were they allowed to dig up botanical specimens, but that on their behalf the Viceroy sent a mandarin forty miles to obtain kaolin and other material used in the manufacture of porcelain.

On the Friday, they were detained all day by violent rain at the head of the river. Next day they left the town of Yushanzhen and set off on their journey down stream. The promised note of compliment from Ambassador to Emperor was delivered to the Viceroy, who, noting the neatness of the Chinese characters, asked who the calligrapher was. 'When I informed him that it was little George Staunton,' Macartney recorded, 'he would scarcely believe that a boy of twelve years old could have already made such a progress. Nor was he perfectly satisfied until he had actually seen him add, at the bottom of the paper in Chinese characters, that it had been written by him.'

The Sunday continued damp and dismal. Depressed by the weather, Macartney departed from his dispassionate assessments:

> We continued our voyage, but so dense a vapour had arisen in consequence of the late rains and overspread the atmosphere that, though the river widened and deepened considerably, our navigation often seemed attended with danger. Our vessels frequently struck upon shelves and sometimes ran foul of each other with a sudden crash, thus contributing not a little to the dismal character of the night, which was still, moist, cold and comfortless. The mist grew every moment darker and heavier, and so magnified the objects around us that no wonder our senses and imaginations were equally deceived and disturbed, and that the temples, turrets and pagodas appeared to us through the fog like so many phantoms of giants and

monsters flitting away from us and vanishing in the gloom. The river became narrower and deeper, being pent up between the mountains which shut it in so closely, and approach so near to each other that till the moment we came to the opening we could scarcely imagine the possibility of a passage. The weather continued cold with no sun until the Tuesday.

At eight o'clock on the Wednesday evening the Viceroy, accompanied by Wang and Qiao, paid a visit to Macartney. They left at midnight. 'The Viceroy uncommonly civil and sociable talked freely on a great number of things, asking several questions relative to Canton, to the value and amount of our trade and that of other nations . . . He suspected great peculation among the public officers at Canton and that the Emperor is much defrauded in his revenue.' With a proper and cautious reserve Macartney answered that he had never been at Canton and therefore could not speak with precision, but he offered to procure any information the Viceroy might want.

At this juncture Changling paused in the conversation to light his pipe. Macartney took a small phosphoric bottle out of his fob pocket,

and instantly kindled a match at it. The singularity of a man's carrying fire in his fob without damage startled [the Viceroy] a good deal. I therefore made him a present of it. This incident led to a conversation, from which it appeared how far the Chinese (although they excel in some branches of mechanics) are yet behind other nations in medical or surgical skill and philosophical knowledge.

Having observed numbers of blind persons, but no wooden legs or deformed limbs here, I concluded that good oculists were very rare and death the usual consequence of a fracture. A conjecture in which the Viceroy conceded.

When I told him of many things in England . . . which I had brought people to instruct the Chinese in, if it had been allowed, such as the reanimating of drowned persons by a mechanical operation, restoring the sight of the blind by extraction or depression of the glaucoma, and repairing or amputating limbs by manual dexterity, both he and his companions seemed as if awakened out of a dream, and could not conceal their regret for the Court's coldness and indifference to our discoveries.

From the manner of those Gentlemen's enquiries . . . and the impressions they seemed to feel, I have conceived a much higher opinion of their liberality and understanding. Whether in these two respects Heshen, the Minister, be really inferior to them or whether he acts upon a certain public system, which often supersedes private conviction, I know not. But certain it is at Zhe-hol [Jehol], when I mentioned to him some recent inventions of European ingenuity, particularly that of the air balloon and that I had taken care to provide one at Peking with a person to go up in it, he not only discouraged that experiment, but most of the others, which from a perusal of all the printed accounts of the country, we had calculated and prepared for the meridian of China. Whatever taste the Emperor K'ang-hsi [Kangxi] might have shown for the sciences, as related by the Jesuits in his day, his successors have not inherited it with his other great qualities and possessions. For it would now seem that the policy and vanity of the Court equally concurred in endeavouring to keep out of sight whatever can manifest our pre-eminence which they undoubtedly feel, but have yet to make the proper use of it. It is, however, vain to attempt arresting the progress of human knowledge. The human mind is of a soaring nature and once having gained the lower steps of the ascent, struggles incessantly against every difficulty to reach the highest. Whatever ought to be will be. The resistance of Adamant is insufficient to defeat the insinuation of a fibre. Time is the great wonder worker of the world, the exterminator of prejudice and the touchstone of truth . . .

I am indeed very much mistaken if all authority and all the address of the Tartar government will be able much longer to stifle the energies of their Chinese subjects. Scarcely a year now passes without an insurrection in some of the provinces. It is true they are usually soon suppressed but their frequency is a symptom of the fever within. The Paroxysm is repelled, but the disease is not cured.

Friday 6th December broke fine and sunny. On the flats each side of the river the mission glimpsed vast plantations of sugar-cane, ripe and fit for cutting. The river itself was sunken, lying twenty feet below field level and giving the Embassy a fine chance to study Chinese mechanical ingenuity (to which the Ambassador was patronizingly to refer).

Water is easily raised by a wheel which the current gives motion to. The nave is made of strong timber but other parts, the fellies, the spokes, the scoops etc., are chiefly made of light bamboo. As this machine appeared to me equally simple and efficient I desired a model and a drawing to be made from it. The quantity of water to be raised by this machine is some one thousand six hundred and eighty gallons per hour, or one hundred and sixty tons of water in one day.

It is not surprising that, as fellows of the Royal Society, Staunton and Macartney – the former more diligent than the other – were both keen botanists and masters of the comparatively new Linnaean system of classification. So they had made sure that, in addition to the two scientists Gillan and Dinwiddie, they were also accompanied on the Embassy by the two botanic gardeners, Haxton and Stronach, whose general task was to collect and classify plant specimens and to obtain the young tea plants for Bengal, as Macartney mentioned in his journal. Prior to departure, the Embassy sought the advice of Sir Joseph Banks, then President of the Royal Society as well as Director of the recently created Royal Botanical Gardens at Kew. He replied with a rather disjointed twenty-page memorandum, addressed to Staunton.

As Macartney and Staunton inspected the specimens they had collected, they recalled the green-fingered wisdom contained in Banks' document.

Sir Joseph Banks on Botany: Hints on the Subject of Gardening suggested to the Gentlemen who attend the Embassy to China

TRUSTING THAT THE GENTLEMEN for whose use these fugitive suggestions are intended will in their passage out have sufficient time to reduce them to such order of arrangement as they may find most convenient to their purpose,

Sir Jos Banks has spared himself the trouble of transcribing them. He has also, to save time, as they will easily observe, been more attentive to dispatch than to accuracy in compiling them, trusting to the Lord or other minds to prevent them from ever appearing in Public.

Accelerating of flowering

The gardeners in Europe are wholly unacquainted with the method of accelerating the blossoming of plants . . . no reasonable doubt can be entertained that the Chinese possess such an art and the acquisition of it would be very desirable to our gardeners here . . .

Dwarf trees

The Chinese have an art of training trees to make them bear all the appearances of ageing individuals of their species and yet produce flowers, fruit and leaves tho' a tree which naturally grows to sixty feet high is kept within the compass of ten inches.

A friend once provided me with the secret in writing of the process by which this singular effect is produced, but unfortunately the ship that brought it was lost and he who had no other copy died before he had advice of the accident . . .

Relative to the collecting of plants for the purposes of Botany, the best advice I can give is that every species especially in China and Japan is indiscriminately dried and preserved for examination in Europe. The most special are the most likely to have fallen under the observations of former visitors and to have been brought home by them, the most obscure and minute are those that have the least pretensions of elegance or beauty and are the least likely to have been before taken notice of. To distinguish with objective certainty whether a plant is new or not is scarce possible to the most sagacious observer without the assistance of a variety of books – more than could be carried on any one voyage. In testimony to the propriety of collecting every species, I can only say that in Madeira where many common plants are mixed among a few African ones, none that could be procured were left behind. The final decision of whether or not each of them was before described was left till our return, where the Botany was our chief object and we had a considerable library of books on board . . .

. . . To leave behind one scarce and curious plant under the mistaken idea of its being a common one will be a source of vexation for ever afterward if the circumstance happens to be discovered. To bring home a hundred common ones will be of no great matter either of labour or inconvenience . . . I should also advise that many individual specimens of each species be brought home in order that different Botanists may be consulted in case of any difficulty, and presents of species made to various professors of Botany on the return of the

Embassy for the honour and credit of those who would have been concerned in it.

The Embassy assiduously carried out Sir Joseph Banks' advice. William Alexander noted that on the journey from Tongzhou to Peking, when the Embassy was mostly riding in carts, 'the gardener went on horseback for the more easily procuring plants'. Subsequently, one of the botanists stayed behind at the Yuanmingyuan, whilst the others went on to Jehol.

Four lists of plants were produced, consisting of (list 1) 107 names from the province of Beizhili, (list 2) some seventy plants collected on the journey between Peking and Jehol, (list 3) 127 plants from the province of Shandong and the environs of Jiangnan, and (list 4) some ninety-seven plants from the provinces of Jiangxi and Canton. All these specimens were duly mounted and pressed on large sheets of cartridge paper, with, at the bottom, a little envelope for the seeds. To this day they can be seen in the plant library of the Natural History Museum in London.

In addition to these highly organized taxonomic forays, individuals such as Sir George Staunton frequently noted their admiration of the flora, fruits, crops and trees that they came upon in the course of the voyage. On the journey to Hangzhou, Staunton had noted:

Several hundred acres of the ground, which is still swampy and surrounds the lake, are covered with Nymphea Nelumbo. The Chinese have always held this plant in such high value that at length they regarded it as sacred. That character, however, has not limited it to merely ornamental and useless purposes; for it is introduced among the articles of the table. Their ponds are generally covered with it and exhibit a very beautiful appearance when in flower. The seeds are somewhat of the size and form of an acorn and of a taste more delicate than that of almonds . . . the roots are sliced and in the summer served with ice. They are also laid up in salt and vinegar for winter . . . Modern attempts to cultivate it in Europe, though with the assistance of artificial heat, seldom have succeeded. In China it often grows spontaneously and is cultivated in the open air with ease, both by the seed and the root.

In his 'Hints on Gardening', Sir Joseph Banks had referred to this plant:

We possess [*Nymphaea nelumbo*] in England but we find it difficult to make it flower in our hothouses but that it has only once been seen in bloom which was at the Duchess of Portland's in the Autumn of 1791, nor can we keep it alive in the winter but by placing it deep in the Bank of a Pit by which the mud in which it grows is kept always as warm as new milk. The Chinese we are told have an abundance of it in the ponds in Peking.

A considerable botanical gardener himself, Staunton made great use of the 'Hints on Gardening' as well as of the book *Icones Kaempferiana* which Banks had included with his memorandum. Of the twenty-two plants that he had listed in his 'Hints on Gardening' 'likely to be more acceptable to His Majesties

Botanic Gardens than the rest', about half were found and listed by Staunton. The rest on the list were Japanese – but circumstances were to prevent the Embassy reaching Japan. One of the listed Chinese plants, *Camellia sesanqua*, was the only one to be recognized with a full-page illustration in Staunton's official account.*

After a party on 18th August 1792, some five weeks before the mission was to leave for China, Banks had written a farewell letter:

> The ceremony of taking leave I have always considered as a painful and unnecessary struggle. I must consequently beg you to explain to all of them, that every good wish I am capable of forming will attend them during the whole course of their peregrinations . . . please God that I should continue a resident of this world at the Time of their return, one who will honour in the extreme the endeavour they make for the promotion of Science, the increase of commerce between two distant nations and the real prosperity not only of their own country but also of that they intend to visit.

---

* *An Authentic Account of an Embassy from the King of Great Britain to the Emperor of China*, 1797.

21

Down River into Canton

9th to 17th December 1793 Although the second portage still lay ahead, the journey through China was entering its final stage. Fields of sugar-cane gave way to fruit groves, the products of which – oranges, grapes, apples, pears, chestnuts, walnuts, pomegranates, melons and lichees – had at one time or another during the mission all appeared at their table.

As they approached the head of the Bei River, they saw vast tracts of hilly land dotted with tea plants. Here their main object of trade, the prime motive for their journey, grew like a common shrub – bushy like a rose tree, and pruned to inhibit upward growth. Three times a year, over a million Chinese were employed to pick, dry and pack the Empire's harvest.

On 9th December, as the trackers hauled them past the terraced hillsides, the Viceroy showed Macartney a further edict from the Emperor. It had been conceived, he explained, in the friendliest of terms, and constituted a follow-up to their earlier conversation. If the King should send a minister to China again, although he would be well received, he should enter through Canton. Macartney replied noncommittally, though he was quick to observe in his journal that this 'implied a disapprobation of our having come up the Gulf of Pe-tche-lee [Beizhili]. Nevertheless, I would not for any consideration [not have done so], as by these means we are now masters of the geography of the north-east coasts of China, and have acquired knowledge of the Yellow Sea, which was never before navigated by European ships.'

Changling then left the party and went on ahead, in order to prepare for the Embassy's arrival at Canton. During the next two days they undertook the portage from Van-gan to Nanzhou, from which point the passage to Canton was usually made in seven or eight days. Observed Macartney:

We shall probably be longer in order to give time to the Viceroy to get there a little before us to prepare for our reception. When he took leave of us he told us he had written to the Emperor in such terms upon our subject that he was persuaded we should leave China, not only without dissatisfaction but with essential proofs of the Emperor's favour. I said that his indulgence to the King my master's subjects would be the most essential and acceptable favour he could possibly confer on me.

Changling's departure left Macartney and his suite in the care of his Chinese friends, Wang and Qiao. From the Viceroy's tone and behaviour, Macartney had realized that the two mandarins had been working hard to promote the interests of the Embassy. Now, with the Viceroy gone, the informal atmosphere led to a series of briefings on aspects of China not hitherto touched on.

Wang, as an old soldier, was able to tell Macartney that he calculated the military force of China at 1,800,000 men. Qiao, the administrator, who had been Governor of several large districts, estimated the population of the Empire at above 360 million and the annual revenue at fifty to sixty million pounds sterling, of which, after civil and military expenses had been paid, nearly £10,000,000 found its way into the Emperor's coffers. Macartney doubted the method of calculation, though. He thought, for instance, that Wang had included troops of the Tartar banners, whilst Qiao in his estimate of population had added the old Manchu dominions of the reigning family and the new conquests of west Tartary. 'When it is considered that China is about eight times as big as France, infinitely more populous in comparison to its extent, far better cultivated and receiving annually for ages a greater commercial balance in its favour, it is possible that my friends may not be guilty of so much exaggeration as one at first sight would imagine.'

With the journey's end in sight, the Embassy's travel-weariness became apparent in their journals. Too much that was new, yet eventually the same, carried with it a sense of repetition which shortened diary entries – except for Macartney's. Since the Embassy needed to give the Viceroy a few days' start, it now had to mark time. Freed from the demands of diplomacy, Macartney decided to pay a visit to the Temple of Pusa, dedicated to the Bodhisattva Guanyin and situated on a clifftop alongside the river. In recounting this visit, Macartney switched from his usual descriptive terseness to the more florid and ruminative prose of one who had time on his hands.

The morning was remarkably fine, the sun rose with uncommon brilliancy, and the whole face of nature was lighted up with cheerfulness and beauty . . . We were attracted to the left by an arm of the river, which . . . had bent and elbowed itself into a deep cove or basin, above which enormous masses of rocks rose abruptly on every side, agglomerating to a stupendous height and menacing collision. The included flood was motionless, silent, sullen, black. The ledge where we landed was so narrow we could not stand on it. We were hemmed round with danger. The mountains frowned on us from on high, the precipice startled us from beneath. Our only safety seemed in the jaws of the cavern that yawned in front. We plunged into it without hesitating, and for a moment felt the joys of a sudden escape. But our terrors returned when we surveyed our asylum. We found ourselves at the bottom of a staircase hewn in the rock, long, narrow, steep and rugged . . . We scrambled up the steps and with much trouble and fatigue arrived at the landing place. Here an ancient bald-headed bonze issued from his den and offered himself as our conductor through this subterranean labyrinth. The first place he led us to was the grand hall or refectory of the convent . . . It is an excavation forming nearly a cube of twenty-five feet. The apartment was well furnished . . . in the middle . . . was suspended a lantern of prodigious size made in London, the offering of an opulent Chinese bigot at Canton. From hence we mounted by an ascent of many difficult steps to the Temple itself, which is directly over the hall, but of a greater extent. Here the god Pusa [Guanyin] is displayed in all his glory – a gigantic image with a Saracen face, grinning horribly from a double row of gilded fangs, a crown on his head, a naked scimitar in one hand and a firebrand in the other. But how little, alas, is celestial or subliminary fame . . . Even the bonzes who live by his worship scarcely know anything of his history.

Opposite to the image is a wide breach in the wall, down from which the perpendicular view requires the finest nerves and the steadiest head to resist its impression. The convoluted rocks above shooting their tottering shadows into the distant light, the slumbering abyss below, the superstitious gloom brooding upon the whole, all conspired to strike the mind with accumulated horror and the most terrifying image.

To this lurid account Macartney later added an apologetic footnote:

Upon reading this account to one or two gentlemen who had visited this place as well as myself . . . though they perfectly agree in their recollection of the principal features of the place, they think them rather heightened and surcharged. I have often thought what amusement might be derived from the perusal of the journals kept by the different persons of the Embassy. Even the journal of a valet-de-chambre might be of some value!

Alas, Aeneas Anderson had next to nothing to say about the Temple of Pusa, but had Macartney had the gift of foresight he would have noted the coincidence that, forty-five years later, on the eve of the so-called Opium War, Commissioner Lin, sent by the Imperial Court to enforce the law and demand the surrender of British opium stocks, was to prostrate himself at the shrine on his way to take up his post at Canton.

Other members of the Embassy whiled away their time with much tittle-tattle and idle comment. Anderson told of a fire on one of the 'inferior junks', and of the improvement in the food due to the increased fertility of the land through which they were passing. Huttner noted the fecundity of the province of Canton, and added that here 'the Europeans are better known than in the rest of China. We are scorned there and we are called Devils, because in the Chinese theatre the devils wear tight fitting clothes like those we use.' Macartney noted the weather: 'sharp with a clear frosty air. The Thermometer at fifty-three this morning and at sixty-three in the middle of the day.' He was impressed by the fertility of the land: 'I believe there is scarcely an acre of cultivable land in China that is not cultivated. Although a general resemblance runs through the whole nation as viewed in the gross, yet almost every province has its own particular industry and varies from the rest in many points.'

Evenings were spent with Wang, Qiao and Mr Plumb. On 16th December Lord Macartney chose to cross-question them on the way of life of Emperor Qianlong. They told him:

He rises about three o'clock a.m.* and then goes to his private pagoda to worship Buddha. He then reads the dispatches of the different officers who are permitted to write to him directly. At seven o'clock a.m. he breakfasts, after which he amuses himself about his palaces and gardens with his women and Eunuchs. He then sends for the First Grand Secretary or Chief Minister, with whom he transacts the current business, and then has a kind of levee which is attended by all the Grand Secretaries and Great Mandarins who have the entree. He dines usually at three o'clock p.m. and then goes to the Theatre or other diversion of the day after which he retires and amuses himself with reading till bed-time, the hour of which is no later than seven o'clock in the evening. A principal eunuch is always waiting during the night in order to conduct him to any of the ladies whom he chooses to call for . . .

. . . He is a man of great parts, learning and application, religious and charitable, affable and affectionate to his subjects, relentless and vindictive to his enemies; much elated with his greatness and prosperity and impatient of the slightest reverse or mischance; jealous of his power, suspicious of his ministers and when angry not easily appeased. He has never admitted any of his sons to the smallest share of his confidence or authority although some of them are upward of forty years old. Nor is it known who he intends for his successor . . .

. . . Some years since the Emperor had pretended that he was weary of the throne, and had fixed a time for his retiring from it, but as the period approached he began to think it better to defer his resignation to a more distant day. At present it stands for 1796, but it is by no means certain it will then take place.

Tuesday 17th December 1793 Stopping at a town some thirty miles from their goal, they found 'large and magnificent barges adorned with a profusion of gilding and glass'. They knew they had reached the end of their journey. These state barges were waiting to take them on the final stage down river to Canton. They had to contain themselves patiently for two days until the Viceroy's preparations were completed. Macartney's comments are revealing:

I can't omit remarking that in the course of one navigation we have had an uncommon profusion of military honours lavished upon us everywhere as we passed along, which I attribute to the Viceroy's having given particular directions for the purpose as he preceded us. As the Chinese consider the province of Canton to be the most obnoxious to invasion from the sea the military posts in it are very numerous. There seemed to be an affected reiteration of salutes . . . to impress us with the vigilance and alertness of the troops . . . Nevertheless they are totally

* The Ambassador would hardly have needed to be reminded of this, given his own experiences.

ignorant of our discipline, cumbersomely clothed, armed only with matchlocks, bows and arrows and heavy swords, awkward in the management of them, of an unwarlike character and disposition, I imagine that they would make but feeble resistance to a well conducted attack. The circumstance of greatest embarrassment to an invader would be their immense numbers, not on account of the mischief they could do to him, but that he would find no end of doing mischief to them. The slaughter of millions would scarcely be perceived, and unless the people themselves soon voluntarily submitted, the victor would indeed reap the vanity of destruction, but not the glory or use of dominion.

22

Last Days in China

Canton, the port that had furnished the Embassy with its prime objective, was now to be a focus for reunions, for recriminations, for final diplomatic endeavour and for farewells. The Embassy arrived in their gilded state barges at 1.30pm on Thursday 19th December. Five days earlier, the *Hindostan* had sailed in from Zhoushan. The *Lion* was anchored nearby off Huangpu with the captured French brig, twice having been beaten back in an attempted voyage to Japan, first by a typhoon and then by dysentery.

Comfortably lodged on the western bank of the Chu-kiang, Anderson rated the present Embassy accommodation 'far superior to any we had seen in our long journey through this country'. Staunton was impressed by the spaciousness of their lodgings, 'fitted up in the English manner with glass and fire grates, found very comfortable in the winter solstice'. But it is Huttner who, never having witnessed such a set-up before, best conveys the claustrophobia engendered by the working conditions at the port:

European trade with China goes through a number of obstacles, one of the most irritating is to go first to the Isle of Macao which is 16 English leagues away [from Canton] and there pay a lot of money for the pilot and written permission without which they cannot enter the Bocca Tigris [the fortified mouth of the harbour]. This detour is extremely disagreeable for ships that have been at sea a long time . . . Low tide prevents the ships which have entered the Bocca going further than . . . three leagues from the town. Between here and Canton there are three toll points. At each one boats are stopped and inspected before they can go to the factories [warehouses].

The factories, built by the Dutch, the English, the French, the Spaniards and the Swedes, are situated on the western bank of the river and can be recognised from afar by the flags flying from tall flagposts . . .

. . . The suburb of Canton in which they are situated because no European dares to enter the town itself, has many streets which consist only of merchant shops of which some are so full of European merchandise that one would think that one was in one of our towns. The Mercaria in Venice and this suburb look very much like each other. Here may be found nearly all the objects that you will find in the ports in Europe. There are especially foodstuffs which leave nothing to be desired either for quantity, quality or price. There is the best meat, vegetables and excellent fruit. The inhabitants of Canton have carried the imitation of furniture, tools and utensils made in Europe of all kinds and especially in England, to the point where they make many of these things, especially in common silver, trunks and so on, as well and more cheaply than in England. Chinese tailors, of which there are a large number in Canton, do the work nearly as well as the English tailors and about half the price. There is much silk and cotton cloth and there is perhaps nowhere that one may be better dressed more cheaply. Laundry is carried out superbly and much more cheaply than in any of our capitals . . .

. . . The greatest circumspection must be used if one does not wish to be deceived in doing business with the inhabitants of the town. The nation has a reputation for a lack of probity to the point of self-congratulation on the ingenuity of the frauds it perpetrates. The inhabitants of Canton are not without exception, indeed the deceptions of the Hoppo and other mandarins are such that Captains of ships are obliged to pay ten per cent more than the official customs dues which the Emperor demands . . . The factories, although constructed at [the Europeans'] expense, do not belong to them but to the owners of the ground on which they are built. Although the Europeans always pay on the spot, either in kind or by barter, they are nevertheless obliged to give their merchandise on credit and to leave without a legal guarantee. In these annual displacements from Canton to Macao and Macao to Canton, they are obliged each time to pay the toll for all furniture and effects they take with them, with a result that they have nothing for which they have not paid the rights twelve times, and sometimes more frequently.

. . . Until the arrival of the English Embassy in Canton there were no means of talking to the Viceroy directly nor by writing . . .

The very lowest of the Mandarins think they are more elevated than a businessman . . . The characteristic I have just quoted proves that the Embassy would have been treated with the same disdain if the attitude of the Viceroy had not prevented it . . . Our two botanists went one day into the country to look at some of the plants. A mandarin from Canton of a fair seniority saw them and either he didn't know who they were or didn't want to know. He ordered a soldier to arrest them. They refused and the soldier struck them. Full of surprised indignation they ran towards the Mandarin who had given the order and obliged him to come with them to the boat where the two Imperial Mandarins [Wang and Qiao] were. He blanched and apologised but such an affront could not remain unpunished. The Viceroy had him beaten with forty strokes of the bamboo. Intervention on our part could not prevent the soldier from having an even more cruel punishment. The end of his ears were pierced with a hot iron. He was savagely beaten and stretched on the rack.

A plethora of observations from the missionaries in Peking fed the recriminations. In letters to Dinwiddie they put forward many reasons for the rapid termination of the Embassy:

Why not accept . . . the Tartar legate [Zhengrui]? He was probably sent by Heshen as a go-between [between] the Ambassador and his master. Why not bribe him? All agree Heshen is one of the most corrupt men in the Empire. A public present he cannot receive, but he expected something considerable in a private way. Is he accessible? Every man is so . . . It was very improper to present young Staunton to the Emperor; he ought not to have been presented at all. What must the Chinese think of the English who make their boys men before their time? . . .

Above all, three reasons account for the peremptory dismissal. First, not complying with the ceremonies of the country; second, not bribing the lower mandarins; and third, one mandarin being degraded one button on his Lordship's account.

During the five days before Christmas, Macartney gave audience to Viceroy Changling, to the Hoppo and to the great mandarins of local and city government. He explained at some length the 'different grievances of our trade', but the Hoppo was against any change in procedure. The Viceroy, on the other hand, thought that any reasonable modification should be made. Viceroy and Hoppo earnestly debated the subject, and intuitively Macartney felt that the Viceroy was getting the better of the argument.

As senior representative of the Embassy, Macartney had to decide the order of sailing of the British merchantmen in port, especially since the news had just come in of the capture of the *Princess Royal* by the French in the Straits of Sunda. There were five ships at anchor ready to depart, and another five new arrivals. One of these would have to take his letters and dispatches to England, and another the duplicates (in case of shipwreck). All this involved hard work and painful decision.

After maturely considering all the circumstances before me, reflecting upon the state of the ships now ready to sail and upon the values of the cargoes provided for the loading of the ships lately arrived and those expected this season (which cargoes, when sold, I can scarcely estimate at less than three million sterling) . . . I have now, however painful to me, been obliged to dismiss from my mind many of the flattering ideas which I had entertained at the commencement of my Embassy, of distinguishing it by some happy discovery, some signal and brilliant success, in the prosecution of our political and commercial interests in these distant parts of the world. I have given up my projected visit to Japan, which (though now less alluring in prospect) had always been a favourite adventure as the possible opening of a new mine for the exercise of our industry and the purchase of our manufactures. All these ideas I have resigned at present, and adopted the measures which appear to afford the most substantial advantages to the public. It is therefore determined that the Bombay Castle, the Brunswick, the Minerva, the Chesterfield and the Bellona shall proceed immediately for England . . . The other ships (probably thirteen) will proceed when ready under the convoy of His Majesty's ship the Lion. Thus by speedy departure of the five ships not only their demurrage will be saved, but if they arrive safe, the Court of Directors [of the East India Company] will be earlier enabled to judge of their China resources. By the Lion's convoying the remainder, an immense property will be secured from danger in these seas and, I trust, reach England in safety.

On Christmas Day and on New Year's Day they celebrated the season by dining with the British exiles in their factory – two occasions of glittering elegance. As a Christmas present, Macartney acceded to a request from the factory that the band of German musicians who had accompanied them on their mission – and whose agreement to the proposal he had secured – remain to entertain them on a permanent basis: 'a valuable acquisition in a country and situation where so little exterior amusement of any kind is obtained'.

The Ambassador arrived for the New Year festivities bearing the latest – and, as it turned out, the last – message from the Emperor. That morning he had received a ceremonial visit from the Viceroy, which had followed the by now well worn pattern: first, the Emperor's salutation of satisfaction on the conduct of the Embassy; second, the repetition of his good disposition toward the English; third, the repetition of all this by Changling, who on this occasion was 'particularly courteous and caressing'. He had issued two proclamations announcing 'the severest punishment against any persons who should try to injure Europeans or practise extortion when dealing with them'. In spite of raising Macartney's hopes the proclamations were soon doomed to be made ineffectual.

Preparations were made for the departure of the Embassy. Macartney felt there was one thing left for him to do. He would use the thaw in relations to obtain permission for the staff of the factory to visit the city. Except for the occasion some two years earlier, when they had delivered to the Viceroy of Canton the letter from Francis Baring, the Chairman of the East India Company, proposing the intended embassy, neither the Commissioners nor their staffs had been inside the city. Macartney had a strong wish to do exactly that. So, entering by the great water gate, the Ambassador, the Commissioners and the British factory exiles traversed the city from end to end. They were impressed by the press of people, and estimated the population at one million. No wheeled carriages or horses were allowed, except those ridden by the Embassy servants. Macartney had seen it all before – in Hangzhou, in Suzhou, in Jehol and in Peking. The expectant, upturned faces made him ponder on the behaviour of the English towards the Chinese.

> We no doubt labour under many disadvantages here at present, but some of them we have it in our power to remove. Instead of acting towards the Chinese in Canton in the same manner as we do toward natives at our own factories elsewhere, we seem to have adopted a totally opposite system. We keep aloof from them as much as possible. We wear a dress as different from them as can be fashioned. We are quite ignorant of their language (which I suppose cannot be a very difficult one, for little George Staunton has long since learned to speak it and write it with great readiness, and from that circumstance has been of infinite use to us on many occasions). We therefore almost entirely depend on the good faith and good nature of the few Chinese whom we employ and by whom we be but imperfectly understood in the broken gibberish [pidgin English] we talk to them. I fancy that the Hong merchants . . . would attempt doing business on the Royal Exchange to very little purpose if they appeared there in petticoat clothes, with bonnet and turbans, and could speak nothing but Chinese or Arabic.

A sudden surge in the crowd jolted Macartney out of his reverie. Who were these smiling faces, many of them bespectacled, pressing on his palanquin? They were all, he thought, reasonably employed, mainly in the making of silk boots and straw bonnets, and in the labours of the forge. The narrowness of the streets and the closeness of the shops made it all something of an ordeal. Speculating on his experience of the last six months, he continued:

Now I am very much mistaken if, by proper management, we might not gradually and in some years be able to mould the China Trade (as we seem to have done with trade everywhere else) to the shape that will best suit us. But it would certainly require great skill, caution, temper and perseverance, much greater perhaps than it is reasonable to expect. I dare say there are a great many hasty spirits disposed to go a shorter way to work, but no shorter way will do it. If the Chinese were provoked to interdict us their commerce, or do us any material injury, we certainly have the means easy enough of revenging ourselves, for a few frigates could, in a few weeks destroy all the coastal communication from the Island of Hainan to the Gulf of Pe-tche-lee [Beizhili], and if I were to indulge the speculation of an ambitious or vindictive politician, I do not doubt that we might vulnerate them as sensibly in other quarters . . . On the other hand let us see what might be the consequence to ourselves. Our settlements in India would suffer most severely by any interruption of their China traffic which is infinitely valuable to them, whether considered singly as a market for cotton and opium, or as connected with their adventures to the Philippines or Malaya.

To Great Britain the blow would be immediate and heavy. Our great woollen manufacture, the ancient staple of England, would feel such a sudden convulsion as scarcely any vigilance or vigour in Government could for a long time remedy or alleviate. The demand of Canton for our woollens alone, can't now be less than five to six hundred thousand pounds per annum, and there is good reason to believe that with proper care it may be in some years stretched to a million. We would lose other growing branches of export to China of tin, lead, copper, hardware and of clocks, watches and similar articles of ingenious mechanism. We should lose import from China not only of its raw silk, an indispensable ingredient in our silk fabrics, but of another indispensable luxury, or rather an absolute necessity of life: Tea. We should also in some measure lose an excellent school of nautical knowledge, a strong limb of marine power and a prolific source of public revenue.

These evils, it would seem, must infallibly follow from a breach with China . . . but all these inconveniences and mischiefs which I have stated as objects of apprehension may happen in the common course of things without any quarrel or interference on our part. The Empire of China is an old, crazy, first rate Man-of-War, which a fortunate succession of able and vigilant officers has contrived to keep afloat for these one hundred and fifty years past, and to overawe their neighbours merely by her bulk and appearance; but whenever an insufficient man happens to have command upon deck, adieu to the discipline and safety of the ship. She may perhaps not sink outright; she may drift for some time as a wreck and will then be dashed to pieces on the shore; but she can never be rebuilt on the old bottom . . .

. . . But to take things solely as they are now, and to bound our views by the visible horizon of our situation, without speculating on probable events (which seldom take place according to our speculations), our present thoughts, our reason, and our humanity equally forbid the thoughts of any offensive measures with regard to the Chinese, whilst a ray of hope remains for succeeding by gentle ones. Nothing can be urged in favour of hostile conduct but an irresistible conviction of failure by forbearance. The project of a territory on the Continent of China (which I have heard imputed to the late Lord Clive) is too wild to be seriously mentioned, and especially if all can be quietly got without it, that was expected to be got with it.

There was nothing to keep the Ambassador in China a moment longer. He felt he had lived off the Emperor's hospitality for long enough. He therefore told the Viceroy a diplomatic half-truth: pleading ill-health and the need for sea air, he had decided to go on to Macao and there await the sailing of the convoy. He allowed Dinwiddie to stay behind at Canton to give his planned course of lectures on natural philosophy to the gentlemen of the English factory, and completed the formal transfer of the German band.

So at 1pm on 8th January 1794, after a reception at the English factory, the Embassy said goodbye to the Viceroy, the Hoppo and the other mandarins. And to the salute and the billowing smoke of the guns, and the shrilling of the bos'ns' pipes accompanied by both the Chinese and the old Embassy band, Macartney boarded the *Lion*'s barge. The pinnaces and boats of the Indiamen, pennants flying and crews all dressed in uniform, carried the rest of the Embassy from Canton. Their two faithful friends Wang and Qiao accompanied them for a farewell dinner on board the *Lion*: 'They shed tears at parting and showed such marks of sensibility and concern as could proceed from none but the sincere and uncorrupted hearts. If ever I could forget the friendship and attachment of these two worthy men, or the services they rendered us, I should be guilty of the deepest ingratitude.'

23

Aftermath

IT TOOK EIGHT WEEKS for the convoy to assemble at Macao. Finally, on 17th March 1794 thirteen ships sailed for England. The two Embassy brigs had been sold – the *Clarence* to a purchaser in Macao, the *Jackall* to the East India Company Marine Service.

The convoy anchored off Spithead on 3rd September. On arrival, despite Macartney's protests, the crew of the *Hindostan* received no shore leave or respite. They were immediately pressed into service with the Grand Fleet – the war against France was now in its second year.

Two days later, Lord Macartney arrived back in London. And, though gratified to discover that in his absence the King had bestowed an earldom on him, he had little time to rest on his laurels. After wintering in Britain he was sent off on another sensitive diplomatic mission – to establish contact in Italy with Louis XVIII and persuade him of the British position in the war against Bonaparte. It was a failure. It was while he was still in Italy that he was appointed Governor of the Cape of Good Hope. But in November 1798 ill health forced him to relinquish this post, and from then on he gradually declined. He died at his home in Chiswick at eight o'clock on the evening of 31st March 1806.

Sir George Staunton had a stroke soon after his return from China. His condition deteriorated, and he died on 14th January 1801. He had managed, however, to compile and publish in 1797 the official record of the Embassy. His son went back to Canton, where in 1796 Macartney's patronage secured him the post of writer for the East India Company. On his father's death he succeeded to the baronetcy. In 1804 he became a supercargo and in 1808 was appointed interpreter. In 1816 he became President of the Select Committee of the East India Company, the most senior post at the Company's Canton headquarters. Subsequently he used his knowledge of the Chinese language to translate the statutes and rescripts of the Qing dynasty. On his return to Britain he became a Member of Parliament and consultant to the government on Chinese affairs.

On his return to Britain, Sir John Barrow helped Sir George Staunton prepare the official account of the Embassy. He produced his own account, *Travels in China*, in 1804. In 1796, he accompanied Macartney to the Cape of Good Hope. In 1804 he was appointed Second Secretary to the Admiralty, a post he held for the next forty years.

Aeneas Anderson published his journal, to the disapprobation of Sir John Barrow, who described it as 'a work vamped up by a London bookseller as a speculation that could not fail'. It was indeed a great success. Between the first edition in 1795 and the second a year later, Anderson had purchased a lieutenant's commission in the Second Royal Manx Fencibles.

After the China mission, Dr Dinwiddie sailed for India in the *Jackall*. With Macartney's dispensation, he was allowed to take his scientific apparatus with him. He also took the Embassy's botanical specimens, tea plants, varnish plants, tallow trees and mulberry trees as well as silkworm eggs, which he handed over to the Superintendent of the Botanical Gardens in Calcutta. Whilst in India, he was able to deliver the lectures so dear to his heart. It is interesting to note that when he left England in 1792 he had been £500 in debt, and when he returned he was worth about £10,000. He died on 19th March 1815.

Lieutenant Parish, in charge of the artillery section of the Embassy, who made excellent plans and drawings of, amongst other memorable monuments, the Great Wall, the lock gates on the Grand Canal, the water-wheel and the Potala Temple at Jehol, was appointed aide-de-camp to the Governor-General of India, Marquis Cornwallis. On the passage out he was swept overboard and drowned.

William Alexander, though paid only half of what Thomas Hickey, professional painter, earned on the Embassy, produced over a thousand drawings, sketches and paintings, from which the engravings used to illustrate the official account of the mission were derived. He published two books of his own, *The Costume of China* and *Dress and Manners of the Chinese*. He was appointed the first Superintendent of Prints and Drawings at the British Museum. He died in 1816.

On the Chinese side, the Emperor Qianlong lived up to his ambition to emulate but not exceed the reign of his grandfather Kangxi. In 1796, the sixtieth year of his reign, on 9th February – the Chinese New Year's Day – at a great ceremony he ostensibly relinquished the throne to his son Jiaqing. However, he continued to 'instruct' Jiaqing until his death on 7th February 1799.

Qianlong's minister Heshen, the great Gelao, survived the Emperor by fifteen days. So corrupt was he, filling the civil service with his placemen, that it can be said that he undermined the dynasty and sowed the seeds of decadence that were to permeate the Chinese Empire in the succeeding century. When Qianlong handed over to his son, it was in fact Heshen who was to take the decisions. However, within forty-eight hours of Qianlong's death, the new Emperor had him arrested; he confiscated all his property and allowed him to commit suicide. Heshen was found to be the richest man in China – worth, at eighteenth-century prices, some £300,000,000.

Zhengrui the Tartar legate – although his demotion during the Embassy for sending the Emperor false memorials was temporary – was to run into more trouble later. After Qianlong's death, on the succession of the new Emperor, Jiaqing, it was discovered that, to avoid being transferred from his lucrative post as Salt Administrator, he had offered a present of two hundred thousand taels to Heshenand; and that, in addition, he owed money to the government. In spite of these and other misdemeanours, the new Emperor made him Grand Minister of the Imperial household, but he was later deprived of this position by Imperial edict. He was subsequently made a Vice-Minister in the Department of Works, but again he angered the Emperor, and lost this post as well as his position in the Imperial household and his right to ride a horse within the Imperial Palace. He died in 1818, in the twentieth year of Jiaqing's reign.

Of the military conducting mandarin, Wang, it is known that in 1796 he was sent to Hebei to suppress bandit sects. He was promoted to provincial Commander-in-Chief in 1798. He subsequently fought rebels in Shanxi and Sichuan. On 12th September 1800, whilst fighting rebels in Shanxi, his force was surrounded. Although wounded he continued to fight until, with his arm severed, he was unhorsed and killed. His friend Qiao continued in the administrative service. In the fifth year of the new Emperor's reign he was promoted to the provincial governorship of Beizhili – an important post, given that this is the metropolitan province in which Peking is situated. In the following year he was given a similar post, presumably retiring from public service in 1804-5.

So much for the protagonists through whom this clash of cultures took place. What was there to show from this meeting of the dynamism of the Age of Reason with the immutability of Confucian culture? Alas, little that was tangible!

Changling, the new Viceroy on whom Macartney worked so assiduously, fell foul of Heshen. He stayed in Canton for only fifteen months. The reason for this short term of office is unknown, but it has been speculated that it was partly due to his friendship with Macartney, and partly due to the fact that he had exposed the falsehood of charges brought by Heshen against various people. After Heshen's death he filled other important posts, and died in 1811.

His spell in Canton failed to improve conditions for the traders. He issued 'proclamations' that had little effect. The first, on 2nd January 1794, promised punishment for anybody 'molesting, plundering or defrauding the English'. The second, three days later, was directed at 'magistrates, military officers and others who might use their position to extort money from Europeans'. Aimed as it was at lower officials, this proclamation failed to fix and standardize the taxes, duties and regulations concerning trade. It was not binding on the higher officials, least of all on the Hoppo. There was always tension between Hoppo, Viceroy and provincial officials, as well as considerable latitude in interpreting the Emperor's delegated powers. When making these proclamations Changling must have known that they would mollify Macartney, encouraging him to think that things were improving whilst at the same time he judged, perhaps wrongly, that they would not cause embarrassment at the Imperial Court.

Captain Mackintosh had direct experience of the ineffectualness of Changling's attempts to regulate trading conditions, as Macartney relates:

> In consideration of Captain Mackintosh having accompanied my Embassy and brought the presents to the Emperor on board his ship, he was assured she would be exempted from all the Emperor's duties payable at the port where she loaded. Being disappointed of the goods expected at Chusan [Zhoushan], he proceeded on the Hindostan to Canton, and took in there a usual cargo for England, but the privilege that had been promised was not understood by us, for after the accustomed duties for all the ships had been paid by the Hong merchants, of which 30,000 taels [£10,000] was the Hindostan's proportion, the Hoppo repaid into Mr Browne's* hand only 14,000 dollars [£4,666] instead of the 30,000 taels as was expected, saying that so much was the exact amount of the Emperor's duties, but not saying nor explaining what became of the remainder.†

Looked at dispassionately, not one of the aims of the Embassy was fulfilled. They negotiated no treaty of commerce, they opened no new ports to extend British trade, and they created no new markets; they failed to negotiate the cession of a piece of land nearer to the tea- and silk-producing areas, and they failed to bring about the abolition of the existing abuses in Canton. But why should this failure on all counts have occurred? Let J.L. Cranmer-Byng take up the tale:

> The real reason for the failure of Macartney's Mission was that from the very beginning it never stood the slightest chance of success. There was never any common ground of understanding between England and China; the two countries possessed two different cultures with totally different outlooks. No treaty of alliance or commerce could be effected while the attitude of those in power in China remained unchanged. To the Emperor and his Ministers the Western Ocean Barbarians seemed especially troublesome, warlike and even dangerous. With such

* One of the senior East India Company Commissioners.

† Prices quoted in eighteenth-century equivalents.

people no relations, except that of suzerain and vassal, made sense. These foreigners must be kept under strict control and allowed to trade only on Chinese terms. To Britain foreign trade was her life's blood. To Qianlong's ministers it brought luxuries and the opportunity of squeeze, which they would have been very sorry to lose, but it was not a matter of national safety. The Ambassador's task became impossible when he reached the barrier of Chinese custom, tradition and exclusiveness.

But there were subsidiary gains. 'We are now masters of geography of the north east coast of China, and have now acquired a knowledge of the Yellow Sea which was never before navigated by European ships,' wrote Macartney in his journal, well aware of the advantages that could accrue should the ports to the north be opened to trade. Secondly, the Embassy returned with a considerable first-hand knowledge of contemporary Chinese culture. Whereas, hitherto, any mission had had to rely on accounts from the Jesuits, other missionaries and other failed embassies, Macartney and his team of experts could now furnish any future embassy with information that could conceivably mean the difference between failure and success. It was the first time that English officials had been in a position to form direct opinions of the mores of their Chinese and Manchu counterparts. Furthermore, young Staunton's mastery of Chinese, as well as initiating the tradition of Chinese language studies in Britain, also indicated the importance of a knowledge of Chinese to those who deal with Chinese officialdom.

These achievements, marginal to the main aims, were very costly. Estimated at £78,000 in eighteenth-century terms, the equivalent today would be many millions.

One last, pertinent question from Cranmer-Byng:

What did the emperor and his advisers – Manchu and Chinese – learn from it? The answer is nothing . . . Thus if England failed to obtain a treaty of trade, or to improve her relations with China, the Chinese Empire equally failed to take her first steps on the road to modernisation which alone could have saved her from the humiliations of the Anglo-Chinese War of 1839-42, the Anglo-French Campaign of 1858-60, her decisive defeat by Japan in 1894-5 and the general economic subservience to Japan and the West during the first forty years of the present century.

Looking back on the Embassy, Dinwiddie expresses most keenly this sense of great opportunities missed, from his berth on the *Jackall* as he waited to sail for India:

Thus the Embassy to me is ended. Its object was noble – the extension of commerce, and the improvement of science. With regard to the first, nothing that looks like an improvement has yet taken place; as to the other, little could be done in the country, while at Peking we were prisoners, and on our journey hurried forward with hardly time to look at an object, and without being able to converse with the inhabitants. To travel through a fine country – to see pagodas, canals and manufacturing towns, without being able to ask a single question, is extremely mortifying. To be conducted . . . by the Gelao . . . to receive a present from the Emperor at parting and the Gelao's farewell speech, without knowing a word he said, and consequently to fall into numerous blunders in our attempt to reply – what information could we derive respecting the arts and sciences in a country where we could not converse with the inhabitants? With what countenance will Lord Macartney return to Europe after his shameful treatment? No apology will satisfy. We go home – are asked what we have done. Our answer – we could not speak to the people.

Appendix A

Edict from the Emperor Ch'ien-lung [Qianlong] to King George III*

You, o king, live beyond the confines of many seas, nevertheless, impelled by your humble desire to partake of the benefits of our civilisation, you have dispatched a mission respectfully bearing your memorial. Your Envoy has crossed the seas and paid his respects at my Court on the anniversary of my birthday. To show your devotion, you have also sent offerings of your country's produce.

I have perused your memorial: the earnest terms in which it is couched reveal a respectful humility on your part, which is highly praiseworthy. In consideration of the fact that your Ambassador and his deputy have come a long way with your memorial and tribute, I have shown them high favour and have allowed them to be introduced into my presence. To manifest my indulgence, I have entertained them at a banquet and made them numerous gifts. I have also caused presents to be forwarded to the Naval Commander [Sir Erasmus Gower] and six hundred of his officers and men, although they did not come to Peking, so that they too may share in my all embracing kindness.

As to your entreaty to send one of your nationals to be accredited to my Celestial Court and to be in control of your country's trade with China, this request is contrary to all usage of my dynasty and cannot possibly be entertained. It is true that Europeans, in the service of the dynasty, have been permitted to live at Peking, but they are compelled to adopt Chinese dress, they are strictly confined to their own precincts and are never permitted to return home. You are presumably familiar with our dynastic regulations. Your proposed Envoy to my Court could not be placed in a position similar to that of European officials in Peking who are forbidden to leave China, nor could he, on the other hand, be allowed liberty of movement and the privilege of corresponding with his own country; so that you would gain nothing by his residence in our midst.

Moreover, our Celestial dynasty possesses vast territories, and tribute missions from the dependencies are provided for by the Department for Tributary States, which ministers to their wants and exercises strict control over their movements. It would be quite impossible to leave them to their own devices.

---

* Translated by Backhouse and Bland in *Annals and Memoirs of the Court of Peking*.

Supposing that your Envoy should come to our Court, his language and national dress differ from that of our people, and there would be no place in which to bestow him. It may be suggested that he might imitate the Europeans permanently resident in Peking and adopt the dress and customs of China but, it has never been our dynasty's wish to force people to do things unseemly and inconvenient. Besides, supposing I sent an Ambassador to reside in your country, how could you possibly make for him the requisite arrangements? Europe consists of many other nations besides your own: if each and all demanded to be represented at our Court, how could we possibly consent? The thing is utterly impracticable. How can our dynasty alter its whole procedure and system of etiquette, established for more than a century, in order to meet your individual views? If it be said that your object is to exercise control over your country's trade, your nationals have had full liberty to trade at Canton for many a year, and have received the greatest consideration at our hands. Missions have been sent by Portugal and Italy, preferring similar requests. The Throne appreciated their sincerity and loaded them with favours, besides authorising measures to facilitate their trade with China. You are no doubt aware that, when my Canton merchant, Wu Chao-ping, was in debt to the foreign ships, I made the Viceroy advance the monies due, out of the provincial treasury, and ordered him to punish the culprit severely. Why then should a foreign nation advance this utterly unreasonable request to be represented at my Court? Peking is nearly two thousand miles from Canton, and at such a distance what possible control could any British representative exercise?

If you assert that your reverence for our Celestial dynasty fills you with a desire to acquire our civilisation, our ceremonies and code of laws differ so completely from your own that, even if your Envoy were able to acquire the rudiments of our civilisation, you could not possibly transplant our manners and customs to your alien soil. Therefore, however adept the Envoy might become, nothing could be gained thereby.

Swaying the wide world, I have but one aim in view, namely, to maintain a perfect governance and to fulfil the duties of the State: strange and costly objects do not interest me. If I have commanded that the tribute offerings sent by you, O King, are to be accepted, this was solely in consideration for the spirit which prompted you to dispatch them from afar. Our dynasty's majestic virtue has penetrated unto every country under Heaven, and Kings of all nations have offered their costly tribute by land and sea. As your Ambassador can see for himself, we possess all things. I set no value on objects strange or ingenious, and have no use for your country's manufactures. This then is my answer to your request to appoint a representative at my Court, a request contrary to our dynastic usage, which would only result in inconvenience to yourself. I have expounded my wishes in detail and have commanded your tribute Envoys to leave in peace on their homeward journey. It behoves you, O King, to respect my sentiments and to display even greater devotion and loyalty in future, so that, by perpetual submission to our Throne, you may secure peace and prosperity for your country hereafter. Besides making gifts (of which I enclose an inventory) to each member of your Mission, I confer upon you, O King, valuable presents in excess of the number usually bestowed on such occasions, including silks and curios – a list of which is likewise enclosed. Do you reverently receive them and take note of my tender goodwill towards you! A special mandate!

* * *

Appendix A

In the Imperial collection of documents dealing with the Macartney mission, this edict exists in draft form and, according to the memorandum attached to it, was dated 3rd August 1793. Therefore it was in existence three days before Macartney set foot in China. It was promulgated on 23rd September of that year and translated into Latin on 3rd October. It was considerably toned down by the missionaries who translated it: as Cranmer-Byng wryly observes, 'It is perhaps as well for subsequent Anglo-Chinese relations that neither Macartney nor the English Government realised quite how condescending was the original Chinese version of the Edict.'

Appendix B

The second edict,* although addressed to George III, is in reply to Macartney's note dated 3rd October 1793 containing the six requests (see page 95) and handed to Macartney when he said farewell to Heshen on 7th October.

You, O King, from afar have yearned after the blessings of our civilisation, and in your eagerness to come in touch with our converting influence have sent an Embassy across the sea bearing a memorial. I have already taken note of your respectful spirit of submission, have treated your mission with extreme favour and loaded it with gifts, besides issuing a mandate to you, O King, and honouring you with the bestowal of valuable presents. Thus has my indulgence been manifested.

Yesterday your Ambassador petitioned my Ministers to memorialise me regarding your trade with China, but his proposal is not consistent with our dynastic usage and cannot be entertained. Hitherto, all European nations, including your own country's barbarian merchants, have carried on their trade with our Celestial Empire at Canton. Such has been the procedure for many years, although our Celestial Empire possesses all things in prolific abundance and lacks no product within its own borders. There was therefore no need to import the manufactures of outside barbarians in exchange for our own produce. But as the tea, silk and porcelain which the Celestial Empire produces, are absolute necessities to European nations and to yourselves, we have permitted, as a signal mark of favour, that foreign *hongs* should be established at Canton, so that your wants might be supplied and your country thus participate in our beneficence. But your Ambassador has now put forward new requests which completely fail to recognise the Throne's principle to 'treat strangers from afar with indulgence', and to exercise a pacifying control over barbarian tribes, the world over. Moreover, our dynasty, swaying the myriad races of the globe, extends the same benevolence towards all. Your England is not the only nation trading at Canton. If other

* Translated by Backhouse and Bland, op.cit.

nations following your bad example, wrongfully importune my ear with further impossible requests, how will it be possible for me to treat them with easy indulgence? Nevertheless, I do not forget the lonely remoteness of your island, cut off from the world by intervening wastes of sea, nor do I overlook your excusable ignorance of the usages of our Celestial Empire. I have consequently commanded my Ministers to enlighten your Ambassador on the subject, and have ordered the departure of the mission. But I have doubts that, after your Envoy's return he may fail to acquaint you with my view in detail or that he may be lacking in lucidity, so that I shall now proceed to take your requests *seriatim* and to issue my mandate on each question separately. In this way you will, I trust, comprehend my meaning.

(1) Your Ambassador requests facilities for ships of your nation to call at Ning-po [Ningbo], Chusan [Zhoushan], Tientsin and other places for purposes of trade. Until now trade with European nations has always been conducted at Macao, where the foreign *hongs* are established to store and sell foreign merchandise. Your nation has obediently complied with this regulation for years past without raising any objection. In none of the other ports named have *hongs* been established, so that even if your vessels were to proceed thither, they would have no means of disposing of their cargoes. Furthermore, no interpreters are available, so you would have no means of explaining your wants, and nothing but general inconvenience would result. For the future, as in the past, I decree that your request is refused and that the trade shall be limited to Macao.

(2) The request that your merchants may establish a repository in the capital of my Empire for the storing and sale of your produce, in accordance with the precedent granted to Russia, is even more impracticable than the last. My capital is the hub and centre about which all quarters of the globe revolve. Its ordinances are most august and its laws are strict in the extreme. The subjects of our dependencies have never been allowed to open places of business in Peking. Foreign trade has hitherto been conducted at Macao, because it is conveniently near to the sea, and therefore an important gathering place for the ships of all nations sailing to and fro. If warehouses were established in Peking, the remoteness of your country, lying far to the north-west of my capital, would render transport extremely difficult. Before Kiakhta* was opened, the Russians were permitted to trade at Peking, but the accommodation furnished to them was only temporary. As soon as Kiakhta was available, they were compelled to withdraw from Peking, which has been closed to their trade these many years. Their frontier trade at Kiakhta is on all fours with your trade at Macao. Possessing facilities at the latter place, you now ask for further privileges at Peking, although our dynasty observes the severest restrictions respecting the admission of foreigners within its boundaries, and has never permitted the subjects of dependencies to cross the Empire's barriers and settle at will amongst the Chinese people. This request is also refused.

(3) Your request for a small island near Chusan where your merchants may reside and goods be warehoused, arises from your desire to develop trade. As there are neither foreign *hongs* nor interpreters in or near Chusan, where none of your ships have ever called, such an island would be utterly useless for your purposes. Every inch of the territory of our Empire is marked on the map and the strictest vigilance is exercised over it all: even tiny islets and far-lying sand-banks are clearly

---

* A town on the Amur River border with Russia.

defined as part of the provinces to which they belong. Consider, moreover, that England is not the only barbarian land which wishes to establish relations with our civilisation and trade with our Empire: supposing that other nations were all to imitate your evil example and beseech me to present them each and all with a site for trading purposes, how could I possibly comply? This also is a flagrant infringement of the usage of my Empire and cannot possibly be entertained.

(4) The next request, for a small site in the vicinity of Canton city, where your barbarian merchants may lodge or, alternatively, that there be no longer any restrictions over their movements at Macao, has arisen from the following events. Hitherto, the barbarian merchants of Europe have had a definite locality assigned to them at Macao for residence and trade, and have been forbidden to encroach an inch beyond the limits assigned to that locality. Barbarian merchants having business with the *hongs* have never been allowed to enter the city of Canton; by these measures, disputes between Chinese and barbarians are prevented, and a firm barrier is raised between my subjects and those of other nations. The present request is quite contrary to precedent; furthermore, European nations have been trading with Canton for a number of years and, as they make large profits, the number of traders is constantly increasing. How would it be possible to grant such a site to each country? The merchants of the foreign *hongs* are responsible to the local officials for the proceedings of barbarian merchants and they carry out periodical inspections. If these restrictions were withdrawn, friction would inevitably occur between the Chinese and your barbarian subjects, and the results would militate against the benevolent regard that I feel toward you. From every point of view, therefore, it is best that the regulations now in force should continue unchanged.

(5) Regarding your request for remission or reduction of duties on merchandise discharged by your British barbarian merchants at Macao and distributed throughout the interior, there is a regular tariff in force for barbarian merchants' goods which applies equally to all European nations. It would be as wrong to increase the duty imposed on your nation's merchandise on the grounds that the bulk of foreign trade is in your hands, as to make an exception in your case in the shape of specially reduced duties. In future, duties shall be levied equitably without discrimination between your nation and any other, and, in order to manifest my regard, your barbarian merchants shall continue to be shown every consideration at Macao.

(6) As to your request that your ships shall pay the duties leviable by tariff, there are no regular rules in force at Canton custom house respecting the amounts payable, and since I have refused your request to be allowed to trade at other ports, this duty will naturally continue to be paid at Canton as heretofore.

(7) Regarding your nation's worship of the Lord of Heaven, it is the same religion as that of other European nations. Ever since the beginning of history, sage Emperors and wise rulers have bestowed on China a moral system and inculcated a code, which from time immemorial has been religiously observed by the myriads of my subjects. There has been no hankering after heterodox doctrines. Even the European [missionary] officials in my capital are forbidden to hold intercourse with Chinese subjects; they are restricted within the limits of their appointed residences, and may not go about propagating their religion. The distinction between Chinese and barbarian is most strict, and your Ambassador's request that barbarians shall be given full liberty to disseminate their religion is utterly unreasonable.

It may be, O King, that the above proposals have been wantonly made by your Ambassador on his own responsibility, or peradventure you yourself are ignorant of our dynastic regulations and had no intention of transgressing them when you expressed these wild ideas and hopes. I have ever shown the greatest condescension to the tribute missions of all states which sincerely yearn after the blessings of civilisation so as to manifest my kindly indulgence. I have even gone out of my way to grant any requests which were in any way consistent with Chinese usage. Above all, upon you, who live in a remote and inaccessible region, far across the spaces of ocean, but who have shown your submissive loyalty by sending this tribute mission, I have heaped benefits far in excess of those accorded to other nations. But the demands presented by your Embassy are not only a contravention of dynastic tradition, but would be utterly unproductive of good result to yourself, besides being quite impracticable. I have accordingly stated the facts to you in detail, and it is your bounden duty reverently to appreciate my feelings and to obey these instructions henceforward for all time, so that you may enjoy the blessings of perpetual peace. If, after receipt of this explicit decree, you lightly give ear to the representations of your subordinates and allow your barbarian merchants to proceed to Chekiang [Zhejiang] and Tientsin, with the object of landing and trading there, the ordinances of my Celestial Empire are strict in the extreme, and the local officials, both civil and military, are bound reverently to obey the law of the land. Should your vessels touch the shore, your merchants will assuredly never be permitted to land or to reside there, but will be subject to instant expulsion. In the event your barbarian merchants will have had a long journey for nothing. Do not say that you were not warned in due time! Tremblingly obey and show no negligence! A special mandate!

Bibliography

BEFORE LISTING THE BOOKS AND PAPERS studied (some more, some less) in the writing of this work, I would like to acknowledge the debt I owe to Professor J.L. Cranmer-Byng, whose masterly edition of Macartney's journal is not only quoted herein but whose editorial notes have guided me through the *terra incognita* of the Qing Court and the East India Company. I can only hope that this work, now out of print and scarce, will soon be reprinted. It deserves a wide audience.

Alexander, William Journal (MS, British Library)

—— *The Costume of China* (William Miller, London, 1805)

—— *Picturesque Representations of the Dress and Manners of the Chinese* (John Murray, London, 1814)

Anderson, Aeneas *A Narrative of the British Embassy to China* (J. Debrett, London, 1795)

Backhouse, E. and J.O.P. Bland *Annals and Memoirs of the Court of Peking* (Heinemann, London, 1914)

Banks, Sir Joseph Hints on the Subject of Gardening suggested to the Gentlemen who attend the Embassy to China (MS 115, Linnean Society)

Barrow, John *Travels in China* (T. Cadell, London, 1804)

—— *A Voyage to Cochin China in the Years 1792, 1793* (T. Cadell, London, 1806)

—— *Some Account of the Public Life and a Selection from the Unpublished Writings of the Earl of Macartney* (2 vols, T. Cadell, London, 1897)

—— *An Autobiographical Memoir of Sir John Barrow* (John Murray, London, 1847)

Collis, Maurice *The Great Within* (Faber & Faber, London, 1942)

Cranmer-Byng, J.L. *An Embassy to China 1793-1794* (Longman Green & Co., London, 1962)

—— Lord Macartney's Embassy to Peking in 1793, from official Chinese documents, *Journal of Oriental Studies* (Hong Kong University), IV, 1-2 (1957-8)

Dinwiddie, James *Biographical Memoir of James Dinwiddie LLD. Astronomer in the British Embassy to China 1792, 1793, 1794*. Compiled from his notes and correspondence by William Jardine Proudfoot (Liverpool, 1868)

Hedin, Sven *Jehol, City of Emperors* (Kegan Paul, London, 1932)

Hsu, Immanuel C.Y. *The Rise of Modern China* (3rd edn, Oxford University Press, 1983)

Hummel, A.W. *Eminent Chinese of the Ch'ing Period* (2 vols, United States Government Printing Office, Washington DC, 1943-4)

Huttner, J.C. *Voyage à la Chine* (J.J. Fuchs Libraire, Paris, 1799)

Bibliography

INDIA OFFICE LIBRARY MANUSCRIPTS

Sketches respecting China and the Embassies sent thither, drawn up by Mr Cobb of the East India House (1792)

Account of Sundry Articles purchased by Francis Baring Esq., Chairman . . . consigned to the care of His Excellency the Right Hon. Lord Macartney (1792)

Note for the Minister in English and Latin translation (1792)

Edict from the Emperor Ch'ien-lung [Qianlong] to King George III

Letter from Macartney to Dundas dated January 1792

List of presents from the Emperor Ch'ien-lung to King George III (1792)

King, Henry C. in association with John Milburn *Geared to the Stars* (University of Toronto Press, 1968)

Lu Gwei-Djen and Joseph Needham *Celestial Lancets* (Cambridge University Press, 1980)

Morse, H.B. *The Chronicles of the East India Company Trading to China* (vol. 2, Oxford University Press, 1925; reprinted Taipei, 1975)

Pritchard, E.H. The instructions of the East India Company to Lord Macartney, *Journal of the Royal Asiatic Society*, Parts II, III, IV (1938)

Proudfoot, *see* Dinwiddie

Robbins, Helen H. *Our First Ambassador to China: An Account of the Life of George, Earl of Macartney* (John Murray, London, 1908)

Siren, Osvald *Gardens of China* (Ronal Press, New York, 1949)

Spence, Jonathan D. *The Search for Modern China* (Hutchinson, London, 1990)

Staunton, Sir George Leonard *An Authentic Account of an Embassy from the King of Great Britain to the Emperor of China* (J. Nicol, London, 1797)

Staunton, George Thomas *Miscellaneous Notices Relating to China* (John Murray, London, 1822-50)

—— Journal of a Voyage to China (MS, Duke University, North Carolina)

Index